Fast Bytes

Windows XP

W. Gieseke

DATA BECKER®

Published by DATA BECKER CORP
154 Wells Avenue
Newton
MA 02459

Author Wolfram Gieseke

Printed in the United States Januray 2002

UPC CODE 6-80466-90204-1

ISBN # 1-58507-109-9

Important note

The procedures and programs described in this book are given regardless of patent. They are intended for amateur and training purposes only.

All information, technical specifications and programs in this book has been produced by the authors with the utmost care. However, the publishers can provide neither a guarantee, nor accept legal responsibility or any other responsibility, for consequences resulting from incorrect information.

The software and hardware designations and trademarks of companies used in this book shall generally remain subject to the legislation covering trade names, trademarks and protection under patent law.

The text contained in this book are suggestions and examples only. They include selective information only with no claims made for completeness.

In addition, although the text has been created with great care, the publisher and the authors shall accept no responsibility for the completeness or correctness, for the contents of the text or for the success of the users actions after following the information given in this manual. Using the information given in the text is solely at the user's own risk.

The names and addresses given in this text are fictitious. Any resemblance to persons alive or dead is purely coincidental and unintentional.

Contents

1. eXPerience – The most important new features at a glance **9**

Logging on and off in Windows XP 9
Turning off Windows XP 11
The new Windows desktop 11
The new Start menu options 15
A better overview for the taskbar 18
Accessing system settings 22
Activating Windows XP 25

2. This is my Windows – Customizing XP **28**

Customizing the desktop background 28
Using different user interface themes 31
Mastering the Windows desktop 33
Great Explorer views for different purposes 35
Creating your own toolbars 39
Transferring your customized settings to other PCs 42

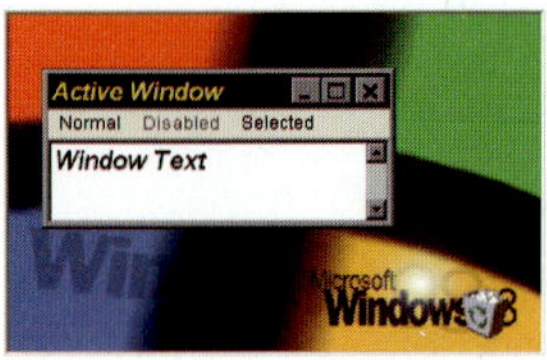

3. Using hardware and software under Windows XP **46**

Immediate measures in the event of program crashes 46
Getting older Windows programs to work 50
Remedying Windows problems through updates 52
Starting Windows in safe mode 55
Solving driver problems with old hardware 57

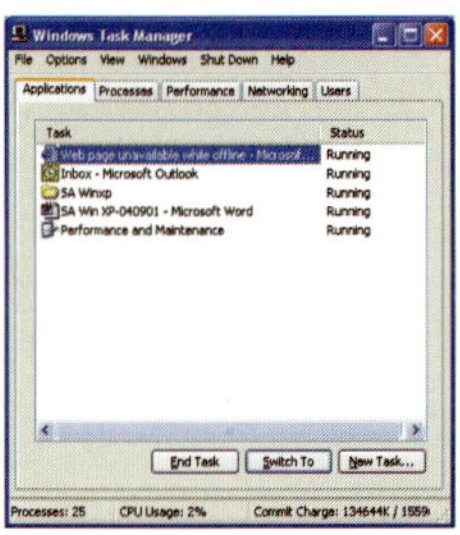

4. Tools - The best Help programs **62**

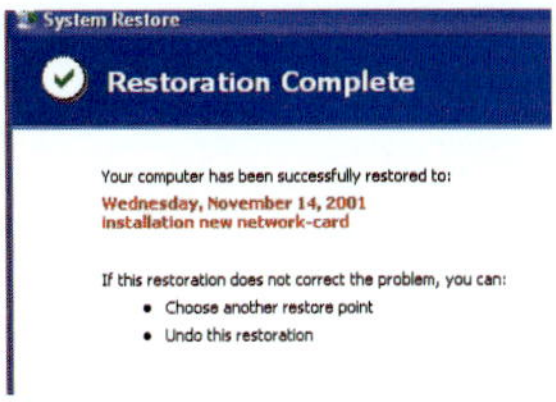

Cleaning up and optimizing the hard drive(s) 62
Saving disk space with Compressed Folders 69
Using the power saving functions 73
Backing up and restoring the XP system 75
Automating maintenance tasks 78

5. Audio, video and more - Multimedia with Windows XP **81**

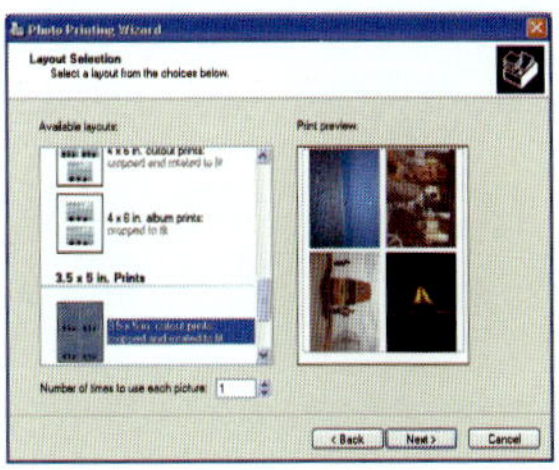

Creating a slide show with a digital camera and a scanner 81
Printing pictures with the Photo Printing Wizard 83
Music and more with Windows Media Player 85
Copying audio CDs to the computer 90
Creating your own audio CDs 92
Burning pictures, documents and files to CD 94

6. Home networking with Windows XP **97**

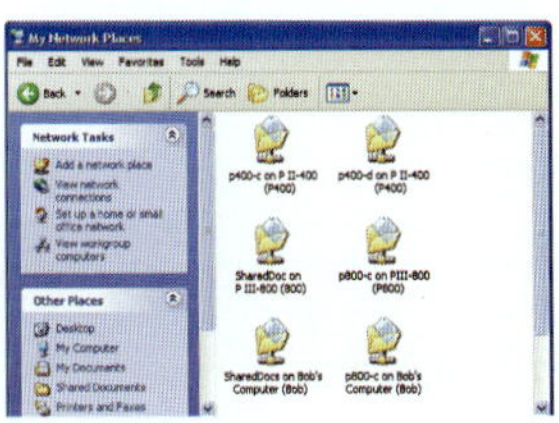

Building a local area network 97
The basic network configuration 98
Sharing your folders with others 102
Accessing other network drives 104
Printing over the network 107
Connecting several PCs to the Internet over a network 109
Monitoring network connections 111

7. World Wide Web! – Online with Windows XP 113

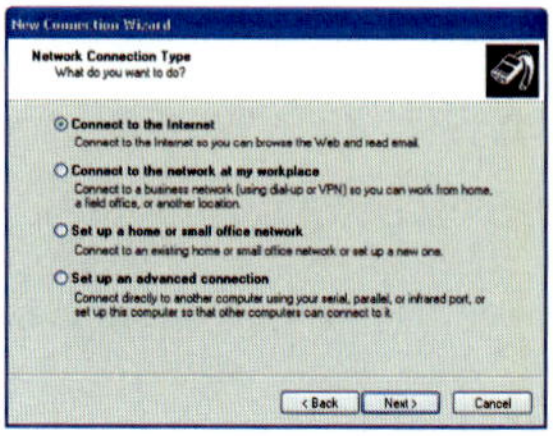

Establishing and optimizing Internet connections 113

Establishing and closing Internet connections automatically 117

Remedying problems with Internet connections 119

When Web sites do not load – What the error messages mean 121

Finding information on the Web 123

Downloading files safely and problem-free 125

Surfing securely with Internet Explorer 127

Protect your privacy from cookies 131

Receiving your favorite station over the Internet 134

8. Worldwide mail – E-mail with Outlook Express 136

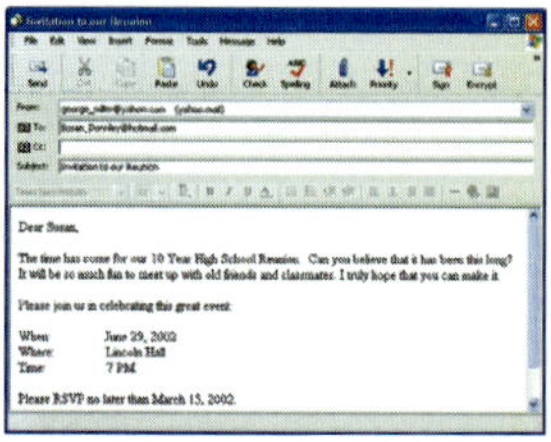

Setting up an e-mail account 136

Sending and receiving e-mail messages 139

Sending files via e-mail 140

Protection from e-mail viruses 141

Confirmation of delivery for e-mails 142

Adding a personal touch with signatures 145

The e-mail is returned with an error message 148

9. Questions, answers, and more ... 150

Why can't I carry out the XYZ function as described in the book? 150

Why can't I record MP3s with Windows Media Player? 151

What do I do if the screen suddenly turns blue? 151

Are there really no more DOS functions? 152

Where can I find more information about the topic of XYZ? 152

Do you still have questions? 154

Internet addresses for Windows XP 154

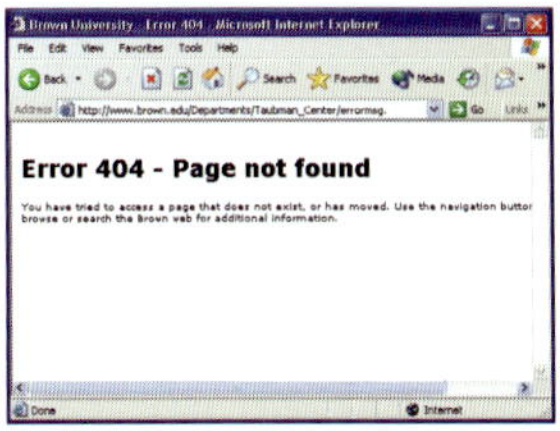

Index 155

1. eXPerience – The most important new features at a glance

According to Microsoft®, the creator of Windows®, Windows XP stands for the completely new experience the users of this operating system will have. And, sure enough, the initial start after the installation proves to be a real surprise to Windows veterans. Windows XP has an entirely new look – and it takes time to get used to it. But a lot of changes have also been made under the hood. Many important settings, for instance, appear in entirely different places because of the task-oriented user interface. The familiar control panel seems to have been made redundant, the start menu looks different, and so on...

In the first chapter of this book, you become acquainted with the most palpable new Windows XP features through a brief overview. These features are noticeable at first glance, and without them, you could hardly use Windows XP efficiently. You learn the differences, and you see that ultimately not all that much has changed. You also discover how you can fall back on beloved habits even in Windows XP, should you prefer them.

Logging on and off in Windows XP

What is immediately striking when working in the new Windows XP are the new log on and log off procedures, as well as the new procedure to turn off your PC.

1 After starting Windows XP, you will first get to a Welcome screen that displays all user accounts, identified by names and a small image.

2 To access your Windows XP account, click your user name and enter the corresponding password. Then press [Enter] or click the green arrow button to finish your logon.

3 Windows then loads your user profile and provides you with your familiar user interface.

Logging off and switching users

Apart from visual changes, there are also functional alterations. Windows does no longer limits itself to managing user profiles; it is now also possible to specify and control which files and documents are accessible to all users and which ones should remain inaccessible. In addition, Windows XP operates a multi-user system, which means that if a user wants to log on, the previous user does not necessarily have to log off. Instead, the previous user's programs and documents can remain open in the background without disturbing the second user. It is possible to switch between the two users without delay instead of logging on and off each time.

1 To log off or to switch to a different user account, click the *Log Off* icon in the Start menu.

2 Then, you can choose if you only want to *Switch User* or if you actually want to *Log Off*. In the first case, your programs and documents remain open, and you can return to them at any time. If you choose the latter option, you log off your account completely, and the PC is available to another user.

3 In either case, Windows XP reverts to the familiar welcome screen. If you chose the option *Switch User*, you can discern from the term *Logged on* underneath the name of the user profile that was used last that it is still active in the background.

Note

The administrator user

With the new user concept, Windows XP introduces a special user type, the *computer administrator account*. This user profile is usually already created during the installation. Only this user can extensively change system settings. This way, it is possible to share your PC with inexperienced users who might otherwise accidentally change the settings. If you don't have access to certain functions and settings in Windows XP, it is most likely because you are using a user profile without administrator privileges. You can, however, grant such privileges to any user by changing the user's profile accordingly.

Turning off Windows XP

1 To turn off your Windows XP PC, use the *Turn Off Computer* icon in the Start menu. To do so, you don't need to log off beforehand. If users are logged on at that time, Windows XP automatically closes their sessions.

2 Windows XP then displays the *Turn off computer* menu. Here, you have the option of putting your PC in *Stand By* mode. This way, the system is "frozen" in its current state and saved on the hard drive so that it can be restored when starting it the next time. Any open programs, documents, and so forth remain the same, and you can continue your work immediately when you turn your computer on again. This mode only works if all hardware components support this mode of operation. It is therefore essential to try out this feature before you use it seriously.

3 Click *Turn Off* to shut down your PC entirely, that is, Windows XP shuts down first and then your computer is turned off automatically.

4 Finally, you have the option to *Restart* your computer. Windows XP shuts down again; the PC is not turned off, however. Instead, a cold boot is carried out so that the computer is restarted from scratch.

The new Windows desktop

With Windows XP, Microsoft has introduced an entirely new visual design to its products. Windows-experienced users notice that rough edges and corners have been replaced by smooth curves and rounded edges. It seems like Microsoft said goodbye to the typical corners and edges. An inclination to colorful elements can also not be ignored. Windows XP is intended to be a very special visual experience. Playful effects such as the fading in and out of menus and message windows top off this new visual design. Let's hope that other areas perform equally well beneath this lavish façade.

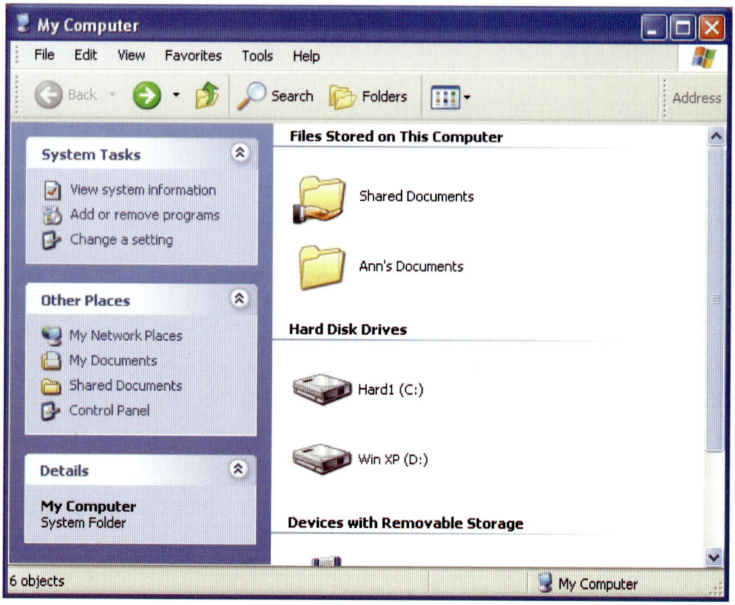

Restoring the classic Windows look

First, the most important aspect: If you don't like the new XP look and you would prefer to have your classic Windows back,it is possible to run Windows XP with its classic look, which has hardly undergone any changes since Windows 95, by activating a special desktop design. You can take a detailed look at designs in chapter 2. For now, proceed as follows to restore your familiar Windows look:

1 Click *Start/Control Panel* to open the control panel (or at least what's left of it).

2 Click *Appearance and Themes*.

3 Select the command *Change the computer's theme*.

4 This leads you to the *Themes* tab of the display properties. Select the entry *Windows Classic* from the *Theme* list box.

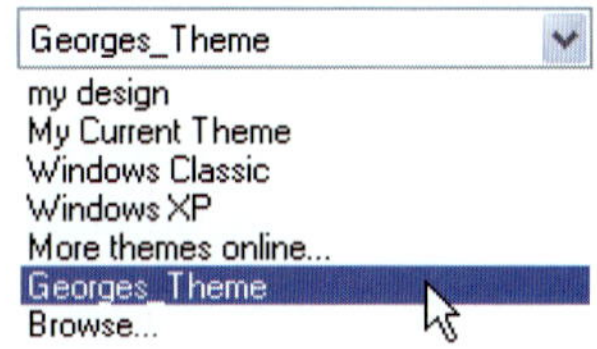

5 Click *OK* to apply your new settings.

6 Windows XP restores the classic look, which might take a couple of seconds depending on your computer. The new (familiar) look is immediately available to you without having to restart the computer.

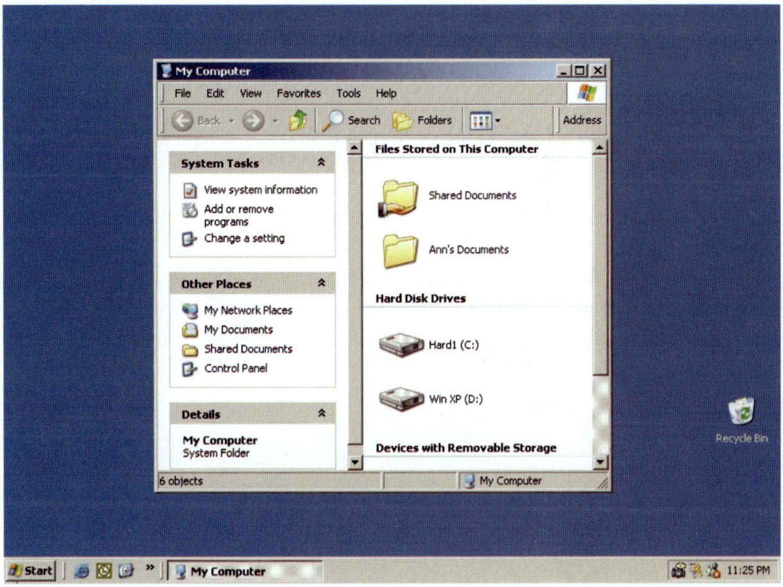

Note

So many choices

You must decide for yourself if it is reasonable to ignore the new Windows look and stick to the classic one. Ultimately, it doesn't take long to become familiar with the new appearance and work environment. In addition, the new Windows look offers a few new functions and advantages, as you discover on the following pages. That's why the new Windows XP look is used continuously in this book. It might therefore be easier for you, if you don't change the new appearance for now. Should you want to change it later on, you can quickly restore the classic look at any time, as previously explained. And who knows – maybe you'll even like the new appearance by the time you get to the last page.

Controlling graphic effects

Apart from the new overall look, a number of dynamic desktop effects soon catch your attention. Menus and ScreenTips are not simply displayed - they fade in gracefully; fonts are artificially smoothed; the mouse pointer and menus cast a shadow on the windows below, and, consequently, the entire desktop obtains a three-dimensional appearance. All this sounds great but if you have an outdated PC with a low processing speed, these effects use substantial resources. Especially the fading in and out of menus takes considerable time. Even if you only want to change a minor setting, it takes a number of seconds until the menu appears and disappears. Fortunately, most of these effects can be set individually.

1 To control the visual desktop effects, go to *Control Panel/Appearance and Themes*.

2 Click the *Display* control panel icon.

3 Click the *Display* tab in the *Display Properties* dialog window. Here you can find the *Effects* button in the lower right corner. The effects menu opens, in which most of the visual effects can be defined.

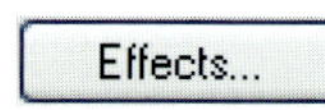

4 The top entry is devoted to the transition effect that is used for the display of menus and tool tips. If you don't want this kind of effect at all, disable the option. Otherwise, you have the choice between the default *Fade effect* and the *Scroll effect*, which you might know from previous Windows versions.

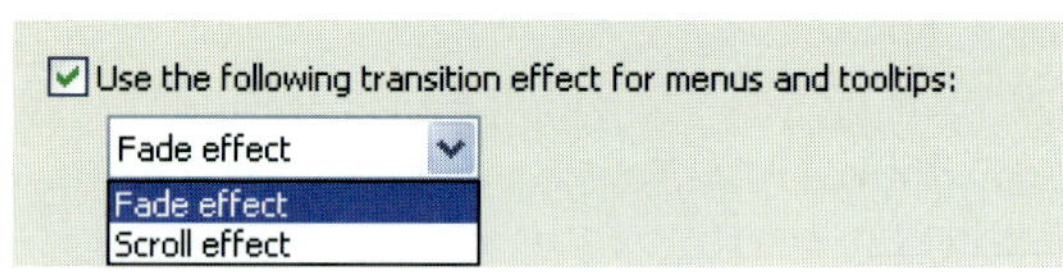

5 The second option allows you to smooth edges of screen fonts. Especially large font types appear considerably more appealing this way. This advantage, however, consumes additional resources, which can lead to a noticeable loss in performance when using outdated computers. In this case, you should disable the option entirely. If you want to apply the smooth edges effect

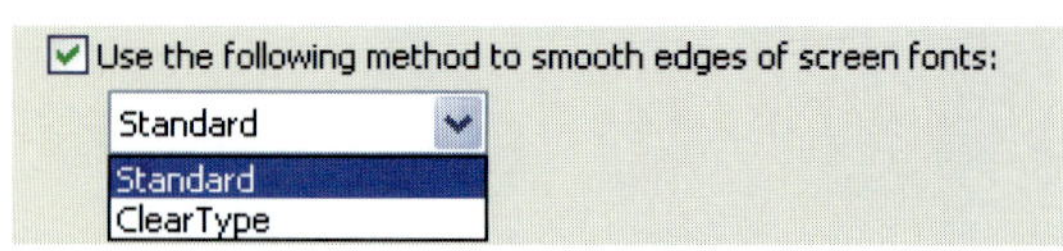

and you use a notebook or a flat screen monitor (LCD), you should select the *Clear Type* option to achieve better results.

6 You can turn off the three-dimensional shadows under menus by disabling the *Show shadows under menus* option.

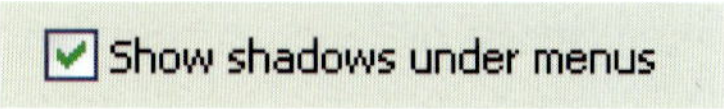

7 The option at the very bottom is another new Windows XP feature: *Hide underlined letters for keyboard navigation until I press the Alt key*. This way you forego auxiliary information about keyboard shortcuts for applications. If the option is enabled, accelerators only appear if you actually use the keyboard controls (for example, Alt).

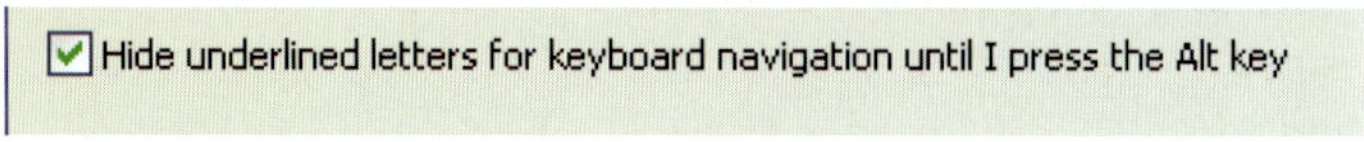

The new Start menu options

The taskbar and Start menu have also been refurbished in Windows XP. The Start menu alterations might be most noticeable. The Start menu is divided into two sections now; programs can be accessed on the leftside and shortcuts to the most important folders and functions are found on the right side of the menu.

Customizing the Start menu

The appearance and functionality of the Start menu can be customized through a number of options to suit your individual habits and preferences.

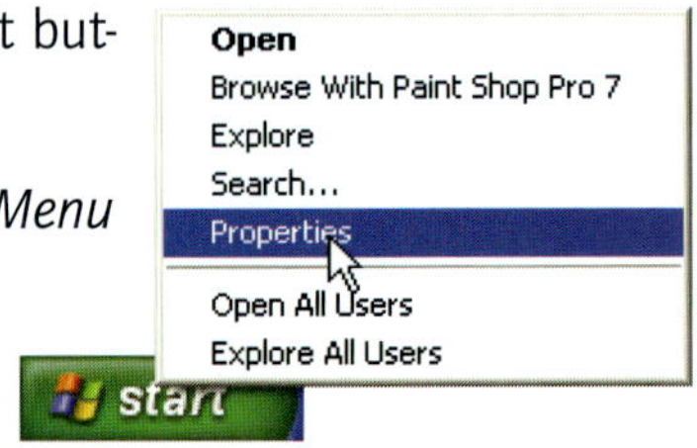

1 To customize the Start menu, right-click the Start button and select *Properties* from the pop-up menu.

2 Click the *Start Menu* tab in the *Taskbar and Start Menu Properties* dialog box.

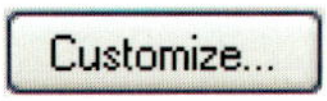

3 Under *Start menu*, click the *Customize* button to define the Start menu settings.

4 *Select an icon size for programs* under *General*. Depending on your personal preferences, monitor capability and your own vision, you can select highly visible *Large icons* or space-efficient *Small icons*.

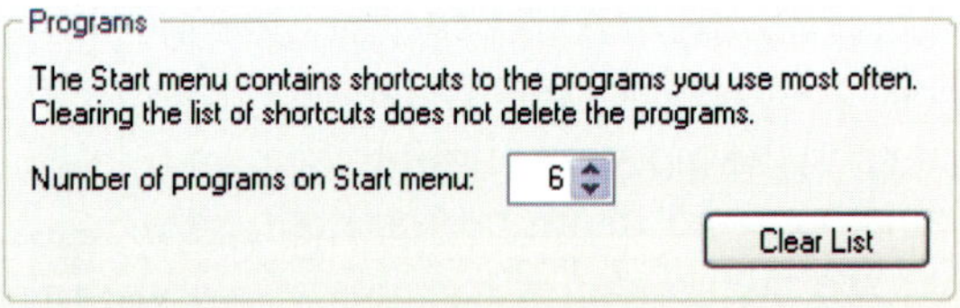

5 Under *Programs*, you can specify how many most frequently used programs should be listed in the Start menu. Please note that the Start menu becomes increasingly larger and complex with each additional program.

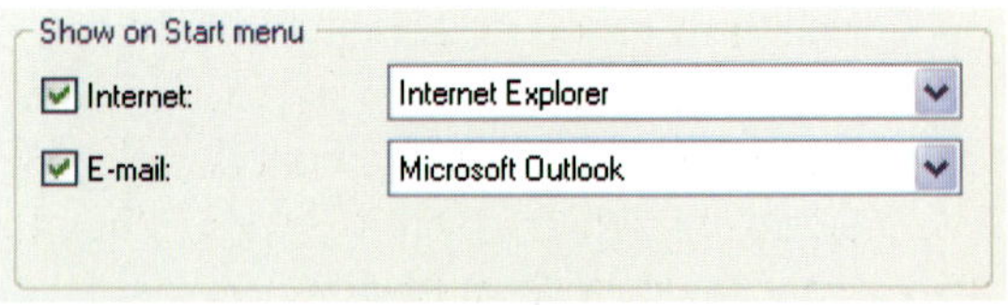

6 The applications that should be used for *Internet* and *E-mail* and that should also be displayed in the Start menu can be defined under *Show on Start menu*. All programs registered for these purposes can be found in and selected from the corresponding list boxes.

7 A number of additional useful settings can be found under *Advanced*. In the *Start menu settings* section, you can enable the option to open submenus when pausing on them with your mouse, for instance. This saves you a mouse click and time. In addition, newly installed programs can be automatically highlighted in the Start menu by selecting the corresponding option.

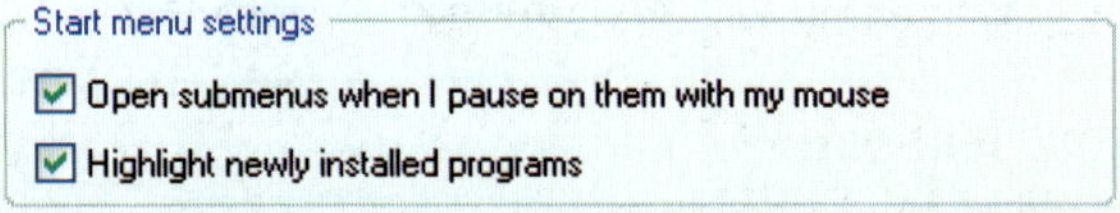

8 Use the *Start menu items* field to define which items should be displayed in the Start menu, and how they should be displayed.

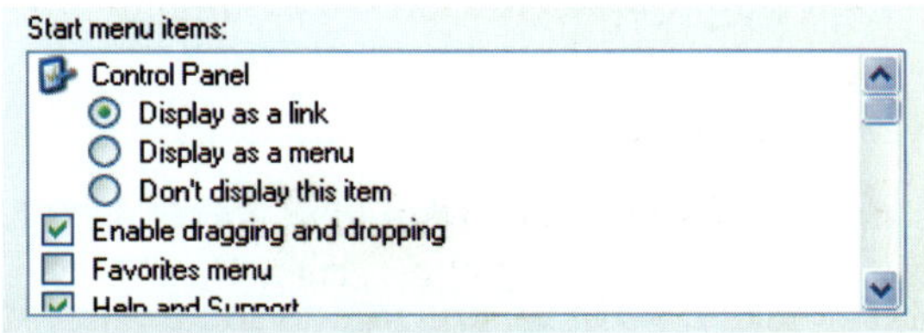

9 Select the option *List my most recently opened documents* to display the menu item *My recent documents* in the Start menu. This menu item provides convenient access to the most recently saved or edited files; its function is similar to the display of most recently used programs. Click *Clear List* to clear the list of most recently opened documents.

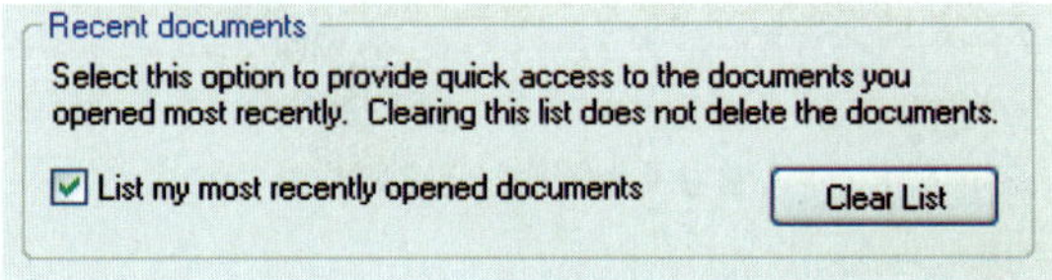

Back to the classic Start menu

As with many other new features, it also takes time to get used to the new Start menu of Windows XP. If you don't want to or cannot adapt to the new Windows look, you always have the option of going back in time. Windows XP can also display the Start menu in its previous appearance. This way, you give up a number of new auxiliary features and functions, such as the automatic display of the most recently used programs. Nevertheless, the classic Start menu allows for some flexibility that is not lost in Windows XP.

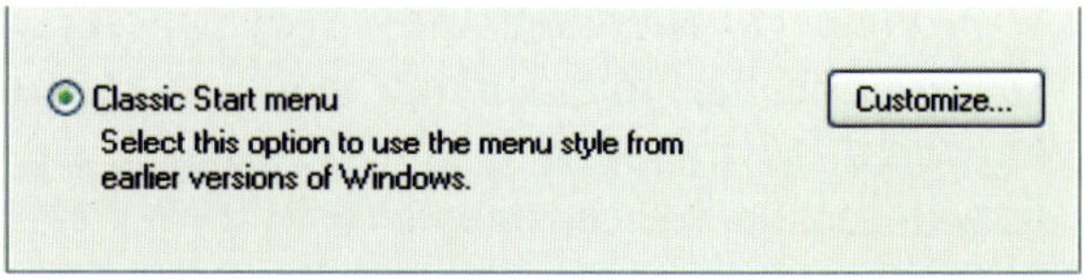

1 To change the appearance of the *Start* menu, right-click the Start button again and select *Properties* from the pop-up menu.

2 On the *Start Menu* tab, select the *Classic Start menu* option.

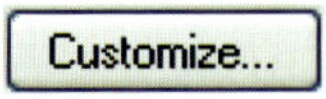

3 Click the Customize button to view the properties of the classic Start menu. Here you find the familiar Start menu options; you also have the option to add or remove elements.

A better overview for the taskbar

The taskbar has also undergone some renovations. It was crucial to the developers to create a taskbar that still provides a good overview, even if the number of running programs and open documents surpasses the average. The display of open programs in the taskbar, as well as the flexibility of the notification area at the right end of the taskbar, was improved.

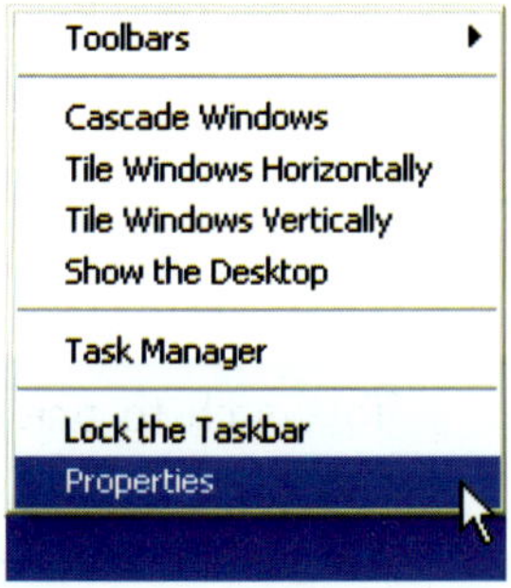

1 You can define the taskbar settings by right-clicking an empty area on the taskbar and by selecting the command *Properties* from the pop-up menu. The *Taskbar and Start Menu Properties* dialog window opens, containing the *Taskbar* section.

2 Here, you find the *Taskbar appearance* section that contains all options required to adjust the taskbar to your work style. Select the option *Lock the taskbar* to lock the taskbar into its current position and size. This function can also be applied to other toolbars.

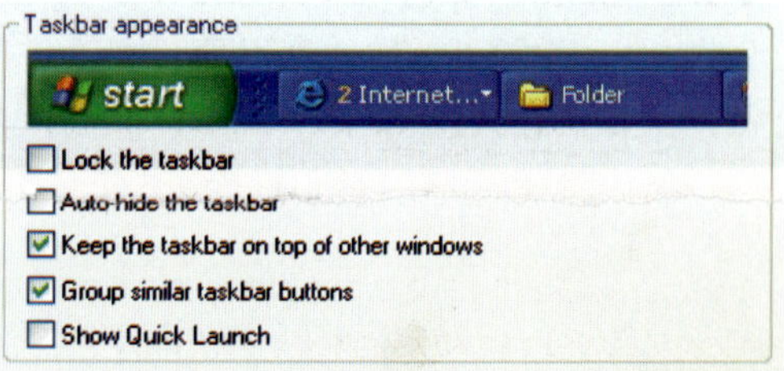

3 The options *Auto-hide the taskbar* and *Keep the taskbar on top of other windows* are already known from previous versions of Windows. They make sure that the taskbar is hidden if it is not used and that it is always displayed on top of other windows.

4 The option *Group similar taskbar buttons* is new, however. You discover in the next paragraph what this function is about.

5 The last option, *Show Quick Launch*, is new as well; it is used to show the Quick Launch bar in the taskbar, which contains shortcuts to frequently used programs.

Grouping elements in the taskbar

Being able to display similar elements in groups is one of the very useful new features of the taskbar. If the corresponding option (see above) is enabled, each document of a certain program is displayed as a separate button in the taskbar. Instead, all documents of the same kind are summarized and displayed as one button. This is done automatically, if the taskbar is full and the buttons would have to be minimized otherwise.

1 In this case, all documents opened in one program are grouped into one button. The prerequisite of this feature is, of course, that several documents are open in at least one program at the same time. You only see one button for this program in the taskbar. In addition, this button contains the number of documents open in this program.

2 To switch to one of the open programs or documents, click its taskbar button as usual. Windows XP does not switch to the program immediately but displays an additional menu offering all documents currently open in this program.

3 Click the desired document to switch to the corresponding program; the selected document is available for editing and viewing.

Similar buttons are only grouped if too many programs and documents are open at the same time, so that Windows XP would not be able to clearly display all of the individual document buttons in the taskbar. Windows XP undoes the grouping of buttons automatically, if you close programs or documents. Alternatively, you can still use the keyboard shortcut [Alt]+[Tab] to switch between programs or documents. This way, all of the open programs and files continue to be displayed at the same time.

Saving space in the taskbar notification area

The notification area on the right side of the taskbar contains small icons that represent programs running in the background. On one hand, the notification area provides an overview of the programs currently running; on the other hand, it allows you to access these programs by clicking the mini-buttons as an alternative to using the corresponding key combination. So far, this is nothing new. Windows XP provides a new notification area feature, however. You are now able to clean up the notification area. In particular, icons for programs that are continuously running in the background without you having to access them regularly might be disturbing and only taking up valuable taskbar space. Such icons can now be removed from the notification area without disturbing the program running in the background.

1 The option of hiding icons that are not required from the taskbar notification area is activated by default. In this case, you usually only see the icons of programs that you use regularly. All other icons are hidden.

2 In addition, a small round button displaying an arrow is shown. Click this button to extend the notification area, so that all icons are displayed. This button appears only if a program icon is actually hidden.

3 Click the round button (whose arrow points into the opposite direction now) again to hide the minimized program icons that are not required.

Optimizing the notification area

The useful cleanup function of the notification area can be customized to suit your needs. You can specify exactly which icons should be displayed and which ones should be hidden. For instance, informative status displays can be displayed permanently, although you might never click them and although it might seem like the programs are not used.

1 Right-click an empty area of the taskbar or the notification area and select *Properties* from the pop-up menu to define your notification area settings. This way you open the properties menu that the taskbar and notification area have in common.

2 Under *Notification area*, you can first specify if Windows XP should *Show the clock*.

3 Use the *Hide inactive icons* option to apply the previously explained automatic cleanup function in the notification area.

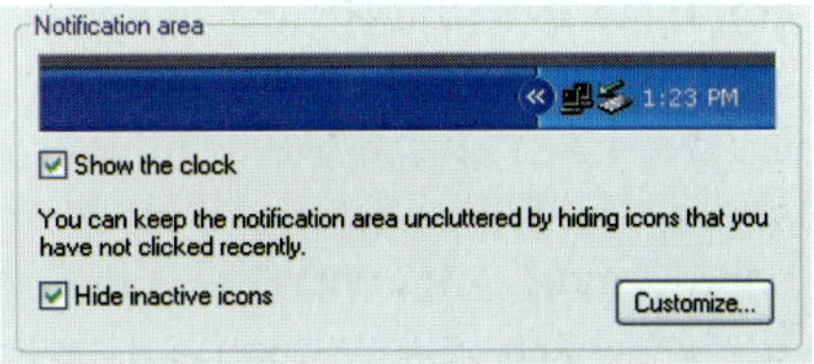

4 Click the *Customize* button to open the *Customize Notifications* dialog window. Use this dialog window to define if and when an individual icon should be displayed.

5 The section *Current Items* shows all icons that are currently displayed in the notification area.

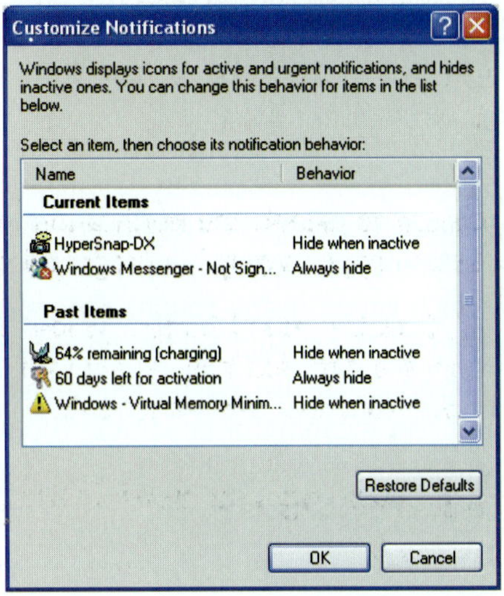

6 The section *Past Items* lists all icons that have been previously displayed in the notification area.

7 Once you choose an icon, you can select a certain *Behavior* from the corresponding selection field to specify when the icon should be displayed in the notification area. You can choose to *Always hide* or *Always show* an icon or leave it up to the automatic function by selecting the *Hide when inactive* default setting.

Accessing system settings

The following new Windows XP feature might have already caught your attention: All of a sudden, the numerous settings required to run your system look entirely different or they are found at entirely different locations. It almost looks like Microsoft rolled a dice to make the changeover to the new operating system as complicated as possible. It's actually not as bad as it seems, however. Most of the settings still look very similar; only the way of accessing them has changed t. This is due to the new task-oriented approach of Windows XP. Users should not have to call up and change a function; instead, they should be able to simply tell the system what they want to achieve. To ensure that you are successful in doing so, you learn where the most important settings can now be found.

1 Windows XP still uses the concept of the control panel that is, the concept of a central control room from which all settings relating to the system and its components can be accessed. The *Control Panel* can be accessed through the Start menu. The corresponding entry can be found approximately in the middle of the right column of the Start menu.

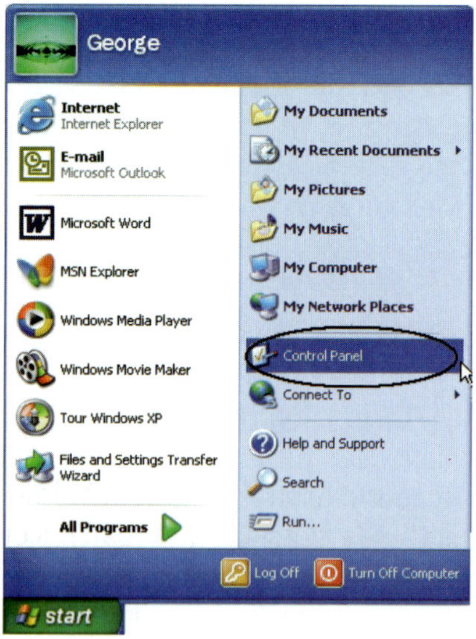

2 Click the entry to open the *Control Panel*. You won't find icons relating to the different control panel modules as you might have expected. Instead, the window is divided into different categories, and you must decide which category the sought-after settings belong to. This should not be too difficult as the categories are divided in a logical manner and contain meaningful headings. The individual categories often contain cross-references to related configurations, which can be helpful should you initially choose the wrong category.

3 Click one of the entries to switch to the corresponding category of the control panel. Here, you find different sections offering you different ways of getting to the desired settings.

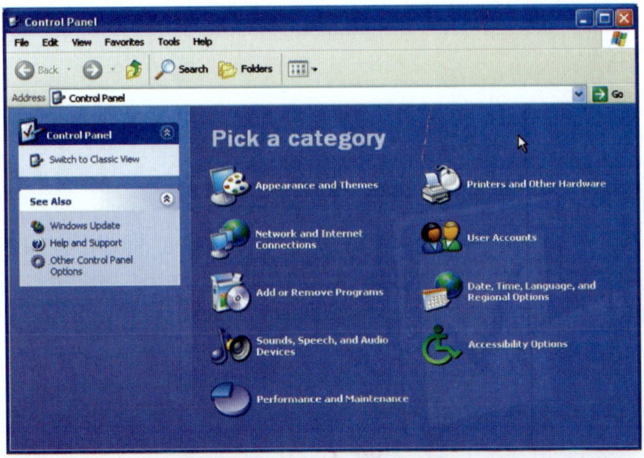

4 First, the *Pick a task* section offers you a selection of tasks relevant for the category you have chosen. If you want to carry out one of these tasks, click the corresponding entry. Windows XP then starts a Wizard or opens a menu containing the pertaining options.

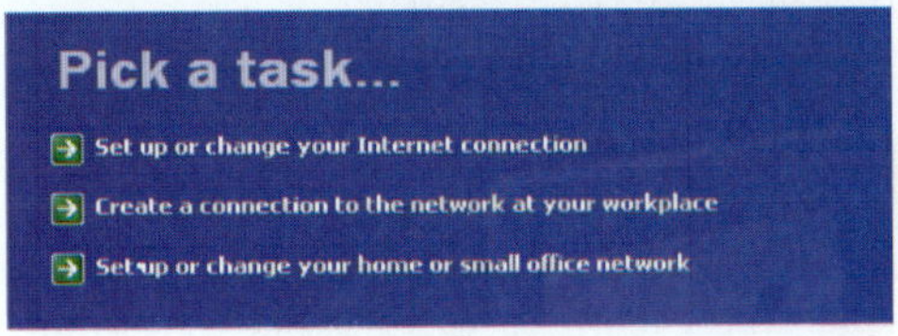

5 Optionally, you can also select a control panel icon. Windows XP either displays the classic control panel icons or the equivalent XP icons that belong to these system configurations. By the time you click one of these icons at the latest, you notice that in many cases few changes have occurred.

6 The *See Also* section on the left side provides cross-references to additional system areas related to the current control panel category. The references can lead to other control panel categories or to specific settings and folders such as *My Network Places*.

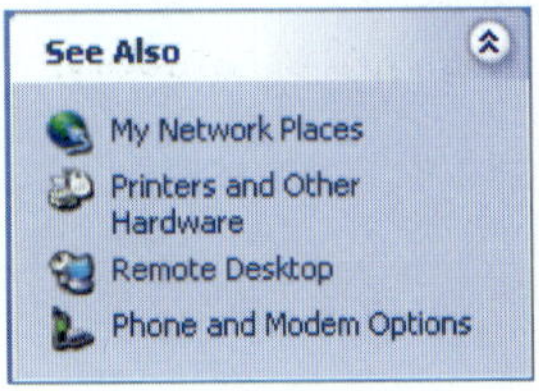

7 Every category contains a specific *Troubleshooters* section where typical problem areas of the corresponding system settings are listed.

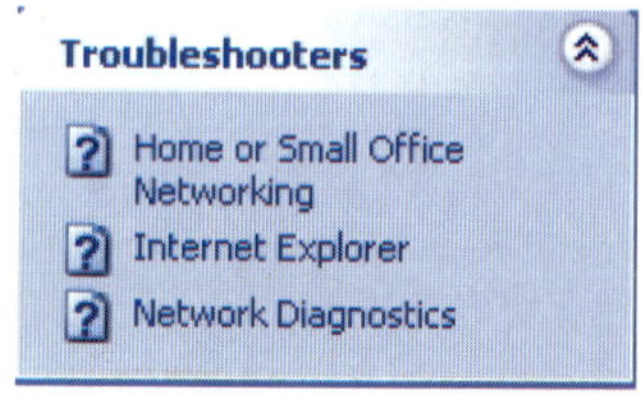

Restoring the classic control panel

It is also possible to revert to the classic control panel appearance of the previous Windows version if you don't want to or can't get used to the new task-oriented design.

1 Go to *Start/Control Panel* again to open the control panel.

2 Simply click the command *Switch to Classic View*, which can be found at the top left of the *Control Panel* section.

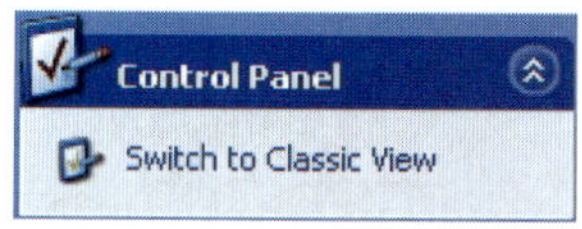

3 Windows XP then switches to the module-oriented look of previous Windows versions. For each category of settings a specific icon displays. Double-click an icon to open the corresponding menu or assistant.

4 If you want to restore the task-oriented view again, click the command *Switch to Category View* in the *Control Panel* section.

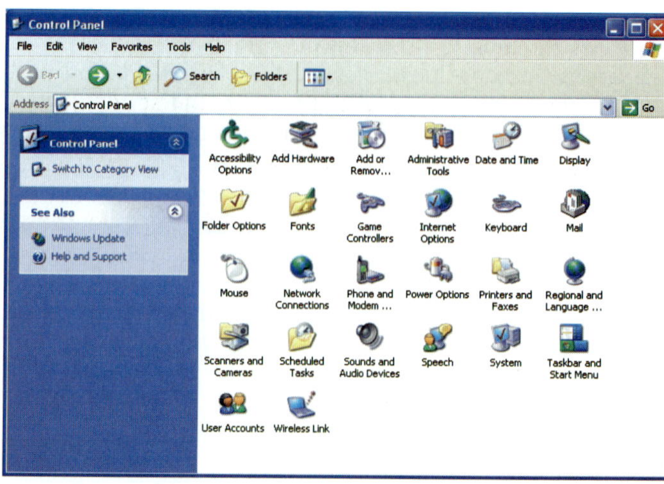

Activating Windows XP

One of the new features of Windows XP, which already stirred up some excitement in the preliminary stages, is the required product activation. As with all current and most likely all future Microsoft products, you must activate the operating system. This activation far exceeds the registration exercised so far. It has to be done – otherwise, Windows XP stops working after some time. In comparison to product registration, product activation is an anonymous procedure, however; no personal data is recorded. According to Microsoft, this technology is used for protection against suppliers of pirate copies that is, to make it harder to use Windows XP unrightfully.

Note

The product activation

When activating your product, you transmit a specific digital code to Microsoft. This code is based on the license number and several generated numbers that, in turn, are based on the hardware configuration of your PC. The code can be transmitted directly over the Internet. Optionally, you can also call the Microsoft Activation Hotline and deliver the information in person. Either way, you receive a personal activation code that can be used to permanently activate Windows XP. The rumor persists that additional data is transmitted to the Microsoft server when activating Windows XP online, whereas the activation over the phone is considered to be entirely anonymous. As independent investigations have disproved these allegations, you can use both methods without any worries.

There's a definite snag to the activation procedure, however: You must reactivate Windows XP if you modify the hardware of your PC on a large-scale. If you suddenly or over time exchange a number of components (for example, new 3D graphics card, bigger hard drive, faster processor, and so forth), you must repeat the activation procedure. If you activate your product online, you can only do so twice. However, you can still activate Windows XP over the phone as often as desired afterwards. Microsoft has agreed to handle/manage the activations generously. Besides, there is no reason to deny you the activation after exchanging a component or a new installation, if you have purchased your license legally.

1 After the installation, the Product Activation Wizard regularly reminds you about the required activation. You can also call up the Wizard manually by going to *Start/ All Programs/Accessories/System Tools/Activate Windows.*

2 During the first step, the Wizard asks you how you want to activate Windows XP. You can choose to *activate Windows over the Internet now* or to *telephone a customer service representative to activate Windows*. Select the method you prefer. You can only choose the online activation twice. First, the activation over the telephone is explained.

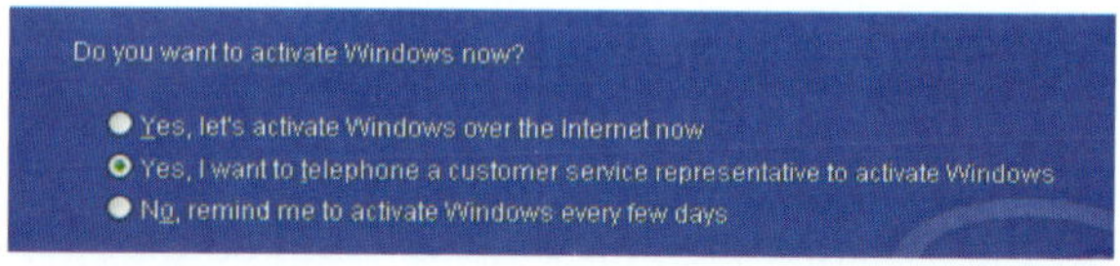

3 The next step is to enter your location. This is important, as it ensures that you contact the correct Microsoft customer service.

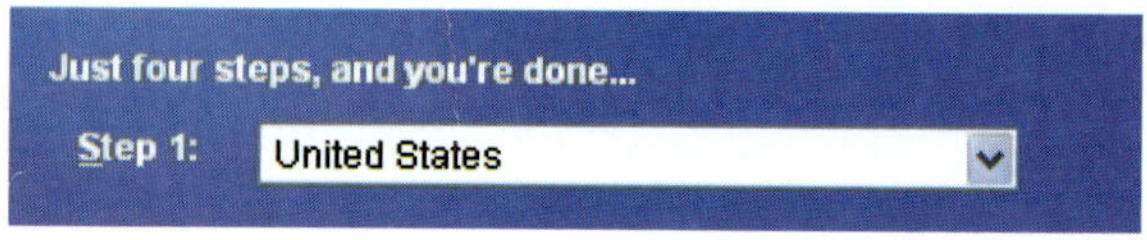

4 Then dial the toll-free number provided.

5 On request, provide the activation hotline customer service representative with the displayed installation ID.

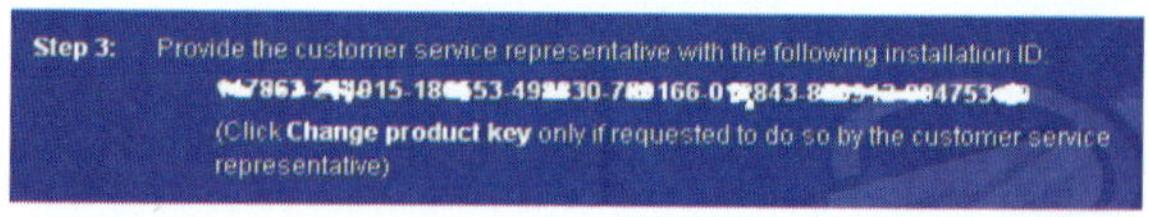

6 You then receive the confirmation ID from the customer service representative. It is advised to enter it immediately in the corresponding fields *A* to *G*.

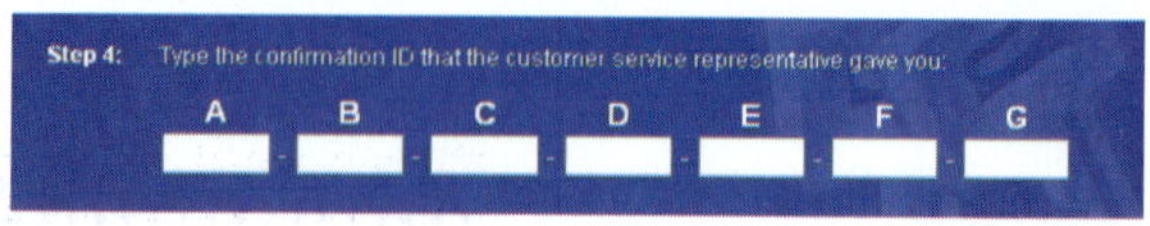

7 Finish your phone conversation and click *Next* to activate Windows XP with the entered code. The message *This copy was successfully activated* confirms the activation.

> **Note**
>
> **Keeping the confirmation ID?**
>
> By the way, there's no point in writing down the confirmation ID and keeping it for any possible activations in the future. The confirmation ID always has to match the installation ID. The latter, however, contains a random component inserted by the Activation Wizard. This way, the installation ID looks different every time, even if your hardware configurations have not been changed.

Activating Windows XP online

Activating Windows XP over the Internet is very similar. It is actually a lot faster and less complicated, as the whole procedure is fully automated and there's no need to read lengthy number codes to one another.

1 The first step is to select the option *Yes, let's activate Windows over the Internet now*.

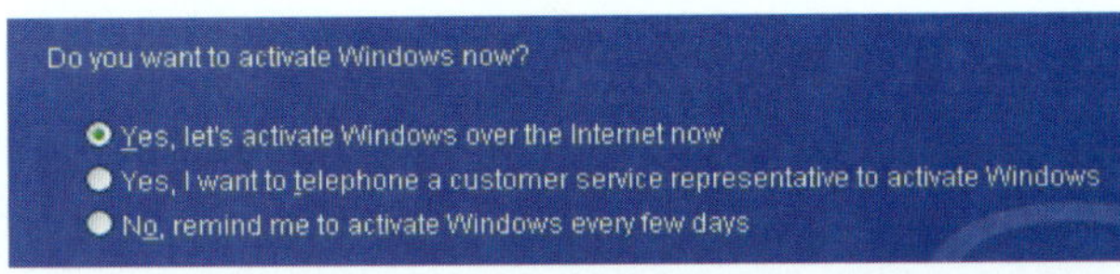

2 You must then decide if you also want to get registered as an XP user at the same time. As this is not necessary, you can decline by selecting *No*. The registration would unnecessarily prolong the entire procedure, as you would have to fill in a whole number of personal data - which is quite different from an anonymous activation.

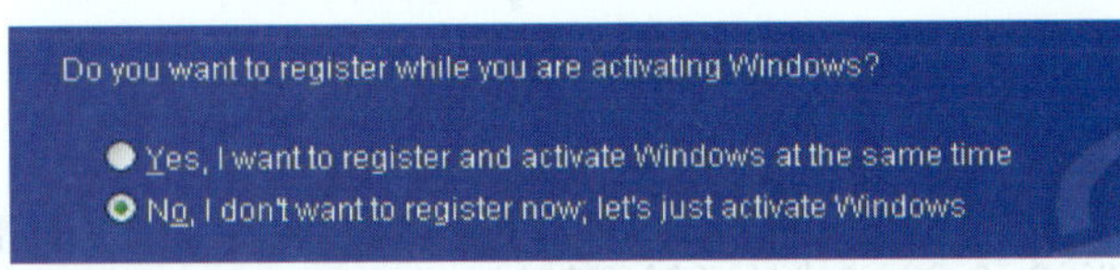

3 Everything else is fully automated. If you are connected to the Internet and you click *Next*, the Wizard accesses the activation server, transmits the installation ID, receives the confirmation ID and automatically activates Windows XP. The entire procedure usually lasts only a couple of seconds.

2. This is my Windows – Customizing XP

Chapter 1 already introduced the XP desktop that is seen as the central user interface from which programs and documents to be processed are opened. In addition, all important functions and settings can be accessed from there. It is therefore important to optimize the desktop according to your personal needs and individual working method. In addition to the desktop, however, Windows XP itself can also be optimized and customized through different settings. You learn the most important settings for creating a perfectly customized Windows system in this chapter.

Customizing the desktop background

You can use background images to personalize the desktop of your PC and make it more interesting. The selection of possible images is wide. Whether it is a picture of your partner, a painting of your favorite painter, or a picture of your dream car – let your imagination run wild! In chapter 5 you learn how to take your own pictures using a digital camera and how to use the pictures on your PC. Even snapshots can be used as desktop backgrounds. If you don't want to take the pictures first or don't feel like looking for images somewhere else, you can always use the pictures provided by Windows.

Note

Background images and memory

Background images not only look nice (most of the time), they also take up a lot of memory on your PC. In addition, the required processing time for recalculating the background image (for example, when opening, closing or switching programs) increases with the size of the picture. Outdated PCs with limited memory and processing resources can be considerably slowed down if a screen-filling background image is used at a high resolution (1024 x 768 and up). In this case, you should probably do without background images. If you are using a newer model with abundant memory and a fast processor, you don't have to worry about it.

1 To select a background picture for your Windows PC, go to *Start/Control Panel/Appearance and Themes* to access the desktop settings of Windows XP.

2 Select the task *Change the desktop background.*

3 The *Display Properties* dialog window opens. Use the *Background* section of the *Desktop* tab to define all background settings. The top half of the dialog window contains a preview monitor that displays the current desktop background. If you change the background settings, you can immediately see the results on the preview monitor.

4 The *Background* section contains a list of available background images. These can be image files as well as Web sites located in the Windows root directory. Select the top entry (*None*) if you don't want to use a desktop background image. Once you select a file, it is immediately displayed in the preview monitor. The monitor also displays the size of the image (minimized) or indicates how much of the desktop area it will cover.

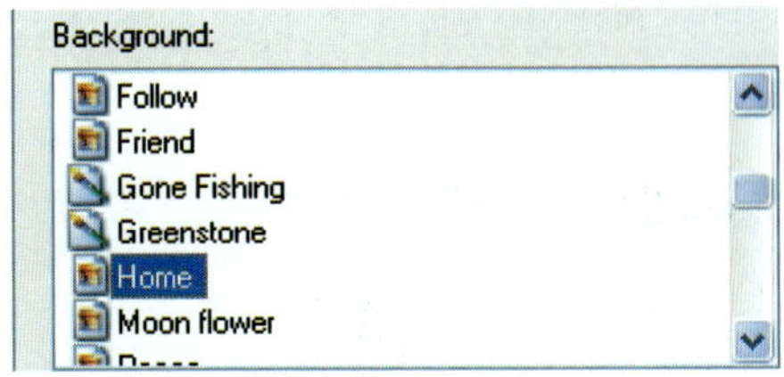

5 To optimize your screen, you can change the *Position* settings of your displayed image. A number of different options are available.

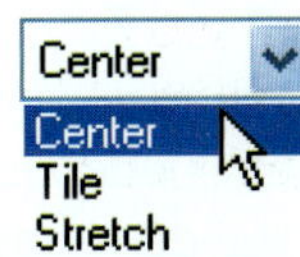

Position	**Result**
Center	The image is displayed in the center of the desktop and its original size is maintained. This option is only suitable for images beyond a certain size. Then the effect can be useful, as there is sufficient space surrounding the image, and any desktop icons placed around the image are visible.
Tile	The image is not placed only once; instead, it is repeated over and over until the entire screen is filled with it. Select this option if you want to use a relatively small image file to fill an area. Images that flow into each other and consequently appear like a single large picture are particularly effective (also refer to the following section describing patterns).
Stretch	This option enlarges the original image to cover the entire desktop. It is not suitable for all images, as the artificial stretching might cause unpleasant effects. Especially small images appear very grainy and unappealing.

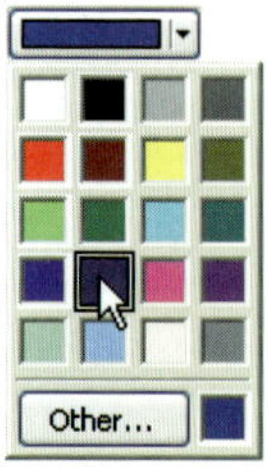

6 If the background image does not cover the entire screen or you don't use a background image at all, Windows XP displays a colored background. You can select the desired color from the *Color* selection box.

7 You can evaluate the results of the different settings on the preview monitor. Click *OK* to apply the new background image or color.

Note

Using images from other directories

The background image list only contains background-capable files that are stored in the Windows root directory (usually *c:\windows*). You can also use files from other directories by clicking the *Browse* button. The *Browse* dialog box opens, from which you can select the desired file. A selected file is temporarily added to the list of background images. Windows is able to display TIF, GIF, JPG, DIB and PNG image files as well as Web sites (*.htm* or *.html*) as desktop background. Consequently, only these file types are displayed in the *Browse* dialog window.

Using images from the Web as background

You may often come across great images that you would like to use as your desktop background when surfing through the World Wide Web in Internet Explorer. You don't have to go through the trouble of saving the image first and then setting it as your background. Internet Explorer offers a great shortcut instead.

1 Once you find a Web site in Internet Explorer containing an image that you would like to use as background, right-click the image.

2 A pop-up menu opens; select the command *Set as Background* to set the selected image as your desktop background.

3 Internet Explorer then saves the selected image as *Internet Explorer Wallpaper* in the Windows root directory (usually *c:\windows*). This image can be found under this particular name in the background list until you select another image from the Internet to be your desktop background.

4 You can also modify the position of this image if desired (see above).

Using different user interface themes

Windows XP has not only changed visually; there has also been an important functional change. Based on the skin function that is already used in MP3 players such as Winamp or Windows Media Player, it is now possible to centrally save and exchange the entire user interface configuration.

Windows XP uses *themes* that summarize all user interface configurations such as screensaver, background settings, color schemes, desktop content, as well as display settings. Instead of using many different menus to configure the settings, you can now centrally control all user interface configurations with the aid of themes.

1 To access the theme function, go to *Control Panel* and select the category *Appearance and Themes* again.

2 Select the task *Change the computer's theme.*

3 Access the *Themes* tab of the *Display Properties* dialog window. Here, you can select a predefined user interface theme from the *Theme* list box.

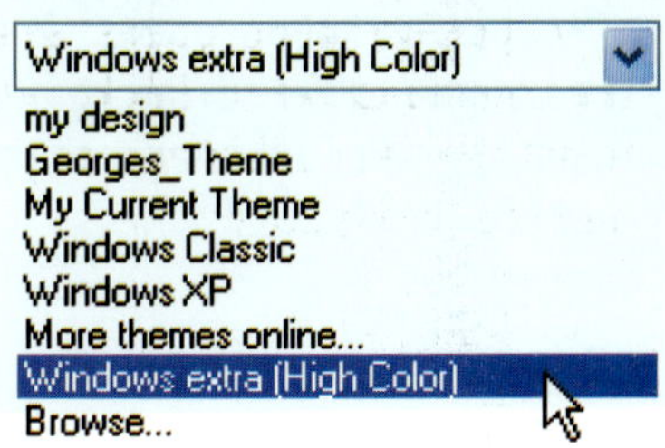

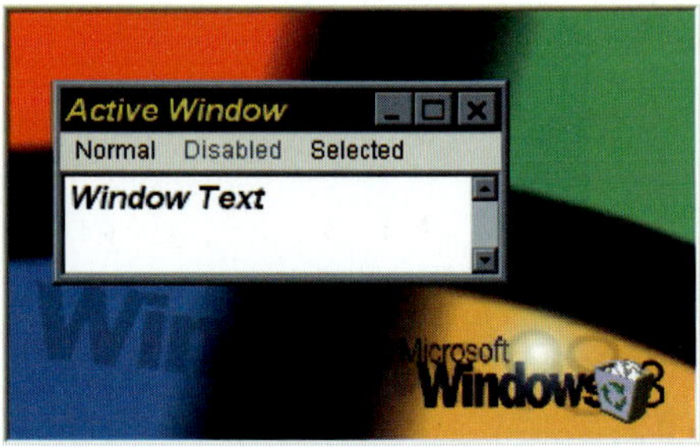

4 The large preview window in the lower section of the tab displays the currently selected theme. This way you can check out different themes without applying the changes to the entire desktop.

5 If you are not happy with the selection of available themes, select the entry *Browse* from the theme list to search your computer for additional themes that are not located in the root directory. You can also select the option *More themes online* from the list box to start Internet Explorer and search the Internet for themes. These themes can then be downloaded and used.

> **Note**
>
> **You prefer the classic theme?**
>
> The list of predefined Windows XP user interface themes also contains the *Windows Classic* theme. By selecting this theme, the user interface reverts back to its standard look, used since Windows 95. If you are used to this look by now and don't want to depart from it, simply apply the classic „retro" look to Windows XP.

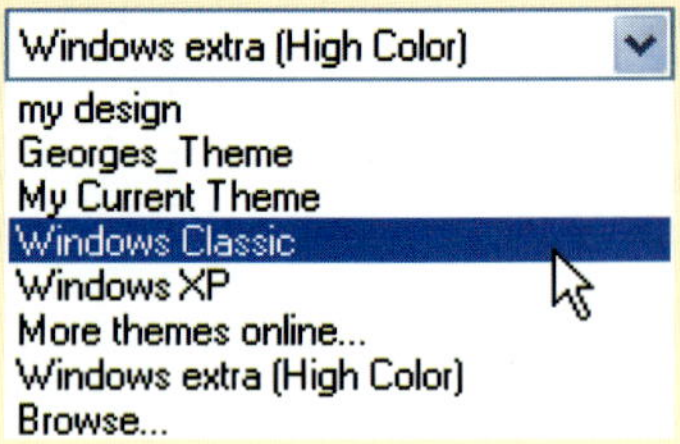

Saving your own themes

If you customize any of the user interface configurations and return to the *Themes* tab, the entry *My Current Theme (Modified)* will be displayed in the *Theme* list box. This customized theme can be permanently saved under its own name. You will thus be able to call up your customized theme at any time in the future.

1 To do so, click the *Save As* button next to the *Theme* list box.

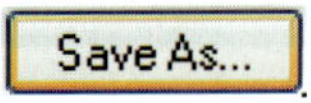

2 Enter a name for your theme in the *Save As* dialog window. By default, it is saved under *My Documents*; however, you can also choose another folder if desired.

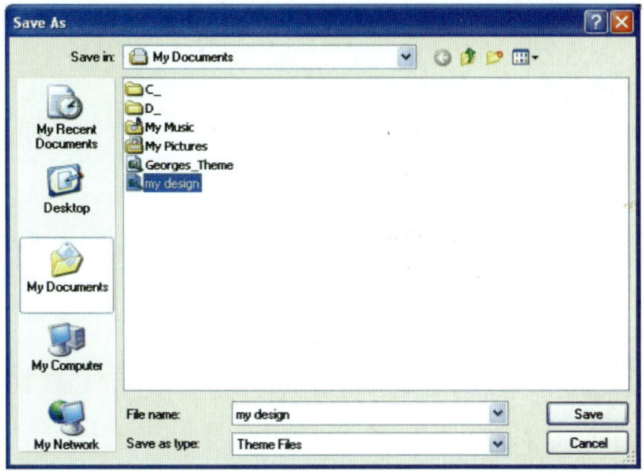

3 If you don't require a theme anymore, you can remove it by clicking the *Delete* button. Make sure that you have selected the correct theme, as no confirmation box appears before the deletion.

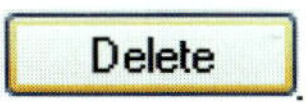

Mastering the Windows desktop

Windows XP uses a somewhat different concept than its predecessors in regard to the organization of the desktop. In the previous versions, the desktop was already decorated with different icons for programs and configurations. Due to the installation of programs and games, a number of icons were probably added to your desktop over time - and before you knew it, your desktop looked like a colorful mess! This fact annoyed many users; therefore Windows XP sets a high value on providing an uncluttered desktop. After the installation of Windows XP, only the Recycle Bin appears on the desktop. Additional icons are only added at the request of the user. In addition, you can also automatically clean up the desktop at any time.

1 To access the desktop configurations, go to *Control Panel/Appearance and Themes*. Then select the task *Change the desktop background*.

2 Click the *Customize Desktop* button located at the very bottom.

3 You can select the standard icons, which should be displayed on the desktop in the *Desktop icons* section of the following tab.

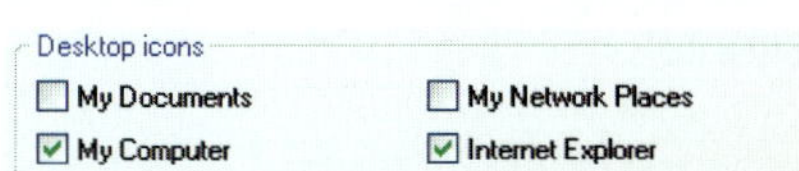

The following icons are available: *My Documents*, *My Computer*, *My Network Places*, and *Internet Explorer*.

4 Use the section below to define the images that should be used for the different shortcuts. Select one of the displayed icons and click the *Change Icon* button. A dialog window opens offering you a number of icons. You can search other files for more icons by clicking the *Browse* button.

5 In the *Desktop cleanup* section, you can select the option *Run Desktop Cleanup Wizard every 60 days* to automatically tidy up your desktop. This Wizard removes all shortcuts from your desktop that have not been used in the last 60 days. You can also call up the Wizard manually by clicking the *Clean Desktop Now* button.

Note

The desktop cleanup

Your desktop icons are simply shortcuts to particular programs, documents, and functions of your computer. They don't represent the actual files. Therefore, you can remove any unnecessary items from your desktop without hesitation, as only the redundant shortcut is deleted. The program or file remains on your computer and can still be opened by using the Start menu or Windows Explorer. The following section explains the desktop cleanup function in detail.

The Desktop Cleanup Wizard

Windows XP offers the Desktop Cleanup Wizard to keep your desktop free of unnecessary shortcuts and to provide a better overview. The Wizard can be used automatically every 60 days or it can be called up manually. It cleans up your desktop in only a few steps. If only keeping your real desk tidy would be that simple!

1 First, the Wizard greets you and introduces itself and its tasks to you. You can skip the introduction by clicking *Next*.

2 The Wizard now analyzes the shortcuts currently displayed on the desktop. It provides you with a list of all shortcuts, which also contains the date the shortcuts where last used.

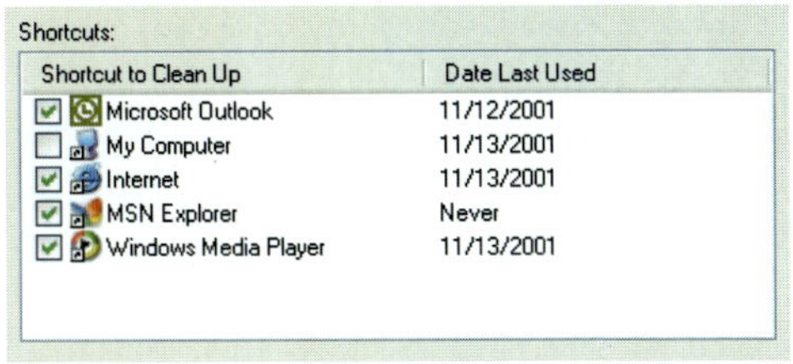

3 A checkmark is placed in front of all shortcuts that have not been used within the last 60 days or that have *Never* been used. The checkmark indicates that the Wizard wants to remove the particular shortcut. Simply remove the checkmark if you want to keep the shortcut. If you want to remove a shortcut that has actually been used within the last 60 days, place a checkmark in front of it.

4 Once you have selected all shortcuts to be removed, click *Next*. The Wizard then shows you a summary of shortcuts to be deleted. Confirm the list by clicking the *Finish* button.

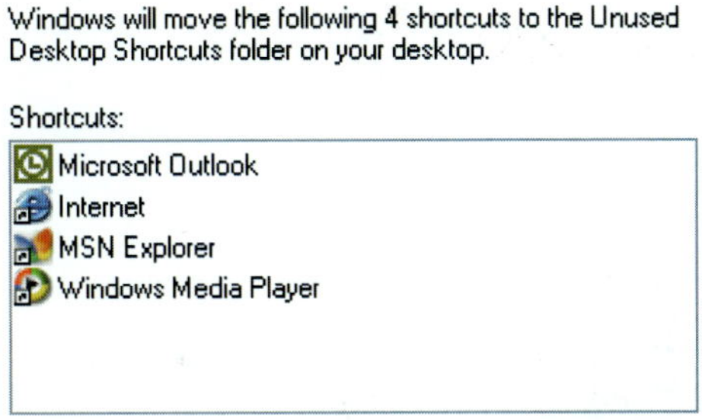

5 The Wizard then removes the selected shortcuts from your desktop. They are not deleted entirely for now; instead, they are moved to the *Unused Desktop Shortcuts* folder. You can quickly access them there if necessary. You can simply delete the shortcut to this folder if you find it disturbing. This way, the shortcuts contained in it are permanently deleted.

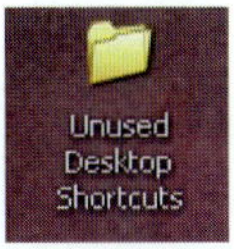

Great Explorer views for different purposes

Windows Explorer is the central tool for working with files and documents. So far, Microsoft has improved and extended this important tool with every new Windows version. The Explorer of Windows XP has also been equipped with new useful functions.

Explorer with task pane

One of the most noticeable new features of the Windows XP Explorer is probably the task pane. Windows XP is generally intended to be more task-oriented, which means that users should not start programs and open files; instead, isusers are supposed to select tasks that should be carried out by Windows.

1 Explorer displays a task pane on the left side, which is context sensitive (that is, the tasks are based on the folder content). If the folder contains a number of simple files, only standard functions are displayed in the task pane(for example, for creating a new folder, copying files, and so forth). To carry out a task, click the corresponding list item.

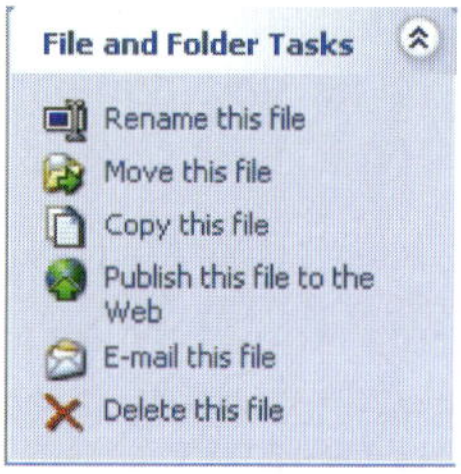

2 If the current folder contains files of certain formats, Explorer offers specific tasks pertaining to these files. If the folder contains image files, for instance, the *Picture Tasks* pane is displayed.

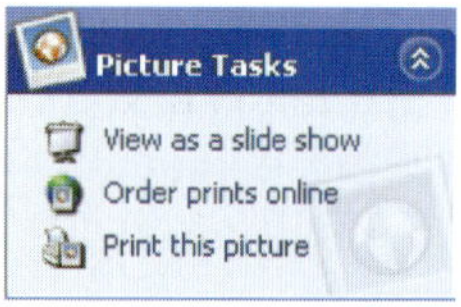

3 The task pane is very sensitive to the objects selected on the right side. If you select a file, the task pane displays file tasks. If you select a folder, however, Explorer immediately switches to folder-specific tasks.

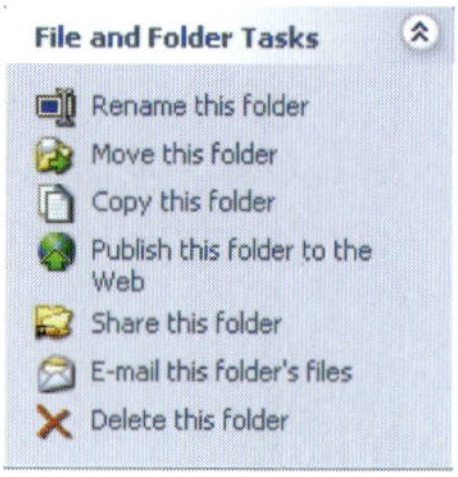

It takes some time to get used to working with the task pane. Once you get familiar with this function, however, you are soon able to save yourself the trouble of clicking around in menus and toolbars or using the right mouse button to open pop-up menus. Most notably, however, you can always keep track of the currently available options, which might be helpful to beginners.

Note

The task pane disappeared?

The task pane only appears if there is enough space available. If the Explorer window is too small (in particular too narrow), no space is left for the task pane, and it is hidden automatically. This is also the case when any of the Explorer bars appear (for example, *Folders*, *Favorites* or *Status*). The task pane is then displaced by the corresponding bar.

Disabling the task pane view

If you can't or don't want to get used to the task pane in Windows Explorer, you can disable the function and consequently free some space in the Explorer window to get a better overview.

1 To do so, select the command *Folder Options* from the *Tools* menu to access the Windows Explorer settings.

2 Here, you can find the option *Use Windows classic folders* in the *Tasks* section of the *General* tab. Select this option to disable the task pane.

3 Apply the changed settings by clicking *OK*.

Different views for working with files and folders

As usual, Windows Explorer offers different views for working with files and folders. Depending on your purpose, you can quickly switch between views.

1 You can click the *Views* button on the toolbar to quickly switch between the different views. Each time you click it, Explorer switches to the next view. If you want to select a specific view, you can also click the small arrow on the right of the button to open the view menu.

2 Alternatively, use the View menu, from which all views can be selected and activated. The following illustration displays the different Explorer views for files and folders:

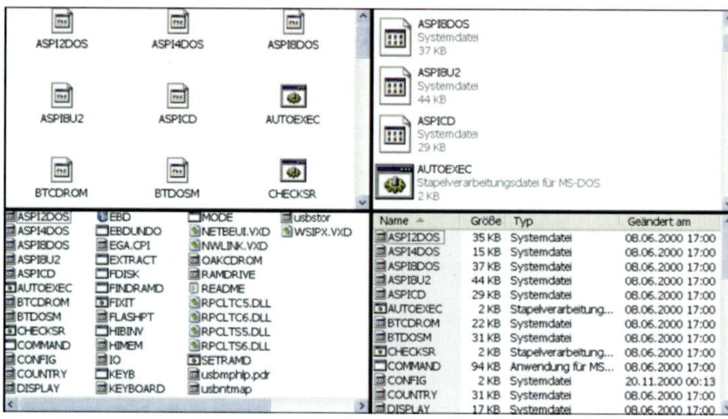

Views for working with pictures

There are two additional views that are specifically designed for working with pictures:

1 The *Thumbnails* view is available at any time, which means it can also be used with folders that do not contain image files. In this view, the folder contents are displayed graphically. „Regular" files appear with their file icons. In the case of image files, a minimized preview of the picture, a so-called thumbnail, is displayed. This way you can keep track of large picture collections without having to open each file individually.

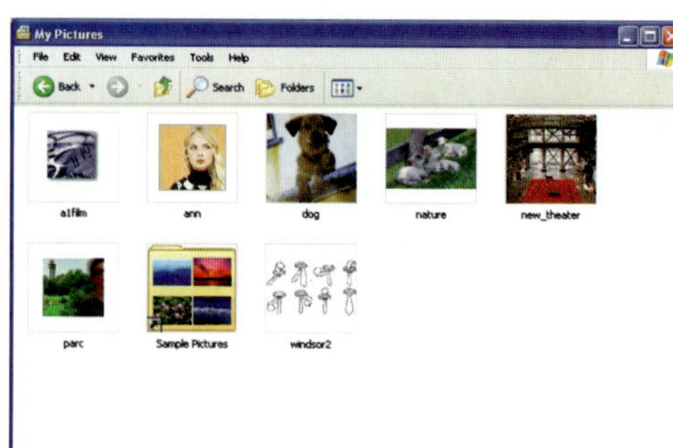

2 The *Filmstrip* view is even more specialized. This view is specifically designed for working with pictures and is only available if the current folder actually contains image files. In this view, all files are displayed as a filmstrip at the bottom of the window. The currently selected picture is displayed in a larger size (depending on the availability of space) in the top section of the window.

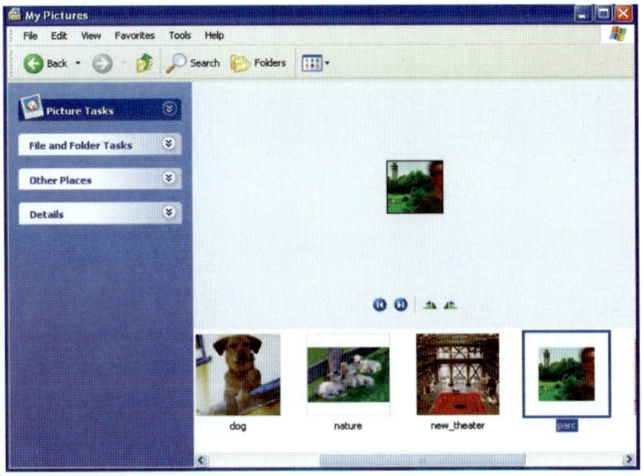

3 Click a filmstrip picture to view it in a larger size. You can also use the *Previous Image* and *Next Image* buttons located below the picture to scroll through the entire picture collection.

Creating your own toolbars

Windows XP offers a number of ready-made standard toolbars; unfortunately, there are limitations to modifying them. You can create entirely new toolbars, however, which work exactly the same way as standard toolbars. The only difference – their content can be entirely customized. You could work more efficiently by creating customized toolbars if, for instance, you frequently use different text documents that are standard templates for letters. You could create your own toolbar containing all letter templates. To type and print a standard letter, you would click the corresponding button on the toolbar. Your word processing program and document is then opened automatically.

Note

The key to success: folders

As in many other cases, folders also play an important role in the creation of toolbars. A toolbar is basically a shortcut to a folder. When creating the custom toolbar, you define the folder the toolbar should link to. If the toolbar is active, the toolbar items consist of the files that are contained in the designated folder. Therefore, your first step in creating your custom toolbar is the actual organization of this folder. You can use an existing folder and adjust its content if required, or you can create an entirely new folder and insert the objects that should be displayed in the toolbar. Note: If the main folder contains files from a number of different folders, it is advisable to create shortcuts to the original files instead of using copies of them. These shortcuts are then displayed in the toolbar. If they are clicked, the original files open.

1 To create a custom toolbar, right-click an empty area on the taskbar.

2 Select the commands *Toolbars/New Toolbar* from the pop-up menu.

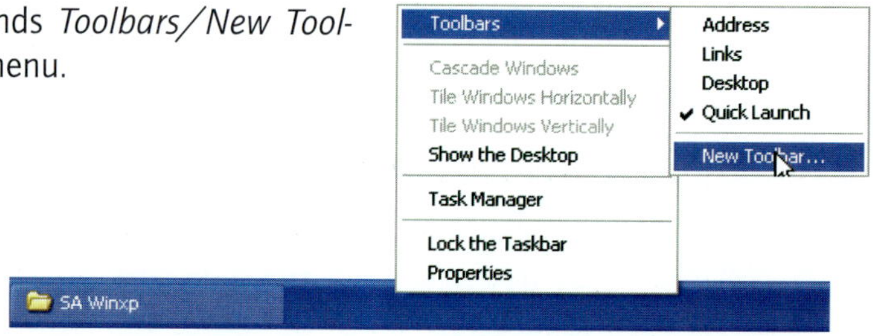

3 You can now select the folder whose content should define the toolbar in the *New Toolbar* dialog window. Simply click it to select it. Confirm your selection by clicking *OK*.

4 The newly created toolbar is initially part of the taskbar. As with any other toolbar, the function and desktop position of your custom toolbar can be individually defined. Simply drag the toolbar to the desired position while pressing the left mouse button.

5 You can also place your custom toolbars at the desktop edge and customize their settings so they only appear when required.

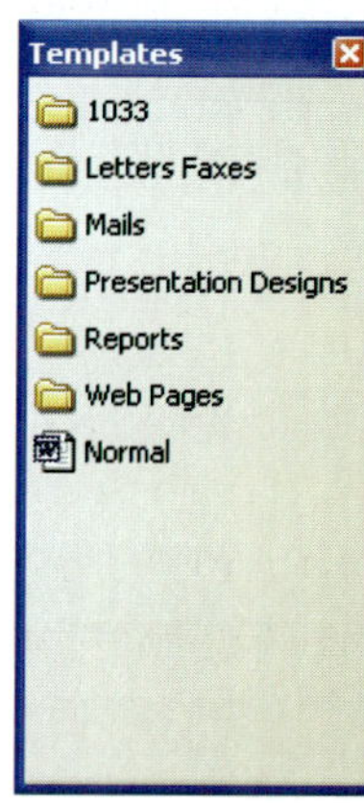

Customizing your toolbars

Once a new toolbar is created, it does not have to remain unchanged permanently. As with standard toolbars, the items of your custom toolbars can be edited and extended as desired. There are two different ways to do so:

- Open the folder that contains the content of your toolbar. Explorer provides you with the familiar file applications for creating shortcuts or moving and deleting items.

- It's even faster to customize the displayed toolbar directly. You can add items from other toolbars, Explorer, and other programs by simply dragging them into your custom toolbar. All changes are automatically applied to the main toolbar folder.

Closing custom toolbars

Custom toolbars might not be required permanently. As with standard toolbars, custom toolbars can also be removed from the desktop. Please note, however, that your own toolbars cannot be turned on and turned off the way standard toolbars can. Once a custom toolbar has been closed, it is gone for good. Should the toolbar be required later on, it has to be created from scratch again.

1 Click the title or on an empty area of your toolbar to open the pop-up menu.

2 Then select the command *Close Toolbar*.

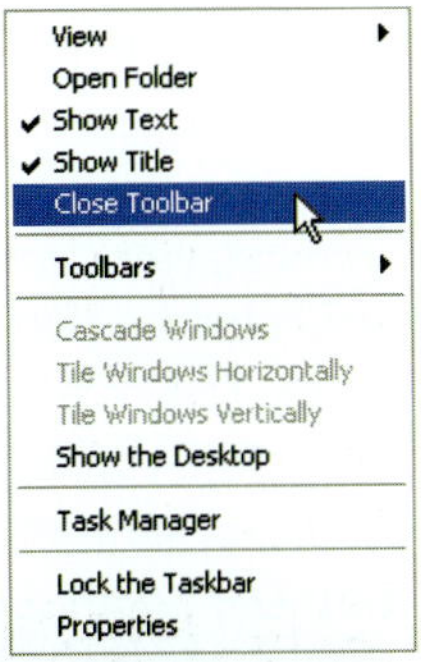

3 Before the toolbar is entirely deleted by Windows, a confirmation message box appears, asking you to confirm the removal. If you don't want this message to appear in the future, select the corresponding option before you confirm the message by clicking *OK*.

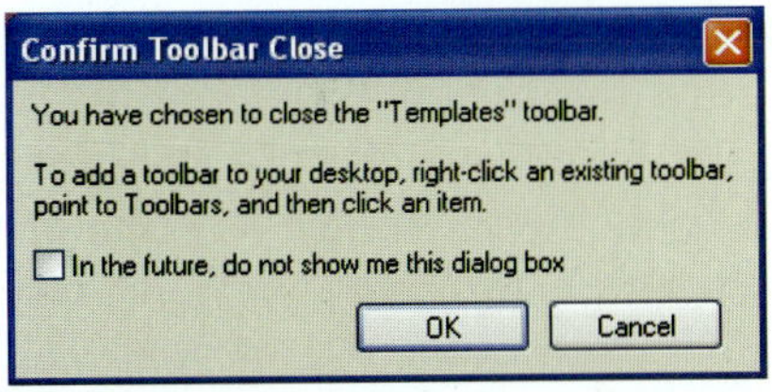

By closing the toolbar, you have simply removed the toolbar from the desktop. The folder containing the toolbar content is not deleted this way. This has the advantage that the toolbar can be recreated at any time. On the other hand, this folder is also taking up space. If you are sure that you won't need the original toolbar, you can delete the corresponding folder as well.

Transferring your customized settings to other PCs

If you frequently work on different computers and would like to work with the same user interface on all of them, you will greatly appreciate another new Windows XP feature. Windows XP provides you with a Wizard that makes it a lot easier to transfer settings from one PC to another. This way, you can conveniently transfer existing settings and files to other computers by using different media (for example, diskette or CD-ROM) or a network.

1 To transfer settings and/or files to another PC, go to *Start/All Programs/Accessories/System Tools/Files and Settings Transfer Wizard*.

2 The Files and Settings Transfer Wizard welcomes you. Skip the introduction by clicking *Next*.

3 First, you must specify if the Wizard is running on the *New computer* or the *Old computer*. If you want to collect files and settings to transfer them to another PC, select the option *Old computer*.

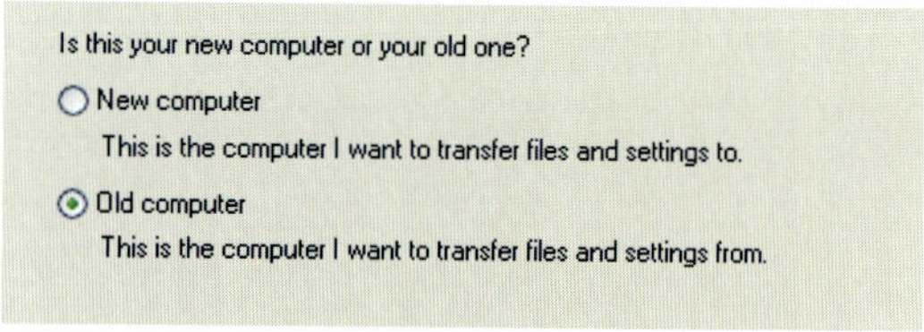

4 Next, the Wizard wants to know how the data should be transferred. The Wizard offers you a choice between *Direct cable*, a *Home or small office network*, a *Floppy drive or other removable media*, and *Other* data carriers as transfer options. Select the suitable transfer method. Please note that diskettes are only suitable for small amounts of data.

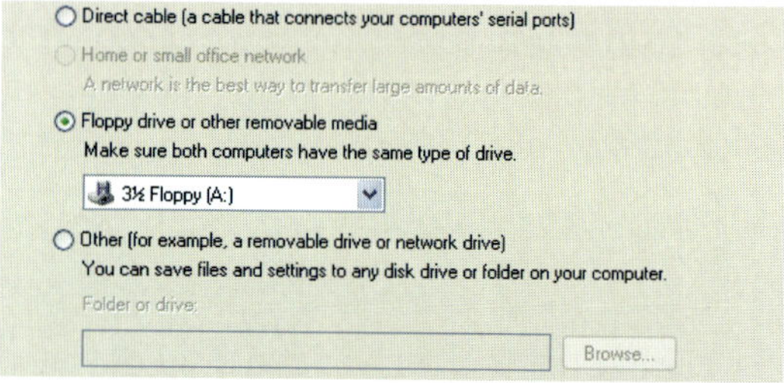

5 You can then choose to transfer *Settings only*, *Files only* or *Both files and settings*. Based on your selection, the corresponding items to be transferred appear in the right half of the window.

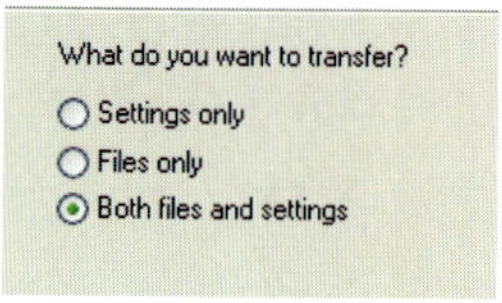

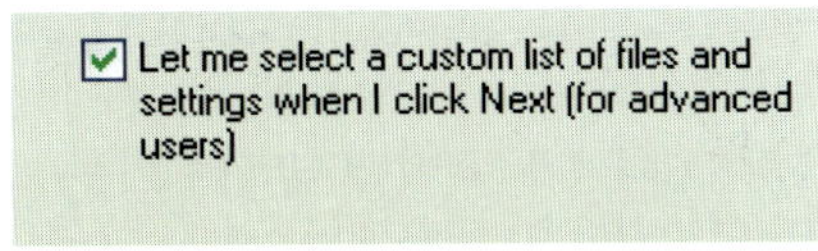

6 If you want to specify the settings or files to be transferred in detail, select the option *Let me select a custom list of files and settings* before you click *Next*.

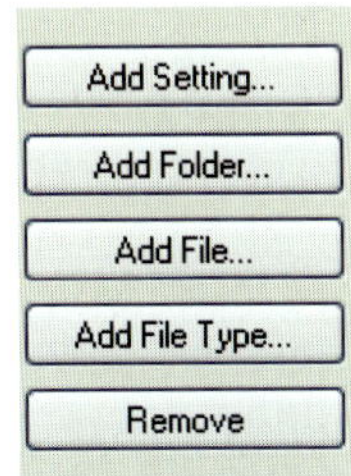

7 If you have selected the previous option referring to user-defined settings, you can now specify the items to be transferred. A list of possible items appears. Use the buttons to the right to edit the list, that is, to remove list items or to add items. A number of predefined items that you can select appears. You can extend the list of files to be transferred by adding entire folders, single files, or certain file types.

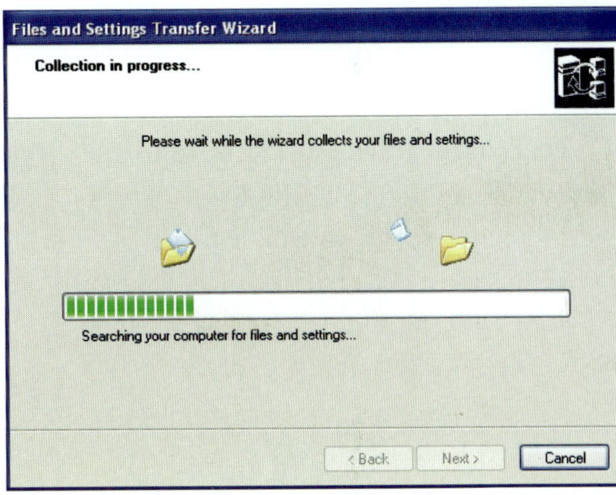

8 After editing the list according to your needs, click *Next* to proceed. The Wizard collects the required data and saves it as a file at the designated location.

9 Click the *Finish* button to close the Wizard.

Note

Transferring settings from other Windows versions

You can also use the Wizard to transfer settings from computers using older Windows versions (starting with Windows 95). To do so, you must transfer the Wizard itself to the corresponding computer first, as it was not supplied with previous Windows versions. The last section of this chapter explains in detail how to perform this procedure.

Restoring the data on the new PC

To restore the data on the new computer, use the Wizard again.

1 This time, select the option *New computer* during the first step, as the files and settings from another computer should be transferred to this one.

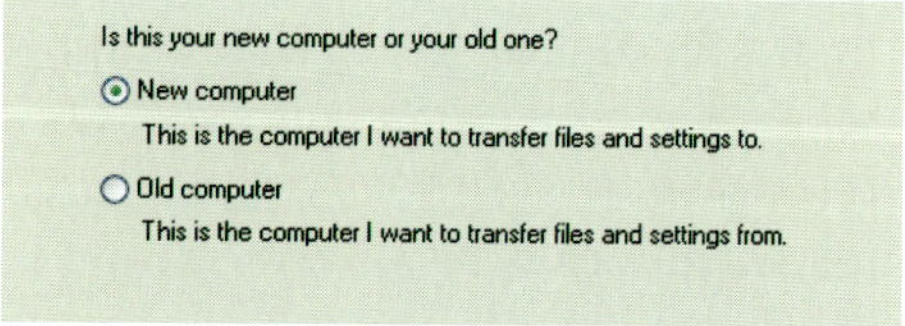

2 If you have already collected all transfer data on the source computer, select the option *I don't need the Wizard Disk* during the next step. Otherwise, you can now create a Wizard Disk for other PCs; this procedure is further explained later.

3 Next, you must define the location from which the Wizard should collect the transfer data. Again, the available choices are: *Direct cable*, *Floppy drive or other removable media*, and *Other*.

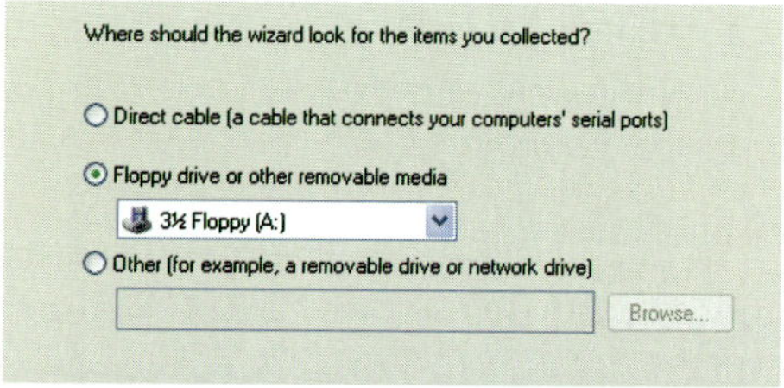

4 The Wizard transfers and restores the files and settings on your target computer.

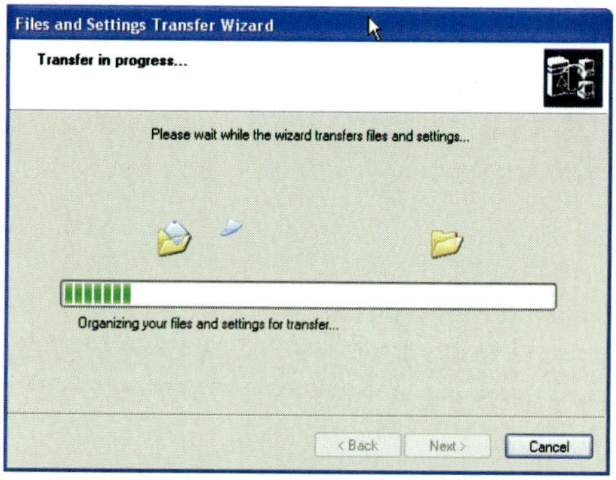

5 Click *Finish* to close the Wizard. You are asked to log off for the changes to take effect. Click *Yes* to confirm the request.

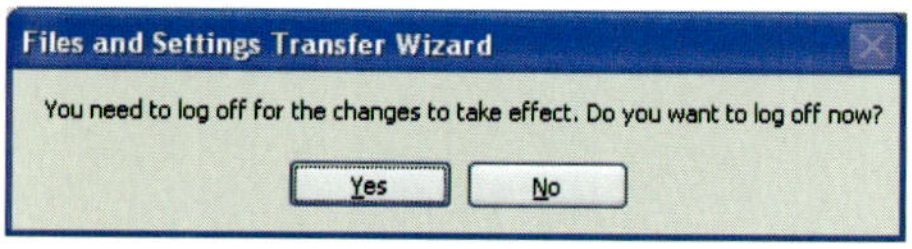

Installing the Wizard on other Windows PCs

The Files and Settings Transfer Wizard is a new feature of Windows XP. Nevertheless, its use is not limited to this system. You can use the Wizard to transfer data from PCs operating under Windows versions 95, 98, 98 SE, ME, NT 4.0, as well as 2000. The Wizard is not intended, however, to transfer data the other way around, that is, from your XP operating system to a previous Windows version. The procedure remains basically the same; however, there's one problem: The Wizard is not supplied with previous Windows versions. This problem can be solved, though, by transferring the Wizard itself beforehand.

1 Go to *Start/All Programs/Accessories/System Tools/Files and Settings Transfer Wizard* again to start the Wizard.

2 Select the option *New computer* in the first step.

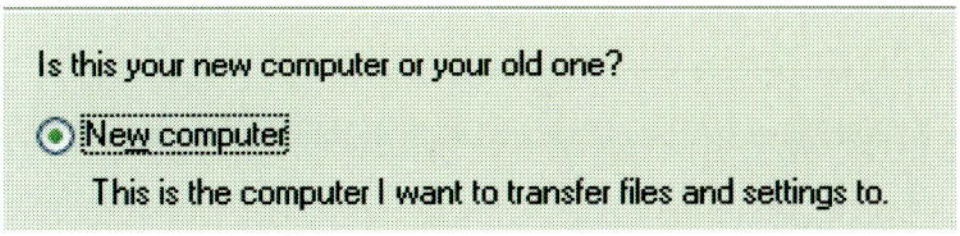

3 You are then asked if the Wizard itself should be transferred to another PC. Select the option *I want to create a Wizard Disk in the following drive* and specify the desired drive. The required files are not that big and easily fit on a regular disk. Click *Next*.

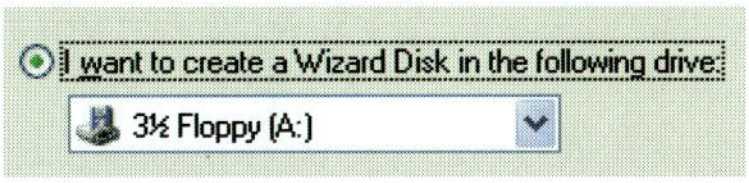

4 Next the Wizard asks you to insert a blank, formatted disk into the drive you selected. After you do so, confirm the message box by clicking *OK*. The Wizard transfers the required data to your disk.

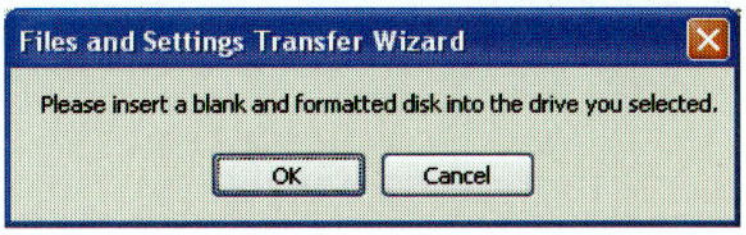

5 Switch to the computer running the previous Windows version and insert the Wizard Disk into the disk drive. View the disk content in Windows Explorer.

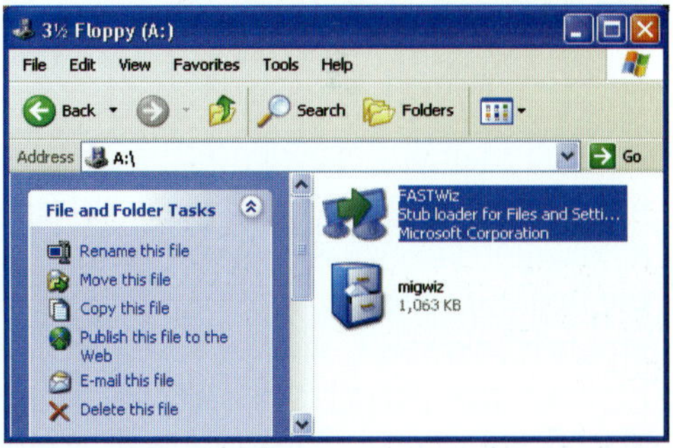

6 Double-click the file *FASTWiz.exe* to open it. This file contains the Wizard installation program. The Wizard starts instantly.

In comparison to the „regular" Windows XP Wizard, this version only allows the collection of data, that is, the selection between *New computer* and *Old computer* is omitted. The computer the Wizard was manually installed on remains the source computer.

3. Using hardware and software under Windows XP

The first two chapters have shown that the user interface of Windows XP has undergone a lot of changes.. Some of these changes are fundamental innovations whereas others are probably more like cosmetic alterations. If you actually take a look beneath the "hood" of Windows XP, you notice, however, that something has happened there. Windows XP's predecessors (up to Windows ME) were still using the good old DOS operating system; although Microsoft tried hard to hide it. Windows XP, however, has an entirely new core, which is based on Windows 2000, the Microsoft operating system for professional use. Microsoft expects significant improvements because of this change particularly with regard to system stability and program stability. This advantage has the drawback of compatibility problems. Software that was developed for previous Windows versions does not simply work under Windows XP. Nevertheless, such problems can be tackled by using a specific Wizard. Using previous hardware under Windows XP can be more problematic, however. It is rarely possible to use the Windows 9x drivers that were supplied with your expansion devices under Windows XP. This means that you must look for the corresponding drivers again to install them.

Immediate measures in the event of program crashes

Judging from our experiences up to this point, Windows XP really does seem to be a significantly more stable operating system than its predecessors. Virtually no application crashes were recorded during our extensive tests, and an entire crash of the operating system was never experienced at all. Once in a while you experience problems; however, Windows XP is not the only one capable of causing these disruptions as especially untidily programmed applications might be the actual cause of crashes. The big advantage of Windows XP is that in previous versions such crashes might have destabilized the entire system and a complete reboot might have been necessary. In Windows XP, however, the faulty applications are usually neatly removed from the memory, and you can proceed with your work immediately. The following are the details of what's happening:

1 If Windows XP notices that an application does not react the way it should, it immediately informs you about it. A message box is displayed informing you about the program involved. (*XYZ has encountered a problem and needs to close.*)

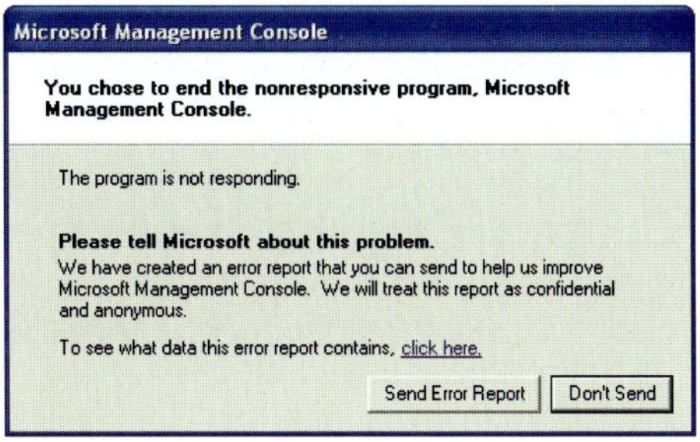

2 A new feature of Windows XP allows you to send an error report to Microsoft. This report is treated anonymously and confidentially; it contains all relevant data pertaining to the crash. Because the error report is sent online, you need a functioning Internet connection.

Note

Are error reports of any use?

Do not expect someone at Microsoft to read your error reports in person and give you valuable advice. This is not even feasible because of the enormous amount of reports expected. In fact, Microsoft collects the error reports automatically and analyzes them statistically. It is possible to deduce from the results if certain programs or situations cause frequent problems. Because these errors then receive particular attention,you certainly stand to gain from error reports because your report (besides others) contributes to the solution of the problem and the publishing of an error correction. Sending an error report to Microsoft every time a program crashes does not really make sense. If you come across certain problems repeatedly, however, definitely send a report. In addition, the orecurring error might already be known and a solution might be readily available. In this case, Microsoft informs you about it directly.

3 If you are skeptical and want to know the exact data the error report contains before it is sent to Microsoft, click the link *click here*. A report preview appears.

4 If you want to send the report, click the *Send Error Report* button. Windows XP contacts a specific Microsoft server and transfers your error report.

5 If the problem is already known to Microsoft and a solution for it is already available, a hyperlink referring to further information about this specific problem is sent to you as a response.

6 Click the *Don't Send* button if you don't want to submit an error report. The faulty program is closed without a further message, and you can continue your work.

Customizing the error report function

Windows XP allows you to customize the transfer of error reports. You can, for instance, entirely disable the function or limit it to certain programs.

1 To define the error report settings, open the *Control Panel* and select the category *Performance and Maintenance*. Then click the *System* icon at the very bottom.

2 Select the *Advanced* tab in the *System Properties* dialog window. Then click the *Error Reporting* button at the bottom right.

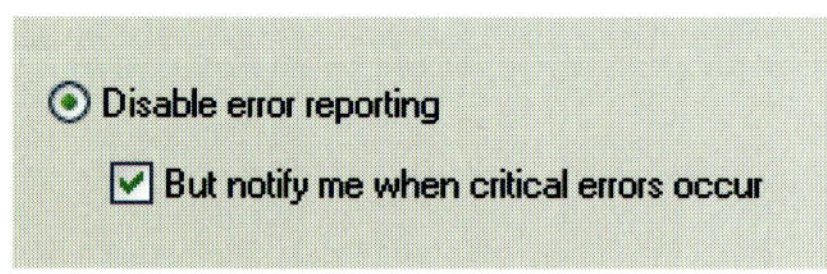

3 The *Error Reporting* dialog window opens. Use the top option to disable the function entirely. You also have the option to limit the function to critical errors only.

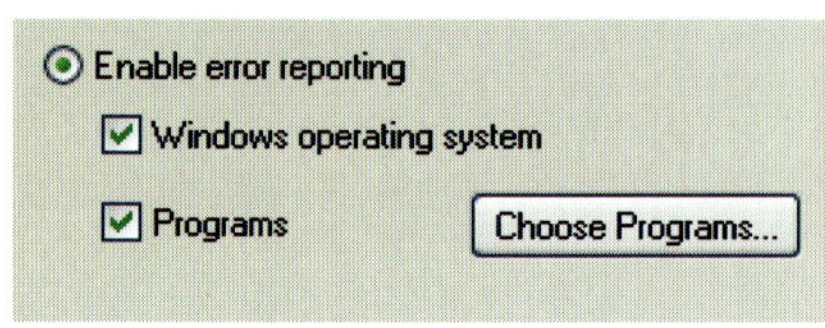

4 Use the option below to enable the error reporting function. You can either limit the function to the *Windows operating system* or include other *Programs* (for example, from other suppliers).

5 In addition, you can specify the programs to be monitored by clicking the *Choose Programs* button.

Removing programs from memory manually

Windows XP cannot always diagnose by itself that an application might not work properly anymore. If it seems to the operating system that an application is functioning correctly but nothing is actually happening in the user interface, you must take action yourself. The revised Windows XP Task Manager allows you to close each running program individually.

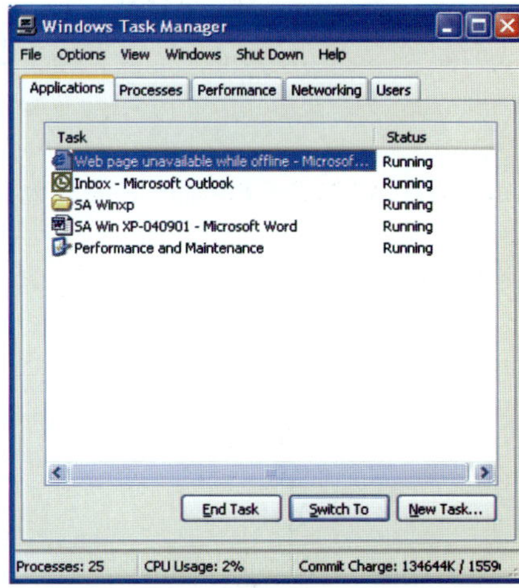

1 If you experience problems with an application, give the "three-finger shortcut" a try: Use two fingers of your left hand to press the Alt and Ctrl keys simultaneously and use a finger of your right hand to briefly press the Delete key.

2 The Task Manager opens. It is a central Windows component that continually monitors and controls running programs. All currently running applications are displayed in the *Applications* tab of the Task Manager.

3 Select the applications that are giving you a headache and click the *End Task* button. The Task Manager thentries to end the applications the regular way.

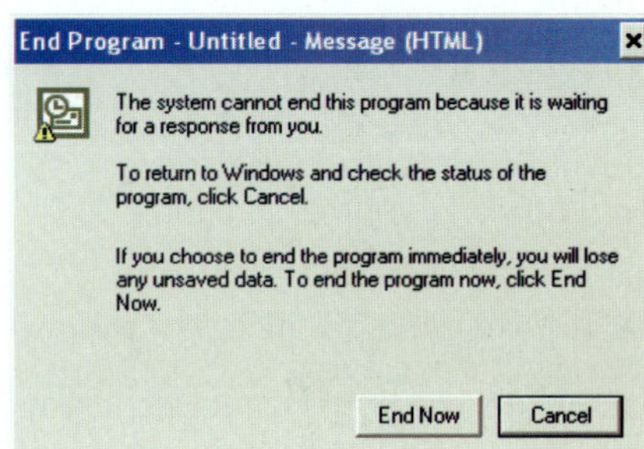

4 If this doesn't work, the Task Manager informs you about the problem and offers you the choice to end the program. Click the *End Now* button, and the Task Manager rigorously removes the application from the memory.

Note

Be wary of losing data

Ending an application by force might lead to a loss of data as you might not be able to save the currently open documents. If the unresponsive application still contains valuable unsaved data, you might want to give the program more time before you take such drastic measures. If the application does not respond at all, your data is lost one way or the other. If the application has an AutoSave function, you might be lucky enough to save at least parts of your work.

Getting older Windows programs to work

As already explained, a lot has happened beneath the hood in Windows XP. Consequently, some applications that were run under previous Windows versions without any hassle might behave petulantly all of a sudden or crash frequently. In some cases, you might not be able to start the program at all. Even if this should be the case, you won't have to do without the program. Instead, you can use the Program Compatibility Wizard of Windows XP, which tries to adjust older applications so that they can be used under the new operating system without any problems.

1 Go to *Start/All Programs/Accessories/Program Compatibility Wizard* to start the Wizard.

2 Skip the introductory window by clicking *Next*.

3 As a next step, you must define how you want to locate the program to be tested. If it is already installed, the option *I want to choose from a list of programs* is your best choice. You can then select the program from a list of installed applications.

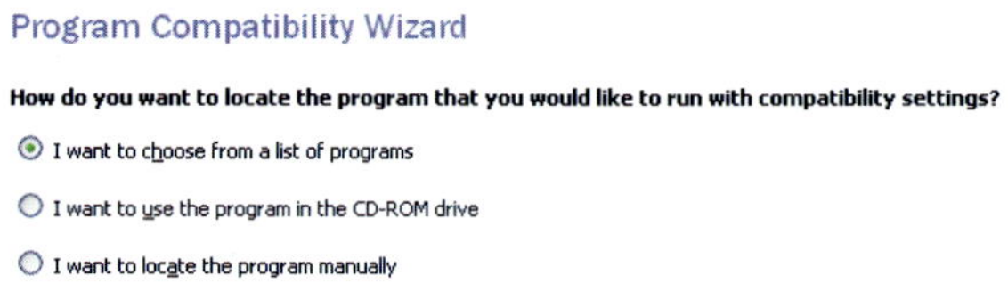

4 If the program is not yet installed correctly, you can access the setup program directly from the installation CD or select the application manually from any folder.

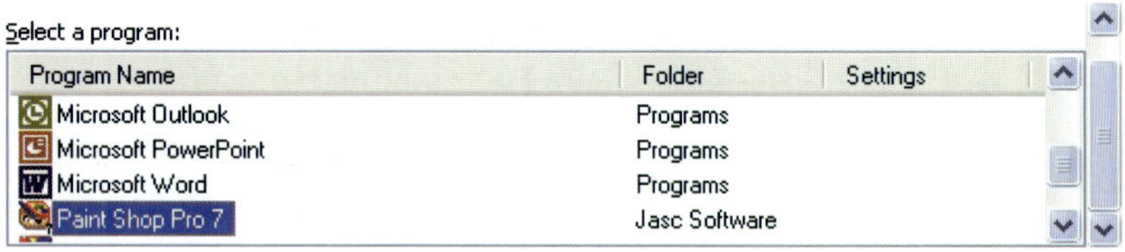

5 If you chose the first option during the previous step, the Wizard now shows you a list of installed applications. Select the program that gives you grief from the list.

6 Next, the Wizard wants to know which operating system supported the application previously. This step informs the Wizard about any possible adjustments it has to make to run the program correctly.

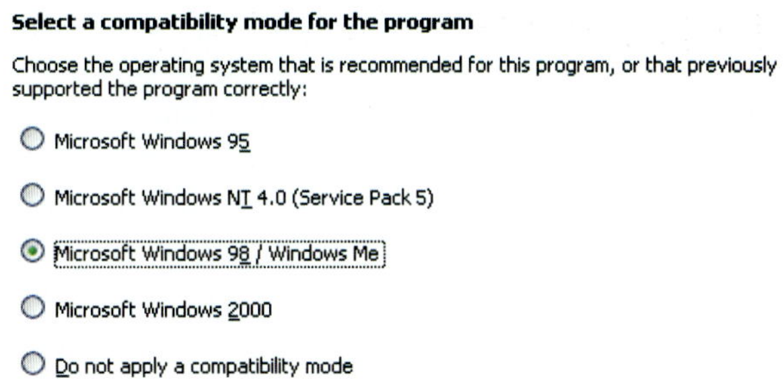

7 If required, you can define additional settings that might facilitate the application of the corresponding program afterwards. The first two options, *256 colors* and *640 x 480 screen resolution* are probably only required with exceptionally outdated programs. The option *Disable visual themes* might be useful with programs that do not conform to the conventional visual themes of Windows. You don't need to get these options right at first. If it doesn't work immediately, simply modify them and try again.

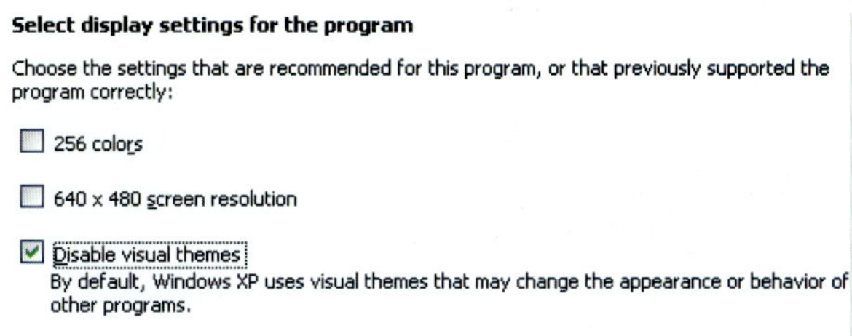

8 The Wizard provides you with a summary of the selected options. If you click *Next*, the Wizard tries to start the application by using these settings.

9 Wait for the result; then return to the Wizard. If the application was started successfully, select the option *Yes, set this program to always use these compatibility settings*. The Wizard then adjusts the settings of this application so that it always starts in the correct mode.

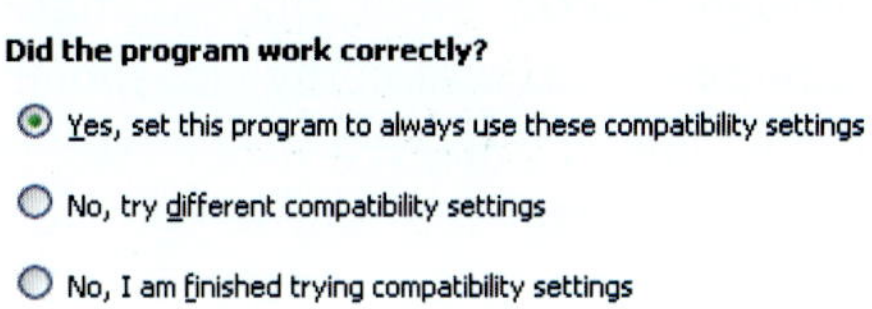

10 If the application didn't run successfully, select the option *No, try different compatibility settings*. Then return to the previous step of the Wizard to try out an alternative configuration.

11 If it still doesn't work after several attempts, close the Wizard by selecting *No, I am finished trying compatibility settings*. In this case, you still have the opportunity to submit the test results to Microsoft in a similar manner to an error report (see above). This is a good idea, for a solution to the problem might already exist. In that case, you are informed about it.

> **Note**
>
> **Program updates for Windows XP**
>
> With all the foresight they showed at Microsoft, we don't expect that you'll have many compatibility problems with running applications under Windows XP, in spite of the new system kernel. If you do have a program that doesn't want to run under any circumstance, you should get in contact with the software manufacturer. If the product is still being offered, there could be a supplement or even a new version specially designed for Windows XP.

Remedying Windows problems through updates

If problems arise with the Windows system or the applications running under it, there is another convenient way of remedying them. Windows XP has a Wizard that you can use to update the system online. To do so, the Wizard connects to a special Microsoft server and determines if any components or applications have been installed on your computer since the installation or the last update for which supplementary files or new versions are now available. The Wizard can immediately download and install such patches. The requirement is a functional Internet connection.

1 During installation, the automatic update function is enabled by default. In addition, it can also notify you sooner or later completely by itself. Notification of the update is displayed in the notification area. If you click this notification, you start the Wizard with the settings for the update function.

2 Confirm the Welcome window by clicking *Next* and determine in the second step how the automatic update should proceed.

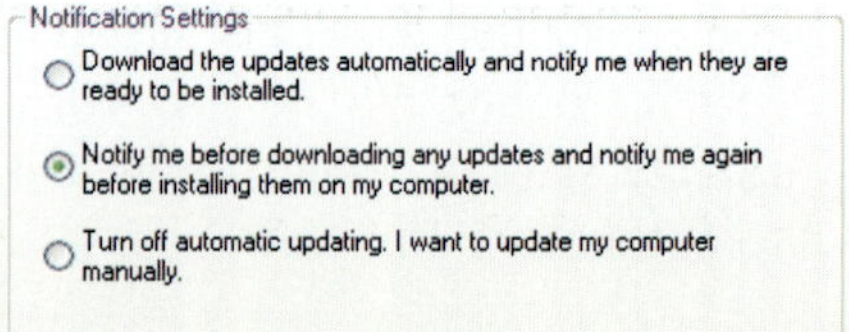

3 By default, the *Download the updates automatically and notify me when they are ready to be installed* option is enabled. Windows automatically downloads the updates when you are online and afterwards offer them for installation. This is a good idea if you are using broadband Internet access or paying a flat rate. In other cases, unnecessary online time and capacity are wasted on downloading data you probably won't even use.

4 Therefore, it is a better idea to select the second option: *Notify me before downloading any updates and notify again before installing them on my computer.* Windows XP then brings any available updates to your attention before downloading, and you can decide what should and shouldn't be downloaded yourself.

5 If you want to abstain completely from using automatic updates, select *Turn off automatic updating. I want to update my computer manually.* You canalways manually check for any current updates at any time.

6 After you have selected the desired option, click *Next* and then *Finish* to close the Wizard and apply the settings.

Updating Windows XP manually

Besides updating Windows XP automatically, you can update it manually at any time. This is particularly useful if you are not normally connected to the Internet often or for a long period of time, so that the system itself cannot search for the required information. In that case, you should regularly undertake making a manual update in order not to miss any important updates.

1 To undertake making a manual update, select *Windows Update* from the bottom left of the Start menu.

2 Internet Explorer now starts, and a special Web site is called up through which the update can take place. However, a special Active X control must be installed to do the update so that the configuration of the existing software on your computer can be determined and the updates can be searched for. This installation occurs directly online and

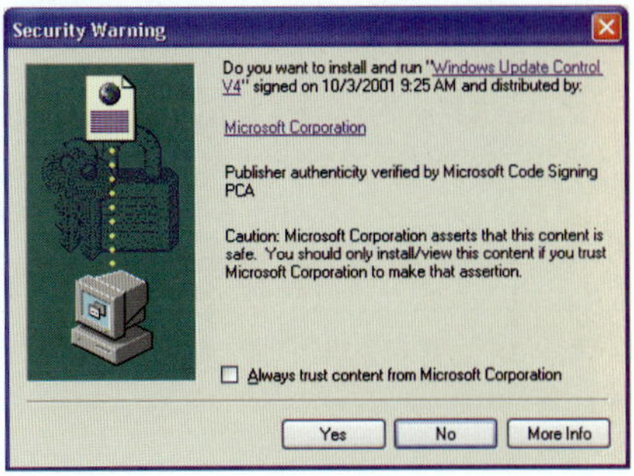

only takes a short time. You must authorize it by acknowledging the security warning with *Yes*.

3 The updating can be done immediately after the installation of the Active X control. While the Welcome message is being displayed, click the *Scan for updates* hyperlink to actuate the process.

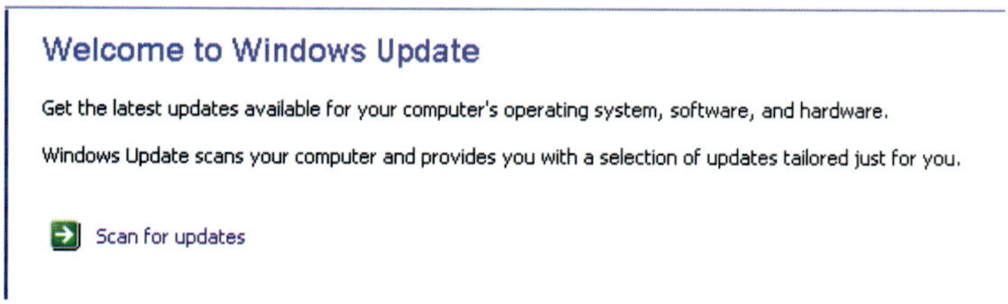

4 The program then searches through the database on the Microsoft server for current updates for the system components, applications and drivers installed on your computer. If an update is found, the message *Windows Update has found X critical updates for your computer* appears. Click this message to obtain more information about the updates and download them.

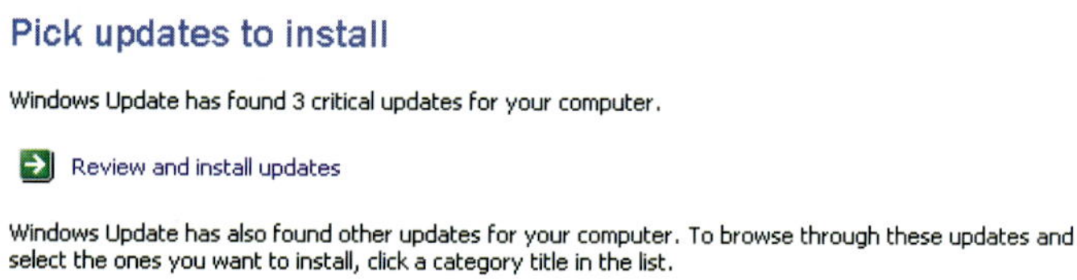

5 You are brought to a list of the components that can be updated. Underneath the summary at the top, you can find a short description for each of the components. In most cases, you can also *Request more information* If you do not wish to update one of the components, click *Remove*. Afterwards, start the download and the installation of the updates by clicking the *Install Now* button.

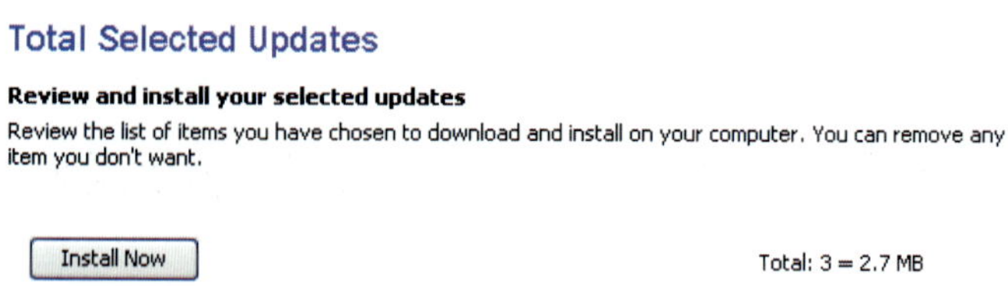

6 Depending on the type of update, you might also have to accept the license agreement. Read through it and afterwards confirm by clicking *Accept*. Otherwise, the download does not proceed.

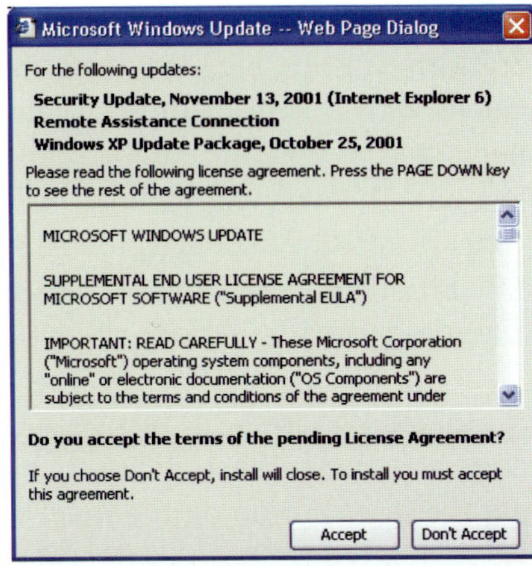

7 The transfer and installation of the updated components begins. You can view how much of the relevant data has already been transferred in a status window.

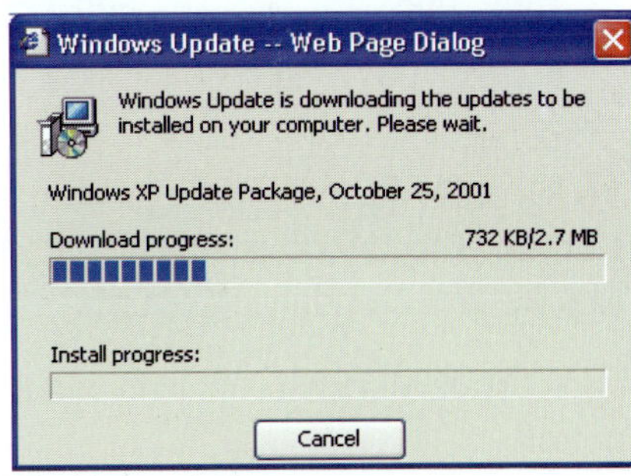

8 Once the updates have been downloaded and installed, restarting your computer is often required, so that the updates can immediately take effect. First, close any documents or applications that are open and then click *OK*.

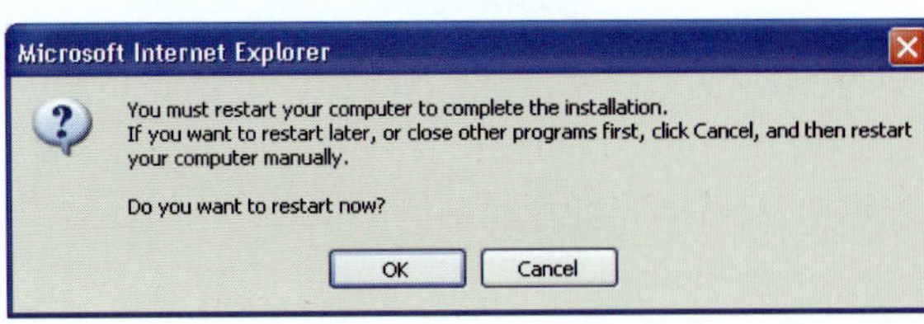

Starting Windows in safe mode

Even with Windows XP, certain circumstances can occur under which the system does not want to start or it does not function correctly after starting. This can be, for example, because of hardware problems that arose after installing or connecting a new device or after the installation of drivers for hardware components. Software crashes, too, can render the system unstable. For such cases, Windows XP comes with a safe mode. Only the core system with its most important components and drivers are then started. Anything that could affect its stability is then left out. This way you can get Windows working again, so you can remove software, or repair or correct problematic settings, for instance. In addition, Windows XP also undertakes a self-diagnosis when starting in safe mode and can then usually recognize and remedy any typical problems automatically.

1 To use Windows XP in safe mode, turn on your computer or restart it if it is already running. When doing so, perform a cold boot, which is best done by pressing the reset button on the main unit.

2 Then, press the [F8] key and keep it depressed during the entire startup procedure. If your computer is making a continual clicking noise through the speakers because you are pressing the key, pay no attention to it.

3 By pressing the [F8] key continually, you keep Windows XP from immediately starting. The *Windows Advanced Options Menu* appears. Here, you can determine exactly how Windows XP starts.

4 To start Windows in safe mode, use the arrow keys to select the *Safe Mode* option.

```
Windows Advanced Options Menu
Please select an option:

    Safe Mode
    Safe Mode with Networking
    Safe Mode with Command Prompt

    Enable Boot Logging
    Enable VGA Mode
    Last Known Good Configuration (your most recent settings that worked)
    Directory Services Restore Mode (Windows domain controllers only)
    Debugging Mode

    Start Windows Normally
    Reboot
    Return to OS Choices Menu

Use the up and down arrow keys to move the highlight to your choice.
```

Safe Mode

5 If you need access to the network to get access to maintenance programs, for instance, you can expand the bare-bones configuration by adding network drivers. For this, select *Safe Mode with Networking*. This is only recommended, however, if you are completely sure that the problem is not associated with the network.

Safe Mode with Networking

6 A very practical option is also the *Last Known Good Configuration* option. Windows XP uses the system restore described in Chapter 4 to return to a system configuration where Windows XP could evidently start correctly. Changes that you have made to the system since that time are lost. Editing done to files and documents naturally remains intact.

7 If you accidentally ended up in the *Advanced Option Menu*, you can *Start Windows Normally* or simply *Reboot* the entire computer.

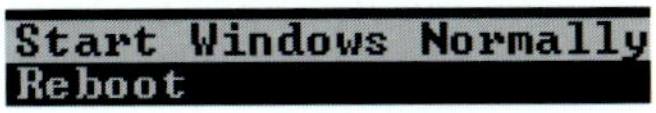

8 If you start Windows XP in safe mode, you quickly notice that things aren't quite normal. First of all, the screen appears unusual. This happens because the system is using the standard graphic drivers. These work with minimal resolution and a low picture refresh frequency. You also find fixed notices in every corner advising you that the computer is in safe mode. Finally, Windows advises you at the end of the startup that the computer is working in safe mode.

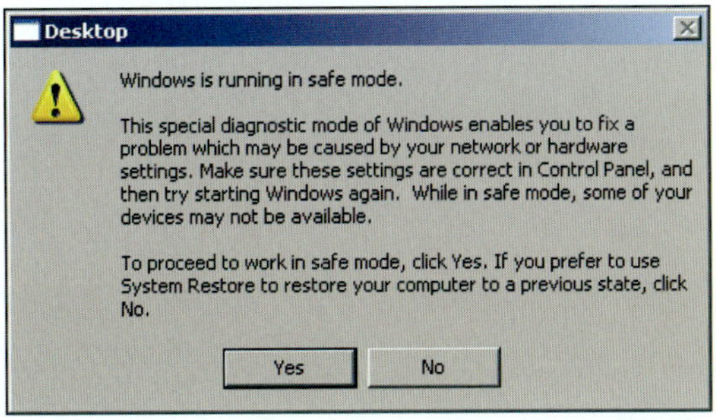

Not all the functions you are normally using are available in safe mode. You, however, have access to the most important system settings and you can configure applications and device drivers, for example. To use the self-diagnostic function in Windows XP, you must exit the system after a Safe startup has taken place and start the computer in Normal mode again. With a little bit of luck, the problem has been solved already.

Solving driver problems with old hardware

The new system kernel for Windows XP can lead to problems in connection with various hardware components. This is because Windows XP no longer shares the driver version of previous Windows versions, where the same driver could often be used for Windows 95, 98, and ME. Instead, Windows XP falls back on the driver version of its professional brother, Windows 2000. This driver version is supposedly better engineered and provides for more stability when dealing with other drivers and the operating system. This is both good and bad news. First, the bad news: Hardware drivers that were created for Windows 9x or ME can generally not be used under Windows XP. To keep the balance, here's the good news: Because Windows XP uses the same driver structure as Windows 2000, you can in many cases use the Windows 2000 drivers for the Windows XP device.

Note

Taking the drivers for a spin

Even Windows 2000 drivers do not always help XP users. In terms of functionality, not all 2000 drivers work under XP. Among other things, products that are usually more basic and rather cheap do not usually come with Windows 2000 drivers. Luckily, Windows XP already includes a number of drivers for standard devices. When you are installing the operating system over an existing one in a computer, a special Wizard checks the installed hardware components to see if suitable drivers exist or can be supplied. If no drivers are available for a device, you must find out how these components can be enabled. The same holds true if you want to post-install devices or connect them to a system running XP. When you are buying a new device, it is absolutely necessary to ensure that it comes with Windows XP drivers or XP-capable Windows 2000 drivers. If you are dealing with an older device, you can search for the XP driver in the Internet or the Web site of the manufacturer. Other possibilities are special Web sites focusing on drivers.

The Windows XP Device Manager

As with previous versions, Windows XP also has a special Device Manager for dealing with hardware components and their drivers. For the most part, its look has changed for the new version of Windows.

1 To use the Device Manager, first call up the system settings by going to *Start/Control Panel* and selecting *Performance and Maintenance.*

2 Once there, click the *System* icon to open the system settings and switch to the *Hardware* tab.

3 Here you can find the *Device Manger* button with which you can open this tool in the *Device Manger* area.

4 In the Device Manger, notice a lot of categories into which the existing hardware components are divided. They are displayed like the folders and files in Windows Explorer. If you click the + symbol before a category, you expand the folder to gain access to the components belonging to it.

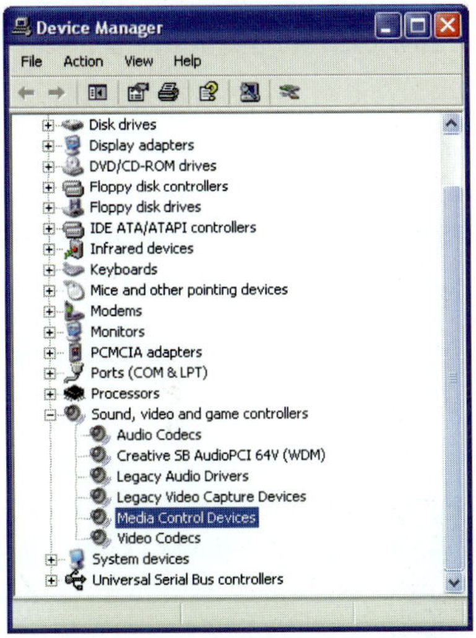

5 To have a closer look at one of the devices, double-click the corresponding entry in the Device Manger. This opens the properties for the device. There, you can find all the information and functions that are available to that device, and if applicable, its drivers. The exact content of the properties depends on the type of the device.

6 If Windows has already determined that a certain device is not functioning normally, the Device Manger automatically indicates this with a colored question mark upon opening the folder. This way, you can quickly track the source of the hardware problem.

Updating drivers for hardware components

If you have come across a new driver for a hardware component that solves existing problems or adds more functionality, you must install it. If the manufacturer provided its own installation routine along with the driver, you should definitely use that. If you only have the actual driver files, however, you can integrate the driver into the Windows system with the help of the Device Manager.

1 To install the driver with the help of the Device Manager, open the properties for the corresponding hardware component and switch to the *Driver* tab.

2 Here, you should first familiarize yourself with the driver details so that you can make sure you are really dealing with an older version of the existing driver and the driver to be installed is newer.

3 Then, click *Update Driver* to replace the existing one with the new version.

4 Doing so starts the Hardware Update Wizard, which first wants to know from where the new driver is installed. If the software is on a CD-ROM or diskette, insert it and select the *Install the software automatically* option. If, conversely, the driver files are already present somewhere on your hard drive, select the second option, *Install from a list or specific location*.

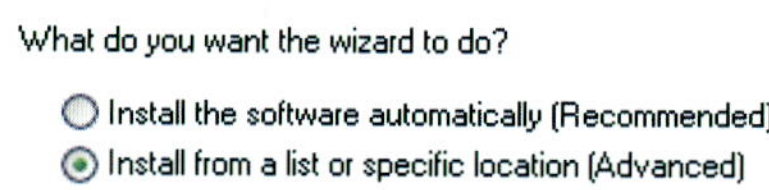

5 In that case, select *Don't search. I will choose the driver to install.* in the next step.

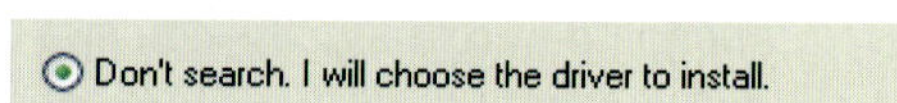

6 Click *Have Disk* in the step that follows. In the file selection window that appears, select the file with the current driver.

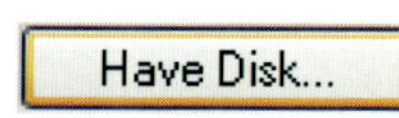

7 If you click *Next* hereafter, the Device Manger installs the desired driver. Depending on the size of the files, this can take a while. Afterwards, you receive a confirmation of installation, as well as a request to restart the computer so that the new driver can be put into use.

> **Note**
>
> **Testing the driver**
>
> If you try to install a driver that was not specially designed for Windows XP but was originally designed for Windows 2000, for example, the Device Manager points this out and notifies you of possible risks if you use that driver. This is valid for all drivers that do not feature a special signature for use with Windows XP. You can install the driver anyway. However, you should take this advice seriously for the sake of system stability, and only install drivers that have been recommended by the manufacturer for use with XP. It is always best, naturally, to locate special XP drivers if they exist.

Uninstalling drivers

If you have determined that the installation of a driver has not given the desired results or has possibly led to new problems, you can return to the previously used driver. Windows XP makes a backup copy of previous driver each time you install a new one, and this copy can be re-enabled at any time.

1 Again, as described above, open the properties of the device in question in the Device Manager and switch to the *Driver* tab.

2 Here you find a button, *Roll Back Driver*, with which you can go back to the previously used driver.

3 Acknowledge the confirmation prompt with *Yes*. Upon doing so, the Device Manager restores the "old" driver.

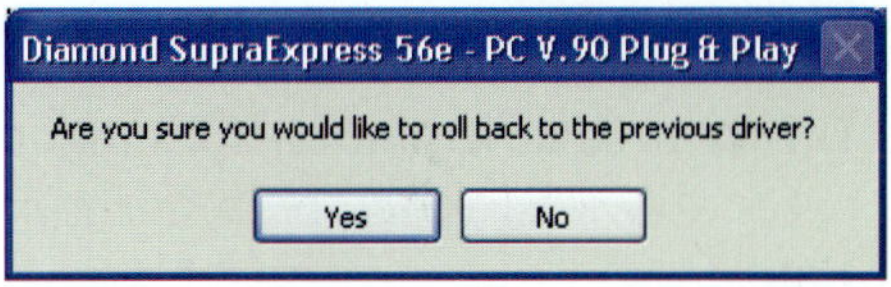

4. Tools – The best Help programs

Windows comes with a rich selection of Help programs and maintenance tools that are supposed to make your work easier. Among others, these include the important tools for maintaining and servicing your hard drive(s), so that the latter can reliably and safely accommodate your information. Therefore, service your drive(s) from time to time to avoid problems or, if in doubt, recognize them in a timely manner before the worst can unfold. The convenient Compressed Folders with which you can save a lot of hard drive space also falls into this area of efficiently handling information. Another important topic is that of the power saving functions with which you can save not only electricity, but also turn the computer on and off more quickly. This chapter also explains how you can secure important files and system information in such a way that they can be restored after encountering problems or loss of data at any time. Finally, you become familiar with the Scheduled Task Wizard with which many of the maintenance tasks that are suggested can be automated, so that they run by themselves in the background without your continual input.

Cleaning up and optimizing the hard drive(s)

The hard drive is one of the most precious computer components. This doesn't necessarily refer to the price, for it has steadily decreased over the last few years. Hard drives are the permanent storage space for applications and documents. Therefore, if anything goes wrong with them, the consequences are often fatal. For this reason, one should regularly maintain and optimize one's hard drives to prevent crashes and be able to spot problems ahead of time.

Spotting hard drive errors in time

Hard drives, too, are only machines, and they may malfunction from time to time. Unfortunately, such errors can have direct consequences, because all your data is saved on the hard drive. In addition, hard drive crashes are usually irreparable, and only a specialist can recover the data for a lot of money, and even then it might not be recovered completely. A good method of prevention is the regular error-checking (known from earlier Windows versions as "ScanDisk"). During an error-check, problems that are caused by crashes or errors of the operating system or of individual applications can be identified and eliminated. At the same time, the program finds bad blocks on the hard drive and marks them as unusable. This way, they won't be used anymore, and data loss is prevented.

Note

What are bad blocks?

Disk drives are organized in blocks. Individual blocks might be damaged by frequent use and might not save data in a reliable manner anymore. If Windows XP finds such damaged blocks during an error-check, it marks them as bad in the hard drive log. These blocks won't be used in the future to avoid the risk of losing data. In the past, bad blocks were not necessarily unusual. In the meantime, the quality of hard drives has risen to where block errors are few and far between. It is a serious warning sign if a hard drive that was reliable in the past suddenly produces new bad blocks at regular intervals. This is often the sign of an impending disk crash of the kind where all data is lost. In such cases, it is definitely recommended that you change the hard drive in time.

1 To check a hard drive for errors, open My Computer in Windows Explorer and select the drive you want to check.

2 Open the drive properties under *File/Properties* and switch to the *Tools* tab.

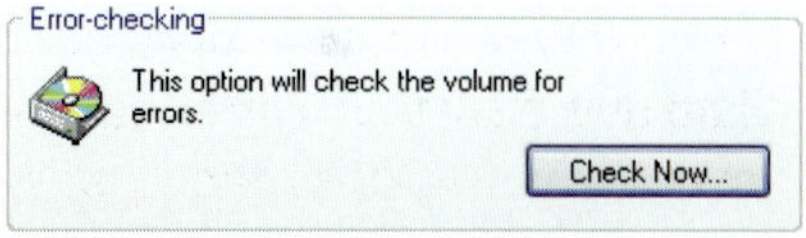

3 In the *Error-checking* category, click the *Check Now* button to start the hard drive check.

4 In the menu that follows, enable the option *Automatically fix file system errors*. This immediately fixes any errors found. Such an adjustment is not always possible if files are open on this drive at the same time. This is a problem especially when you want to check the Windows system drive, in which case Windows notifies you of the situation and offers to automatically run the check when you start the system next.

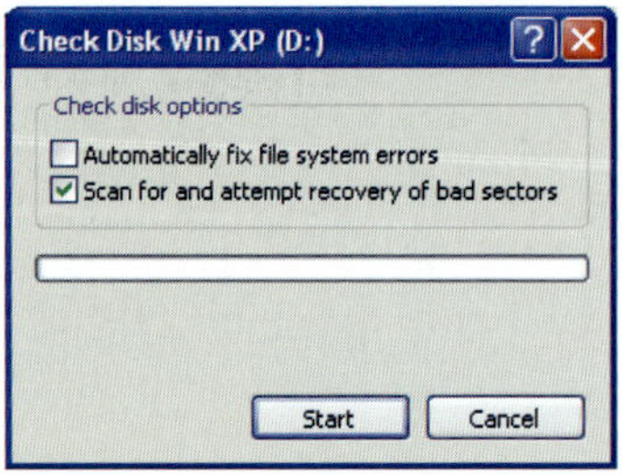

5 The option *Scan for and attempt recovery of bad sectors* leads to a more thorough check. If the option is disabled, only the management of the logical drive is checked, that is, the directory structures, file allocation tables, file entries, and so forth. If the option is enabled, on the other hand, the program checks the physical hard drive for bad blocks. This takes considerably longer (especially for modern hard drives of many GB), yet you should do it from time to time.

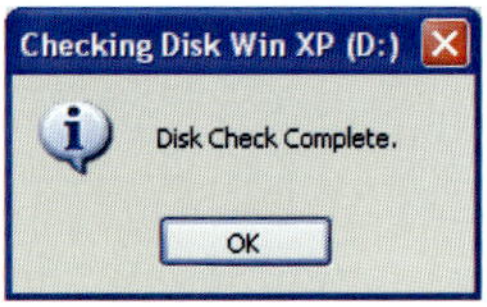

6 Click *Start* to begin checking. You can monitor the checking process in the status display. When the check has been completed, the program notifies you with the message *Disk Check Complete*.

Optimizing the hard drive speed

An unpleasant effect of hard drives that are already pretty full is the fragmentation of data. This perceptibly slows down access and increases the risk of data loss. For this reason, Windows XP comes with a program for defragmenting drives, which reorganizes the content of your hard disk to restore the usual access speed.

Note

What are fragmented files?

The storage space on your hard drive is divided into many little blocks. To save a file, the operating system divides the file into several bits corresponding to the size of these blocks and distributes the bits over several free blocks. Usually, a file is distributed over several adjacent blocks. When a hard drive is full, this is not possible, however, because not enough free adjacent blocks are available. Then, the operating system searches for any free blocks and saves the data on them. Such files, which are distributed over different blocks that are not adjacent, are labeled fragmented. The fragmentation has a negative effect on the access speed. Because the read and write heads on the hard drive must search for the data in different areas, accessing files takes longer. The defragmentation program reorganizes the files on the drive and reunites all fragmented files.

1 To optimize a drive, open its properties under *File/Properties* or by clicking *Properties* in the pop-up menu.

2 In the drive *Properties*, switch to the *Tools* tab. Here, you find the *Defragmentation* category. Click *Defragment Now* to start optimizing the drive.

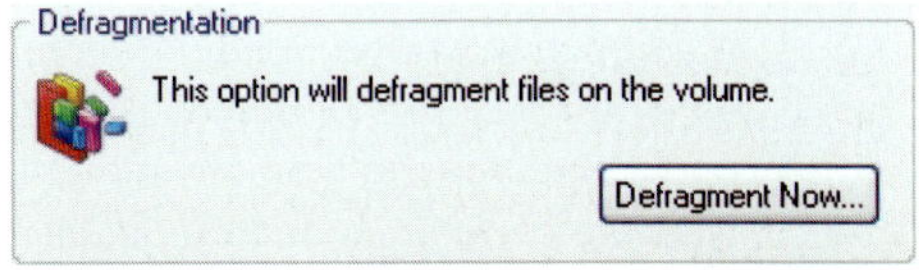

3 This opens the defragmentation program. Here, you should first check whether an optimization is even necessary and makes sense. Select the drive in question from the list at the top and click *Analyze* at the bottom.

4 The program then analyzes the structure of the data on the hard disk and determines the degree of fragmentation. This might take some time, depending on the size of the drive. You can monitor the progress in the status bar at the bottom of the window. If the degree of fragmentation is below a certain threshold, the loss of performance is so low that the optimization is not worth the effort. The program communicates this to you, but you can perform the optimization in spite of it by clicking *Defragment*.

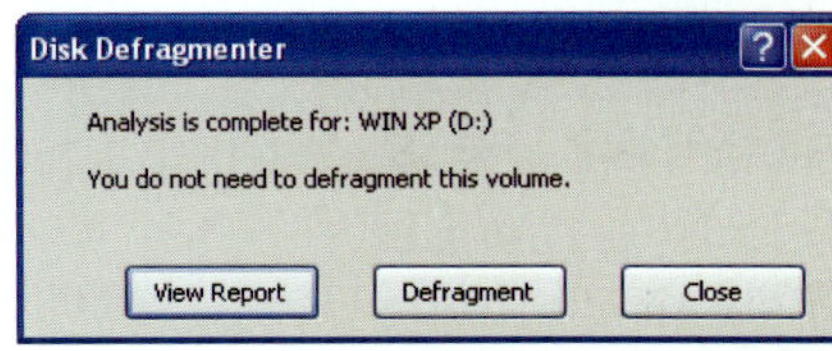

A complete optimization might take a few hours, depending on the size of the drive. After all, the program has to read in every single block, find a suitable new storage place for it, and write it to the hard drive again. In addition, it is trying to relocate blocks that belong together to the same area. You can view the progress on-screen. You can interrupt the process at any time during defragmentation by clicking *Pause.* Don't worry about messing something up; the computer always sets up the file system safely. However, it can take a few seconds until the process stops, so you should give the program a bit of time after you click *Pause*. If you need to use the computer for a short while, you can always interrupt the defragmentation. The program freezes its activity for a while, after which you can resume it.

Note

Caution during defragmentation!

During defragmentation, the optimization program first creates a major mess with the data on the hard drive to organize it that much better afterwards. During this restructuring period, your computer is highly sensitive. A crash at this point could mean heavy data loss. For this reason, it is best to leave the computer alone and not run other applications during defragmentation. Besides, working on the computer simultaneously with the defragmentation program is only possible within certain limits, because the program itself uses a lot of the computer's capacity.

Cleaning up the hard disk

Modern Windows applications have the nasty habit of filling the available disk space with temporary files, cache data, and immovable files. These superfluous space fillers should actually disappear automatically, but the applications are not very reliable when it comes to removing them. If you remove these files regularly, you can save a lot of space. Cleaning up doesn't have to be tedious manual labor. Disk Cleanup searches your drives and folders and makes suggestions about which files are superfluous and can be removed without worry.

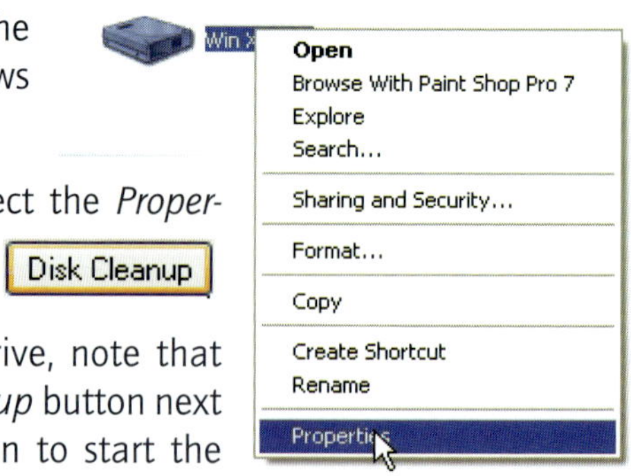

1 To start the disk cleanup, open the drive you want to clean up in Windows Explorer.

2 Right-click the drive entry and select the *Properties* menu item.

3 In the *Properties* menu for that drive, note that the *General* tab displays the *Disk Cleanup* button next to the drive statistics. Click the button to start the cleanup.

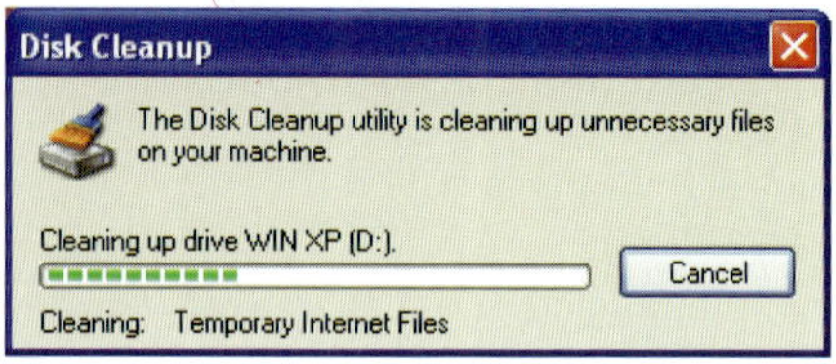

4 The Disk Cleanup now checks the selected drive and uses different strategies to determine all the files that can be cleaned up. For instance, it checks the temporary file folder and searches for the files that were not removed in the regular way (for example, because of a system crash) and that are now occupying space unnecessarily. The program also checks the folder for temporary Internet files. If you surf a lot, you might have collected a lot of data here that you don't really need to save.

5 Once Disk Cleanup has finished checking, it presents a summary of its findings. At the very top, you can see the maximum amount of storage space that can be freed.

6 The field *Files to delete* displays the kinds of files found by Disk Cleanup on the drive. Select the file types you want to remove. If, for instance, you want to save the *Temporary Internet Files* for offline viewing, uncheck the corresponding entry. In the bottom half of the window, you note a short description for each category of files.

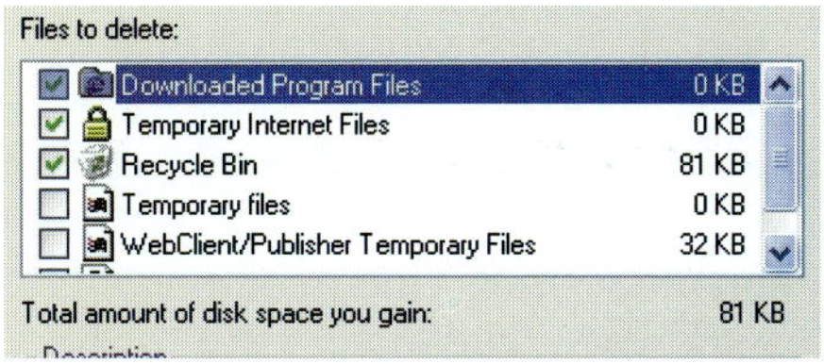

7 If you are unsure about whether you can delete one of the categories without worries, you can click the *View Files* button in the *Description* category to open an Explorer window displaying the individual files. Thus, you can check with which files you are dealing exactly.

8 Once you have determined the files you want to delete, click *OK*. At the prompt, confirm your decision to perform the cleanup by clicking *Yes*.

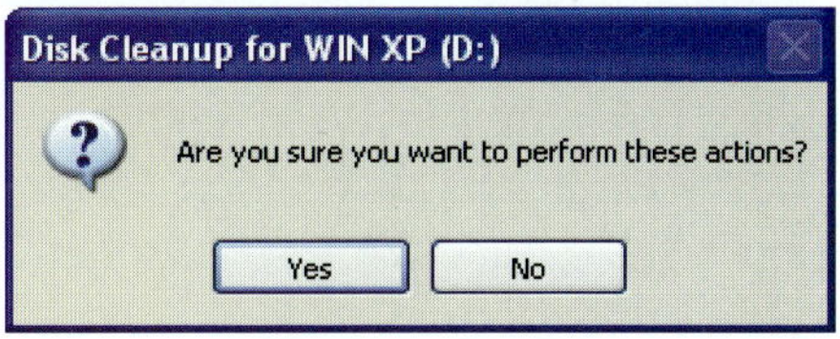

Freeing more disk space

Maybe the disk cleanup described above wasn't as successful as you would have wished. If you want to free a specific amount of hard disk space (for instance, to install a new application on your computer), Disk Cleanup gives you another option.

1 In the Disk Cleanup menu, switch to the tab *More Options*.

2 Here, you can free additional storage space in the *Windows components* category by removing unnecessary Windows components. . To do so, you should check whether you really don't need all the installed Windows components. During a complete installation, numerous Help programs and program add-ons are set up, which you might not need at all and which only take up space. Click the *Clean up* button.

3 This starts the Windows Components Wizard, which lists all the Windows components. All installed components are checked off. To uninstall components, uncheck them. When you have unchecked all superfluous components, apply the new configuration by clicking *OK*. Windows then removes the components freeing up space. Restarting the computer might be necessary after this operation.

4 In the Disk Cleanup window, you also have the option of carefully reviewing the *Installed programs*. Perhaps there are some programs that you have installed only to try out and which you have long since given up. These, too, might be wasting precious disk space. To remove them, click the *Clean up* button in this category.

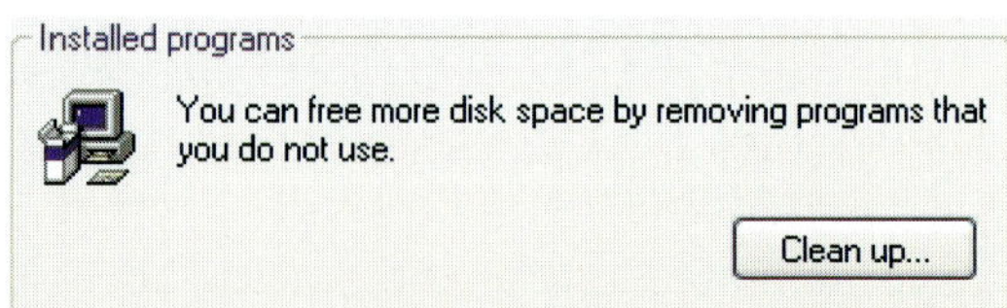

5 This takes you to the *Add or Remove Programs* category of the *Control Panel*. All installed applications are listed here by name and the amount of space they occupy (*Size*). In addition, the *Used* information tells you how often this application has been used lately. To uninstall an application, select its entry and click *Remove*. This opens the uninstall function for the program in question. If you have uninstalled all applications you don't need anymore, close *Add or Remove Programs* by clicking *Close*. Here, too, you mightneed to restart your computer.

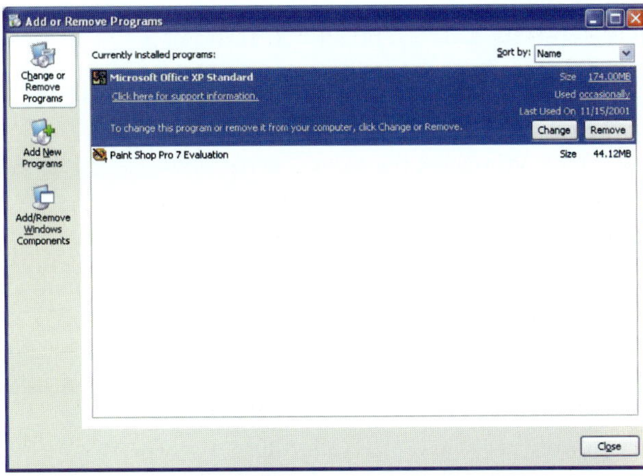

6 Finally, Disk Cleanup also offers you the option of deleting the *System Restore* information to free additional disk space. The system restore function is explained in more detail later in this chapter. Before deleting such data, you should read the corresponding passages.

Saving disk space with Compressed Folders

Another possibility for increasing the available storage space on your computer is provided by the Windows XP Compressed Folders function. Compressed folders make it possible to save large files in a compact format to the hard drive or other storage media. Compressed data generally takes up considerably less space, and you still have unlimited use of the packed documents and programs without having to manually extract them every time. Compressed folders are integrated into Windows Explorer as if they were perfectly normal directories.

Note

The ZIP format

There are a number of different compression methods. The ZIP process is the one dominating the PC market. Previously, you needed additional software like WinZip to zip up Windows files. This is no longer necessary for compressed folders in Windows XP. They integrate the compression into Windows Explorer, while also being 100% ZIP compatible. The advantage is that you can exchange compressed folders with other users using a disk or the Internet, even if these have a different Windows version without compressed folders.

Creating compressed folders

Before you can compress files, you need to create a compressed folder.

1 Open Windows Explorer.

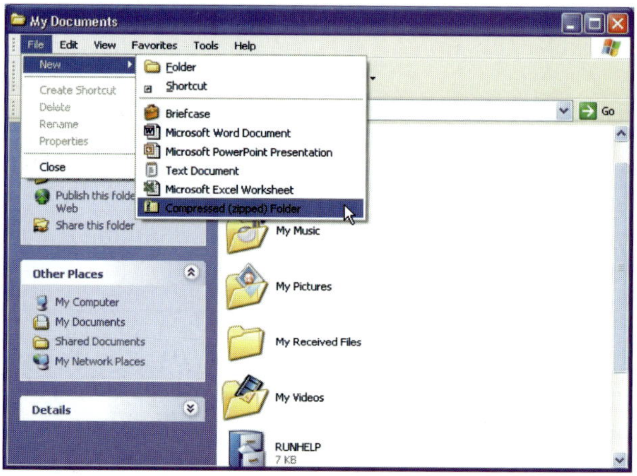

2 Select the directory in which you want to set up the compressed folder.

3 Go to *File/New/Compressed (zipped) folder.*

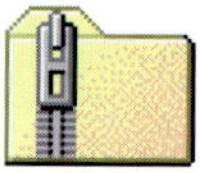

4 Windows Explorer then creates a new compressed folder in this directory. You can recognize a compressed folder by the zipper on the folder icon.

5 The new archive is first labeled *New Compressed (zipped) Folder.* Enter your own customized name. If you want to send the folder through the Internet, you should stick to the 8+3 name rule from the days of DOS and Windows 3.x. Even if Windows XP allows much longer names, you ensure compatibility with other system.

Creating folders for existing files

If you need a folder to compress one or several already existing files, you could create an empty folder as described above and then copy the files into it. However, there is an easier way:

1 Start Windows Explorer and open the directory containing the files you want to compress.

2 Select all files you want to insert into the compressed folder.

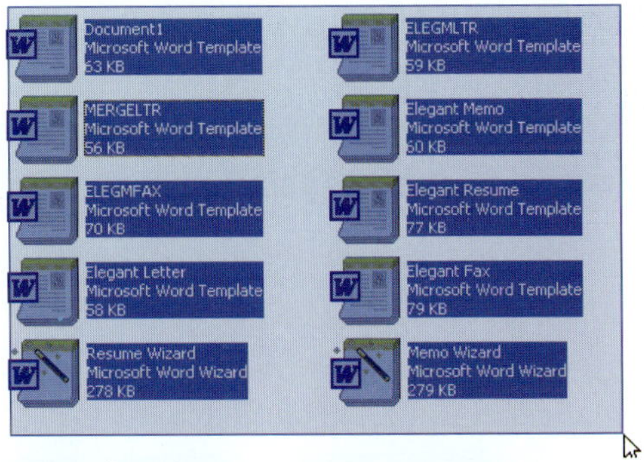

3 Right-click the selected folders to open the pop-up menu. Select *Send To/Compressed (zipped) Folder.*

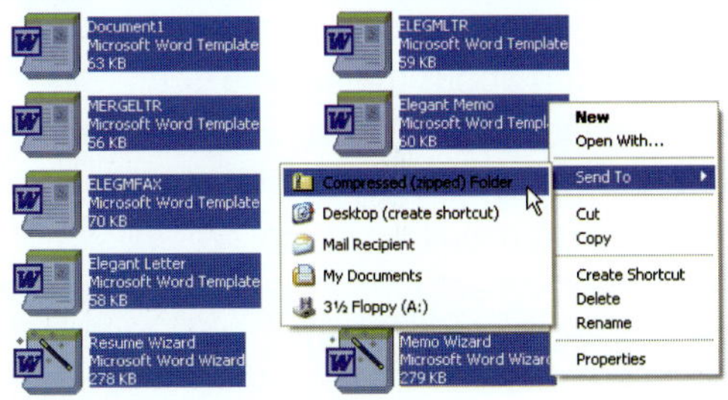

4 Windows Explorer then creates a compressed folder with the selected files in the current directory. The compressed folder receives the name of the first selected file, but you can rename it as you would any other file or folder.

5 If you want to save the files only in their compressed version, you should delete the uncompressed versions.

Opening and using compressed folders

Technically speaking, compressed folders are simply files in ZIP format. Windows Explorer in Windows XP was expanded to use files of this format without the help of additional ZIP software. Windows Explorer establishes itself as the program responsible for ZIP files. The advantage of this arrangement over external ZIP programs is that compressed folders (which are files, strictly speaking) behave like normal folders on the surface.

1 To open a compressed folder, select the directory containing it in Windows Explorer and double-click the compressed folder icon.

2 Windows Explorer then opens a new window displaying the contents of the compressed folder. In the right window, you can see an overview of the contained files and subfolders. The left panel displays the most important compressed folder functions.

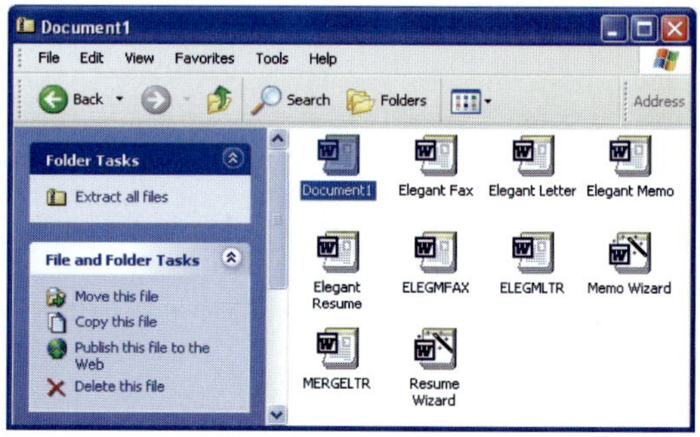

3 To obtain additional interesting information about the archive's contents, enable the detailed view by going to *View/Details*. In addition to the usual information, you need to obtain the following information for each file: whether the file *Has a password* (encrypted, yes or no), what its *Packed size* is (compressed size), what its actual *Size* is (uncompressed size), and what the *Ratio* is (how much the file was compressed).

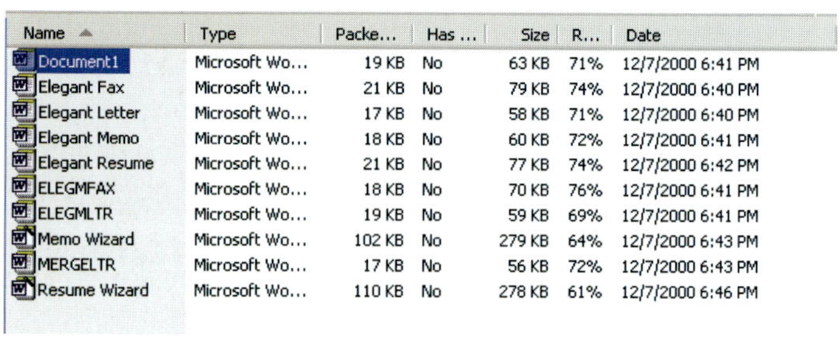

Name	Type	Packe...	Has ...	Size	R...	Date
Document1	Microsoft Wo...	19 KB	No	63 KB	71%	12/7/2000 6:41 PM
Elegant Fax	Microsoft Wo...	21 KB	No	79 KB	74%	12/7/2000 6:40 PM
Elegant Letter	Microsoft Wo...	17 KB	No	58 KB	71%	12/7/2000 6:40 PM
Elegant Memo	Microsoft Wo...	18 KB	No	60 KB	72%	12/7/2000 6:41 PM
Elegant Resume	Microsoft Wo...	21 KB	No	77 KB	74%	12/7/2000 6:42 PM
ELEGMFAX	Microsoft Wo...	18 KB	No	70 KB	76%	12/7/2000 6:41 PM
ELEGMLTR	Microsoft Wo...	19 KB	No	59 KB	69%	12/7/2000 6:41 PM
Memo Wizard	Microsoft Wo...	102 KB	No	279 KB	64%	12/7/2000 6:43 PM
MERGELTR	Microsoft Wo...	17 KB	No	56 KB	72%	12/7/2000 6:43 PM
Resume Wizard	Microsoft Wo...	110 KB	No	278 KB	61%	12/7/2000 6:46 PM

Extracting files from compressed folders

Files that have been saved in an archive folder in compressed form can be restored to their original format. This is useful, for instance, for files that you have compressed to send over the Internet but which you want to use again uncompromised. Because Windows XP treats compressed files like normal directories, you can simply drag and drop individual files into other folders or move them to a different spot by copying and pasting them. The file is then automatically extracted and saved in uncompressed form. In addition to retrieving individual files, you can also extract the contents of an entire folder. For that, there is a special function in Windows Explorer.

1 Open the compressed folder whose contents you want to extract.

2 In the left column, select *Extract all files* from the *Folder Tasks* to restore the compressed files.

3 Windows Explorer then starts a Wizard to help you set the necessary parameters.

4 As a second step, establish the directory in which you want to save the decompressed files in the field *Files will be extracted to this directory*. Enter the path directly into the text entry field or select it from a dialog box after clicking *Browse*.

5 If the files are password protected, click *Password* to enter it.

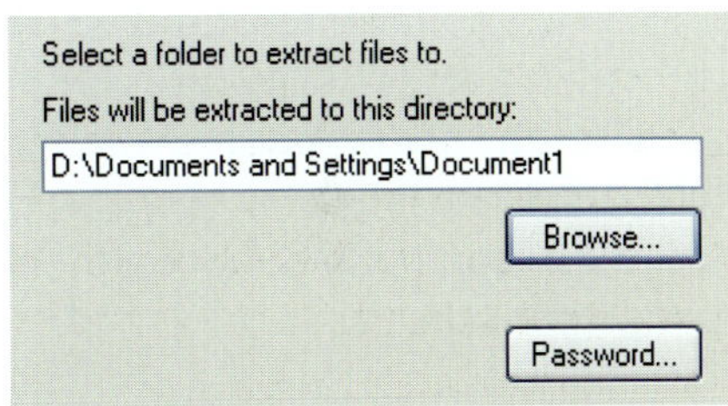

6 Click *Next* to start decompressing and restoring the files. Windows Explorer then unpacks the files from the compressed folder and writes them into the selected directory in their original format.

7 As a final step, the program confirms the successful restoration of the files and offers to display the extracted files immediately. To see the files, enable the option *Show extracted files*. Windows Explorer shows you the directory with the restored files.

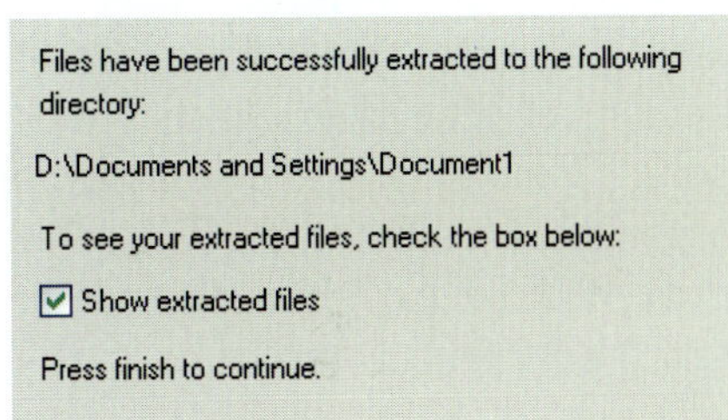

Using the power saving functions

Windows XP has a power saving concept with which you can significantly lower power consumption depending on the current use. In addition, it supports a new standard for power efficient usage through the integrated ACPI (**A**dvanced **C**onfiguration and **P**ower **I**nterface). The ACPI specifications make it possible to bring a computer almost to a standstill at the touch of a button to minimize power consumption. The computer can still be awakened within seconds at a corresponding signal. This signal doesn't have to come from the keyboard or a mouse but also from a modem or a network card. Thus, PCs can be used as energy-efficient network servers or faxes, for instance.

1 To manage the power saving functions of your PC, open the system settings by going to *Start/Control Panel*. Select the *Performance and Maintenance* category.

2 Open the *Power Options*.

3 First, stay in the *Power schemes* tab. In the field of the same name, select the most appropriate standard from the pre-set schemes.

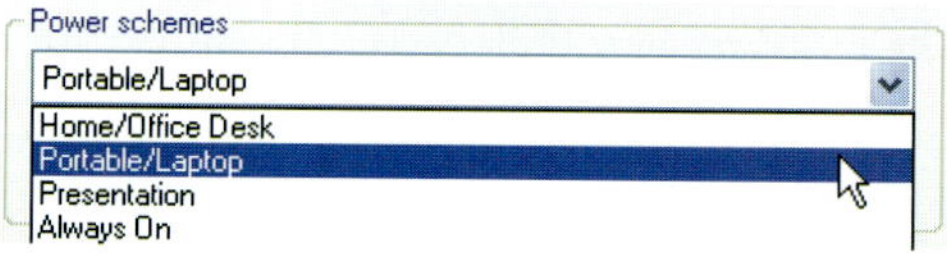

4 If you are not happy with any of the schemes, simply create your own. In the lower portion of the window, enter the amount of time after which the computer should enter into *System standby* or should *Turn off monitor/Turn off hard disks*. With *Save As*, you can save these settings as your own scheme that you can reuse.

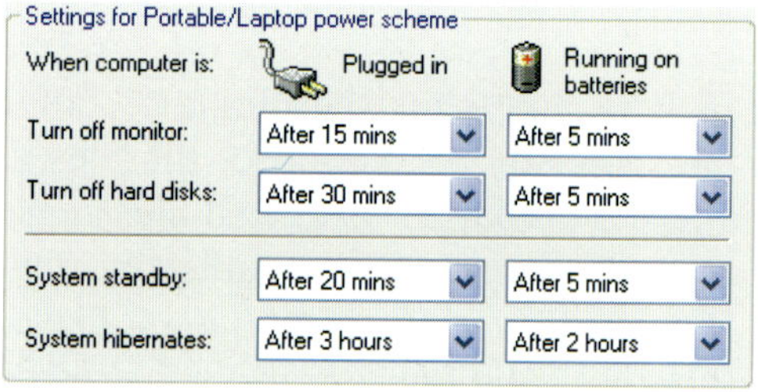

Note

Saving power for hard drives

Turning off the hard drives after the computer has been idle for a certain period is a great way to save power. In addition, it considerably lowers the noise level of a computer that is not in use at the moment. However, it also has a disadvantage you should know about: hard drives built for everyday use are meant to be shut down and brought back up only a few thousand times. Normally, this is no problem if you turn on the computer in the mornings and off at night. However, if the powers saving functions lead the hard drive to turn itself on and off ten times a day, for instance, the computer's life span can be seriously shortened. For this reason, you should choose a period of time after which the hard drive turns itself off that is long enough to prevent unnecessary wear-outs.

5 You can choose further options in the *Advanced* tab. Use the option *Always show icon on the taskbar* to place a special power management icon in the information area of the Start Menu bar. This is useful if you change the settings regularly. The function *Prompt for password when computer resumes from standby* offers an additional protection mechanism.

Backing up and restoring the XP system

If you already have some experience with older Windows versions, I'm sure you've run into the following problem: you only changed a setting or installed a program yet suddenly nothing functions as it did before. Sometimes this even happens after your computer crashes or without any reason whatsoever. Then it's time for painstaking error searching and fumbling with the settings, but most of the time the only thing that helps is completely reinstalling the system and all the headaches associated with that. With Windows XP, such nightmares are a thing of the past, for it comes with a clever system for saving all operating system settings. If the computer should act up one day, you can simply return to a previous state when everything was still functioning. This return to a previous state only applies to the system settings, of course. The documents created or edited in the meantime are saved in their entirety.

Saving the system state

For Windows XP to restore something, the state of the operating system needs to be saved from time to time. Normally, this happens automatically through so-called restore points. Windows XP automatically creates restore points every time you start the system or when you install a new application, for instance. However, you can create such restore points yourself at any time. This is recommended right before you change important settings or when you want to make manual changes to the registry, for instance.

1 To create restore point, go to *Start/All Programs/Accessories/System Tools/Backup* to open the Backup Utility Wizard.

2 In the first step, select *Create a restore point* as the task you want to perform and click *Next* to continue.

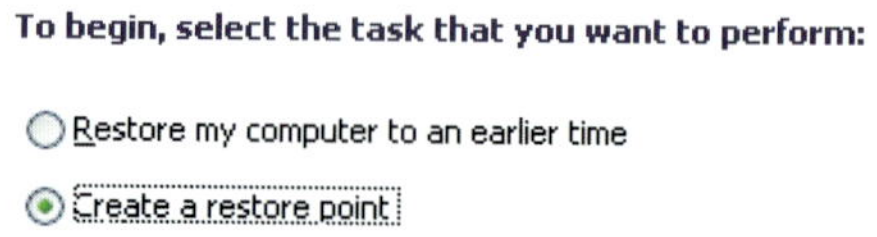

3 In the text entry field, enter the *Restore point description*. Enter the reason for which you want to create this restore point. You don't need to enter the date and time, for this information is added automatically.

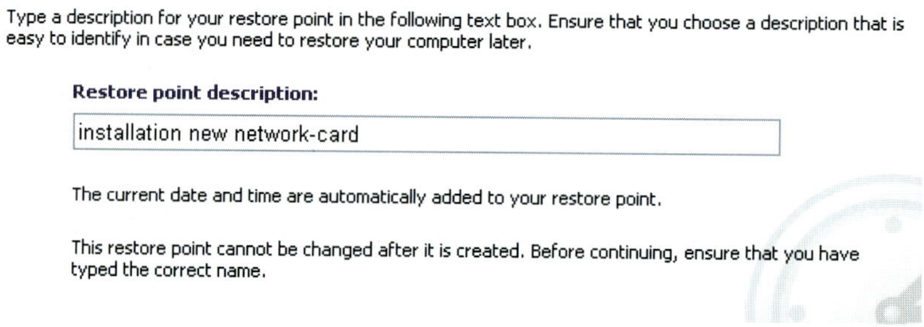

4 Click the *Create* button to complete the backup.

5 The Wizard then saves the entire current contents of the registrations database in one restore point. It then notifies you of the successful backup of the system data. You can close the Wizard or return to the beginning.

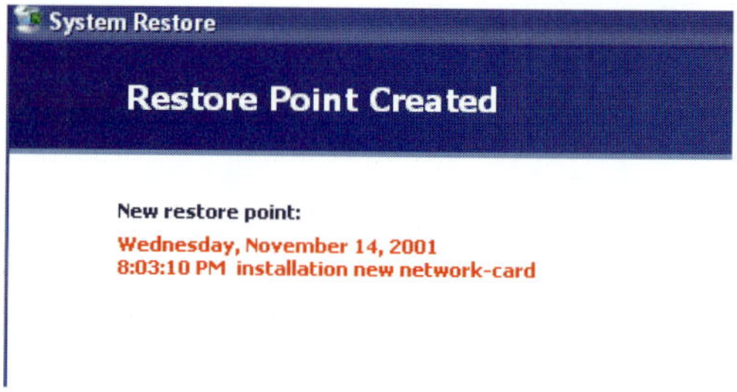

Restoring the system state

If you have concrete problems with Windows XP – certain features don't work correctly anymore, you can't establish a network or Internet connection, and so forth – go back to a saved system state when the system was functioning as it should.

1 Call up the Backup Utility Wizard again, by going to *Start/All Programs/Accessories/System Tools/Backup*.

2 Select the task *Restore my computer to an earlier time.*

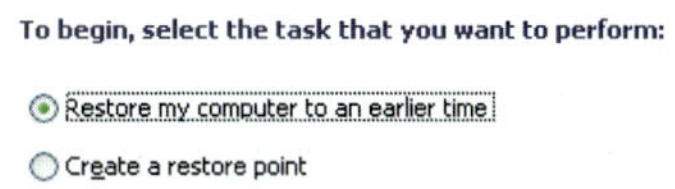

3 For the next step, select the point in time to which you want the system to be restored. Think about when the disturbances started and select a previous date from the calendar window on the left. The bold print indicates restore point dates.

4 When you select a date, its restore points are displayed in the field on the right. Select the point to which you want to return. Be aware that restore points automatically created in conjunction with a program installation were created before the installation. Thus, returning to them means that the installation is undone.

5 Next, the Wizard asks you to confirm the selected restore point and notifies you that rebooting the system is necessary for system restoration. If you have any documents open, you must first close these. Then, click *Next* to initiate the restoration.

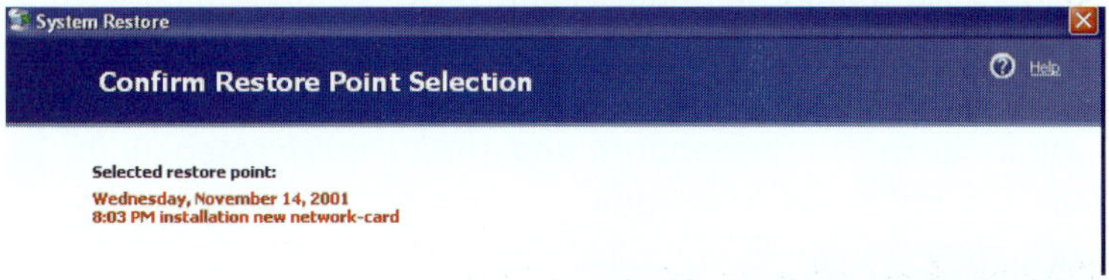

6 Windows XP completes the system restore and restarts. After it reboots, it checks whether the restoration was successful and confirms this with a short confirmation message.

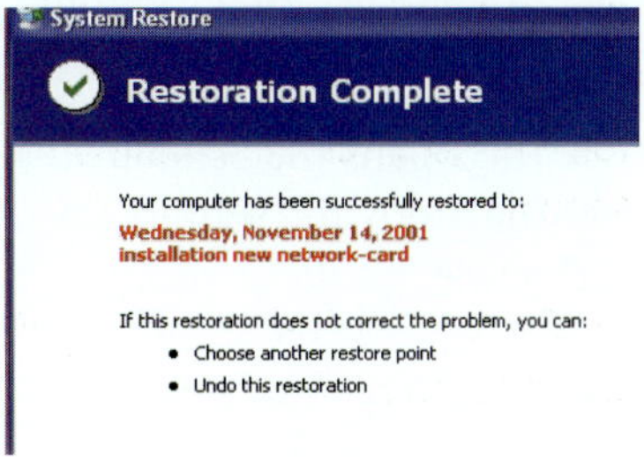

If the restoration shouldn't be successful, you should try another, earlier restore point. If the system state has become even worse, you can undo the restoration. To do so, select the option *Undo the last restoration* from the first step in the Backup Utility Wizard.

> **Note**
>
> **When Windows won't start at all**
>
> Sometimes the problem is grave enough to keep Windows from opening. Then the Backup Utility Wizard doesn't help you much, because you can't even access it. In that case, start Windows in safe mode first (see chapter 3). If that doesn't work either, you should select *Last Known Good Configuration* from the *Windows Advanced Options Menu*. Windows returns to the last successfully saved restore point and starts with those settings. The system should now work again. If necessary, you can return to another (maybe even better suited) point.

Automating maintenance tasks

Windows XP comes with different tools and help programs for maintaining the operating system and the Windows components. The most important tools include Disk Defragmenter and Disk Cleanup presented in this chapter. For the safety and optimum performance of your PC, you should regularly call up and use these maintenance tools. Thanks to the *Scheduled Tasks* feature of Windows XP, you can now allow such regular maintenance tasks to be performed automatically.

1 Open the special *Scheduled Tasks* folder. You can find the folder in the *Performance and Maintenance* category in the *Control Panel* or by going to *Start/All Programs/Accessories/System Tools/Scheduled Tasks*.

2 Double-click *Add Scheduled Task* to allow a maintenance task or another application to be run automatically.

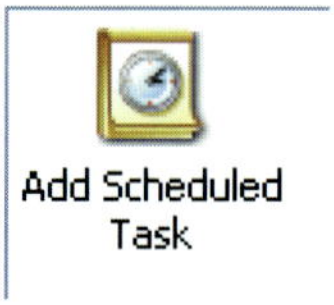

3 This opens the Scheduled Task Wizard, which takes you through all the steps for setting up the automatic process. Click *Next* to acknowledge its greeting.

4 As a first step, determine which application you want to run regularly. Select one from the list of registered Windows XP programs. The list also features maintenance programs like Disk Cleanup. If the application you are looking for should be missing from the list, you can select it from a file selection dialog box by clicking *Browse*.

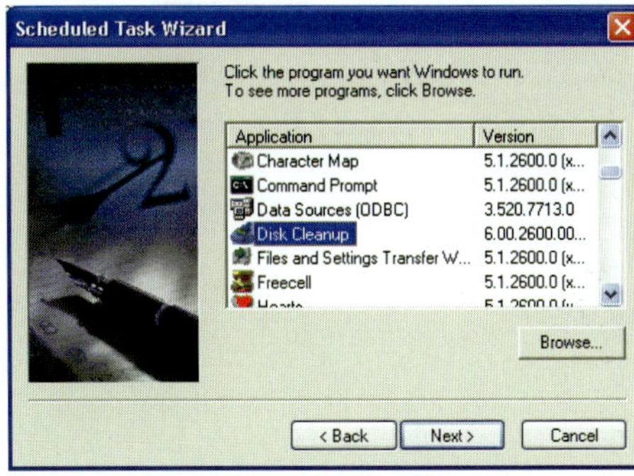

5 Determine a name for the task. The Wizard takes the name of the selected application by default. You can replace the name with one of your choice.

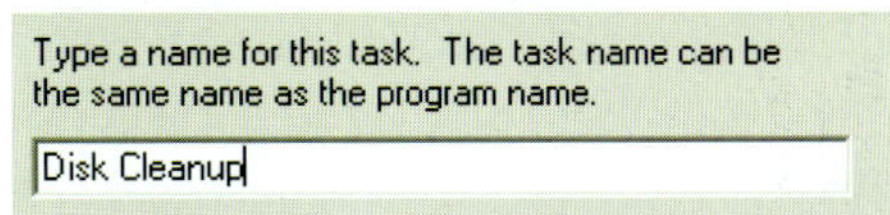

6 Next, determine how often you want to perform this task. Your decision should depend on how often each task should be performed. If you are always tight on available hard drive space, it makes sense to run the Disk Cleanup *Daily*. If, on the other hand, you have a lot of space available, a *Weekly* or *Monthly* performance should suffice. In addition to the time definitions, you can schedule the task to be performed *One time only*, *When my computer starts*, or *When I log on*.

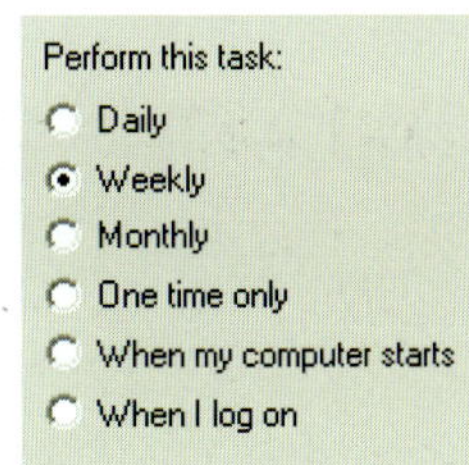

7 Depending on the options you have just chosen, you can now refine the schedule for performing the task. In the example, the task is performed weekly. Decide on what days and at what hour to run the application. In addition, you can restrict the performance for every other or every third week. Thus, you can be flexible with your schedule. Which setting options are available at this point depends on the option chosen in the preceding step, however.

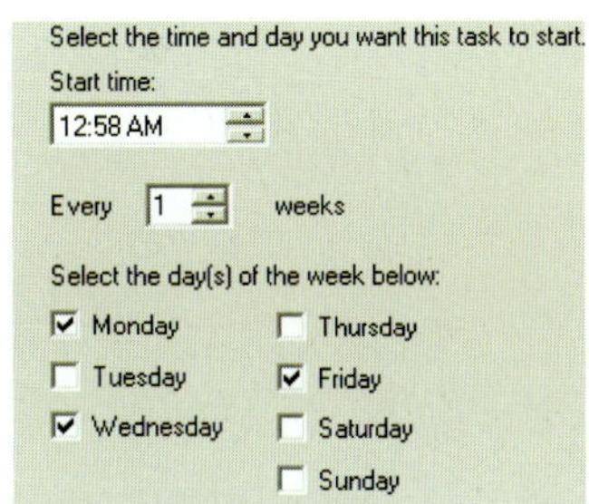

8 You now must enter the user name and password necessary for starting the application. Confirm the password by entering it again.

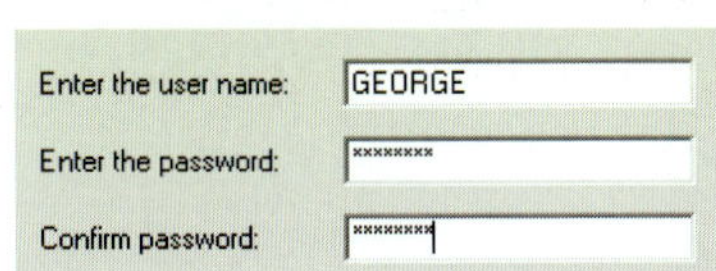

Note

Automatic tasks and the users

The user system of Windows XP makes it necessary to assign each application to a user. Normally, the user to which an application is assigned is the one who called up the application. Because in this case the application is started automatically, the user entered here is assigned to it. This is important, because the application has access only to data to which this user has access. Important: Some system tools can only be run if they are assigned to a user with an administrator account. If that is the case with your application, enter the name of such a user.

9 Finally, the Wizard displays a summary of the planned task. Make sure that everything is configured according to your wishes; then click *Finish* to set up the task.

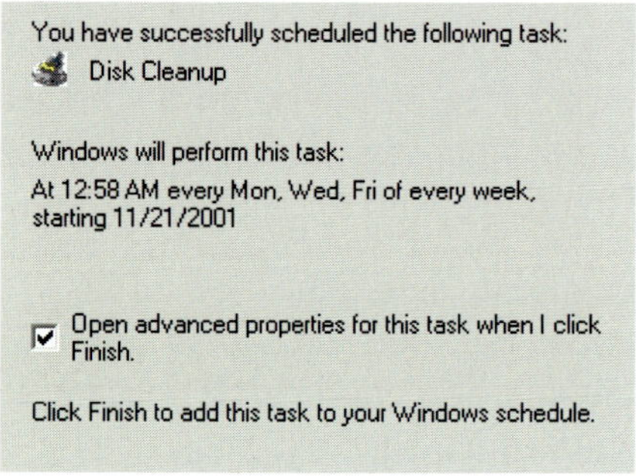

5. Audio, video and more – Multimedia with Windows XP

These days, just about any modern PC is media compatible, that is, it can display pictures and videos in full color, rapidly and loudly. A color monitor, a sound card and loudspeakers, a CD-ROM (or even better, DVD) drive and average storage capacity are the accessories of any multimedia PC. The quality of the multimedia display (for example, for videos and 3D images) depends only on the processor speed. Windows XP comes with multimedia tools. The new system supports especially amateur photographers with digital cameras. A better, expanded version of Windows Media Player is also included. In addition, Windows XP offers creative types the opportunity to produce their own pictures, videos, and sounds, and to effortlessly save their works of art with the help of an attached CD burner.

Creating a slide show with a digital camera and a scanner

Scanners have been popular with PC users for a few years now, and digital cameras are now finding their ways into the hearts of amateur photographers as well. Owning a digital camera only makes sense, however, if you have a computer capable of downloading, editing, printing, or saving pictures on CD. Furthermore, it is only fun if the computer can support these features optimally. Windows XP acknowledges this by seamlessly embedding features for working with scanners and digital cameras into the interface and by supporting these with handy Wizards. Trying to figure out the software of the device manufacturers thus becomes pretty much superfluous.

Connecting a digital camera to the PC

Windows XP supports digital cameras with USBs admirably well. As soon as you have connected the camera to the PC, a Wizard automatically opens, offering you different possibilities for transferring and editing pictures. You can even automate this selection, for instance to the effect that all pictures from this camera are always transferred to a certain directory.

1 When you connect a digital camera to the USB port on your computer and turn it on, Windows XP automatically launches the Removable Storage Wizard. The Wizard recognizes that the device is a digital camera, and offers you the appropriate options.

2 Click *Print the pictures using Photo Printing Wizard* to print the pictures on a connected printer. You can even choose special formats like contact sheets. For more details on printing pictures, see the next section.

3 If you want to get an overview of the pictures first, or only mean to look at them, choose *View a slideshow of the images.* Windows XP then displays the pictures one by one in a simple presentation.

4 If you want to save the pictures on your PC and edit them further, you can let the Wizard transfer the picture files to a folder of your choice. Click *Copy pictures to a folder on my computer* to start the Scanner and Camera Wizard. More details on this Wizard later.

5 Click *Open folder to view files* to display the contents of the camera in the usual folder view. Here, you have access to any pictures and can copy, rename, or delete individual ones. You can also manually transfer files to other folders or directories.

6 If you want to edit the pictures with a different application (perhaps the software that came with the camera), select the last option, *Take no action*, to close the Wizard.

7 No matter what action you take, you can enable *Always do the selected action* to automatically select that option when you connect the camera to the PC in the future.

Transferring pictures from the camera to the PC

If you have selected the option *Copy pictures to a folder on my computer* in the *Removable Storage* menu, the Scanner and Camera Wizard is now started, with which you can conveniently transfer your pictures to the PC.

1 First acknowledge the Wizard's greeting by clicking *Next*.

2 The Wizard then shows you an overview of the pictures located in the camera. Select which pictures you want to transfer. All pictures are selected by default, but you can deselect individual pictures by removing their checkmarks. In addition, you can establish, with the help of the icons on the bottom left, if individual pictures need to be rotated.

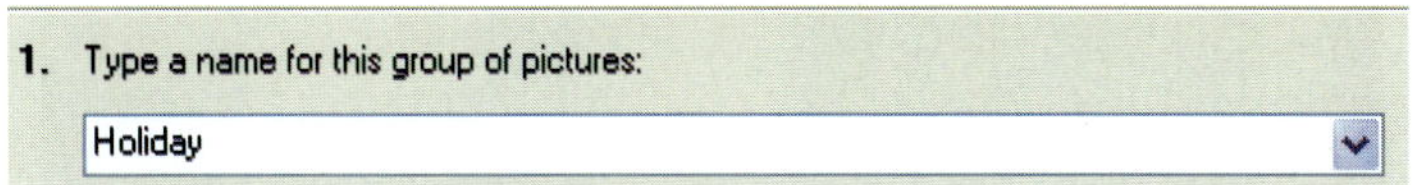

3 In the next step, *Type a name for this group of pictures*. This name is saved as the name template for the picture files. The index number of each picture is added to each individual picture name.

4 Next, *Choose a place to save this group of pictures*. Windows XP saves the pictures in the folder *My Pictures* by default, but you can enter a different folder by clicking *Browse*.

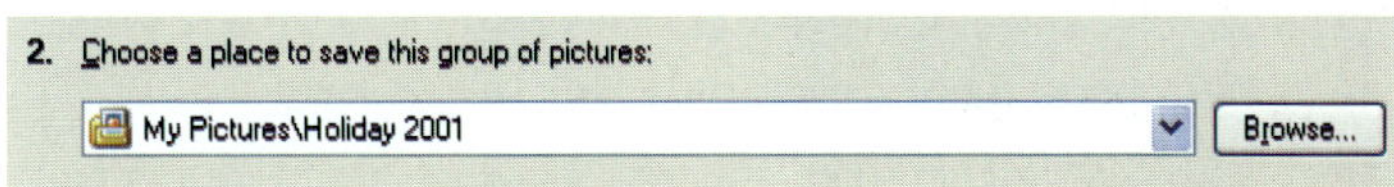

5 Click *Delete pictures from my device after copying them* to automatically free up space on the digital camera after copying your pictures to the computer.

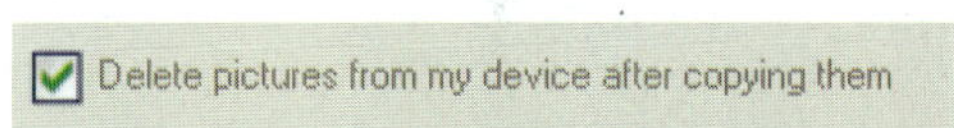

6 Click *Next* to start transferring the pictures from the digital camera to the PC.

Printing pictures with the Photo Printing Wizard

The Photo Printing Wizard makes printing pictures directly from a scanner or digital camera easy. c. You can start the Wizard automatically when you connect a digital camera to your PC through a USB port.

1 Select *Print the pictures using Photo Printing Wizard* from the *Removable Storage* menu.

2 Disregard the Wizard's greeting by clicking *Next*.

3 The Wizard then displays an overview of the pictures located in the digital camera. Here, you can select which pictures you want to print. All pictures are check-marked by default. If you don't want to print a picture, remove the checkmark by clicking it.

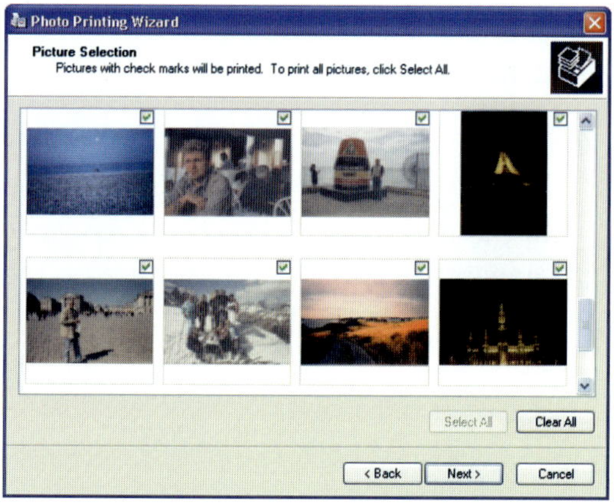

4 In the next step, select the printer with which you want to print. Both local devices and networked printers are listed here (see chapter 6). In addition, you can adjust the most important printing options for the selected printer under *Printing Preferences*.

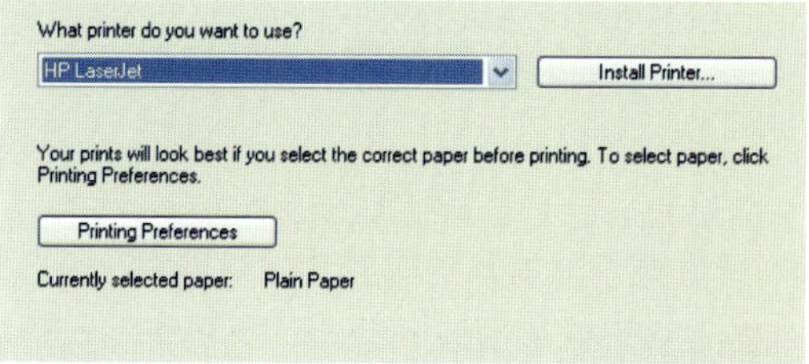

5 The next step is the *Layout Selection*. Here, you can determine how and in what size you want to print your pictures. You can print a picture to cover an entire page or to correspond to a standard size. In addition, you can print contact sheets or print several pictures on one page. The Wizard automatically computes the size of the pictures to optimally

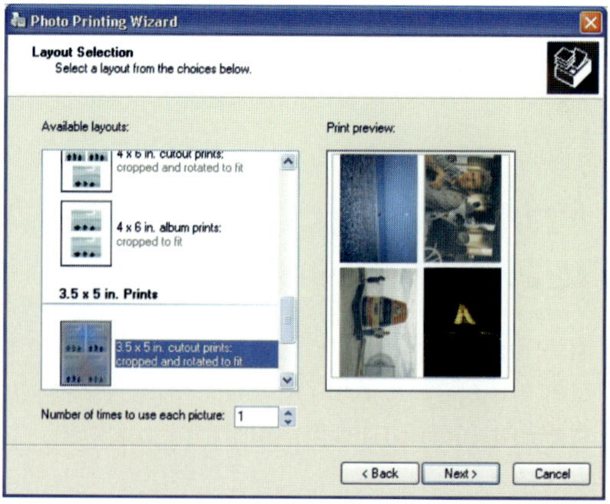

adapt them to each format. For this reason, it might take a few moments to display the preview for some of the formats.

6 The Wizard prepares the pictures according to the selected settings and sends them to the chosen printer.

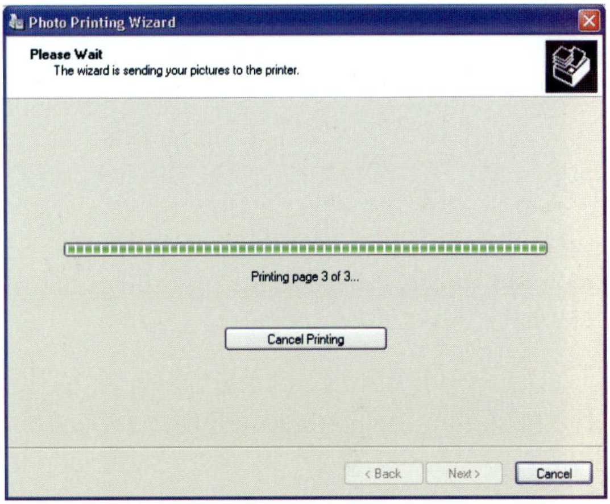

Music and more with Windows Media Player

The version of Windows Media Player integrated in Windows XP is a powerful multimedia tool, offering you many practical and convenient features in addition to the playback of audio and video files. It is compatible with virtually all usual audio and video formats. In addition to playing AVI and MPEG videos, it also plays MP3 clips and audio CDs. With Windows Media Player, you can even create your own audio CD, which you can then burn with an attached CD burner.

Note

About skins

One of the outstanding features of Windows Media Player is the customizable interface through so-called skins. Just like with Windows XP itself (see chapter 2), you can almost entirely customize the look of the program. Several skins are included with the program, but you can download other skins from the Internet for free in the future and even create your own. The different skins are somewhat problematic for our description of the program, for the interface and controls differ from one design to the other. In the following, you use the full view mode of the default Windows XP skin that was installed with Windows XP. Stay with this setting for right now. Once you are acquainted with the program, you can try out other options. You will rapidly become familiar with other looks of the controls

The Windows Media Player controls

While Windows Media Player is running and playing a file, the following controls are at your disposal in the form of buttons:

1 The large *Play* button starts the playback of an open file. When Windows Media Player is called up by Internet Explorer or Windows Explorer to play a file, the playback of the file is started automatically.

2 During playback, the *Play* icon changes to a *Pause* icon with which you can interrupt the playback of the file. Click the *Play* icon again to resume playback.

3 The *Stop* button stops the playback of the current file. The file is set to the beginning but not closed. If you are streaming data from the Internet, Windows Media Player maintains the connection. This allows you to resume playing almost immediately.

4 *Previous* rewinds the current media clip to the beginning. If you are playing a playlist composed of several clips, this button takes you to the previous clip in the list. Click the button once to return to the beginning of the current clip. If you click again at this point, you jump to the beginning of the previous clip.

5 *Next* is useful only in connection with playlists composed of several media clips. Click this button to jump to the beginning of the next clip and start playing it.

6 The *Mute* button disables the playback of audio for media files. In contrast to the *Pause* button, this doesn't stop the playback of the clip. To hear the sound again, click the same button. If this button is disabled, your sound card doesn't support the mute feature.

7 The *Volume* slider controls the volume level of the clip being played back. This slider is only enabled if your sound card supports this feature.

8 Use the *Seek* slider to scroll back and forth or jump to a particular spot in an audio or video clip while it is playing.

9 Use the *Shuffle* button at the top right (you may know this button from your CD player) to play the songs on the playlist or CD in random order. Click this button again to exit this mode.

10 Click the *Switch to skin mode* icon at the right of the control buttons to switch from the default full-screen view to the skin view in which Windows Media Player is displayed on-screen as an independent design object instead of a classic window.

11 In the skin view, the controls look very different depending on the chosen skin. Generally they are the same buttons, however, and even the icons are at least similar, so it won't take long for you to adjust.

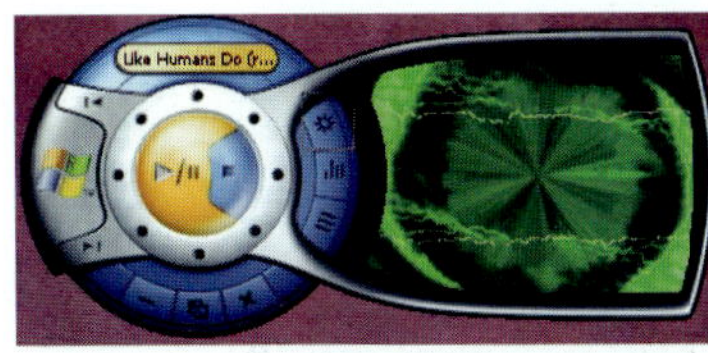

Capturing existing media clips

For Windows Media Player to manage your media collection and make it accessible to you, it must first know where files are located. Therefore, it needs to search your hard drive and capture multimedia files. It then analyzes the results and structures the data so you can access it more easily.

1 To search the hard drive, go to *Tools/Search for Media Files* in the Media Player. The program automatically calls up this feature when it is started for the first time. Afterwards, you need to initiate the search yourself at regular intervals to keep the program up-to-date. If you generally only use Windows Media Player for your multimedia files, however, the program automatically registers all changes and new files, which renders further searches superfluous.

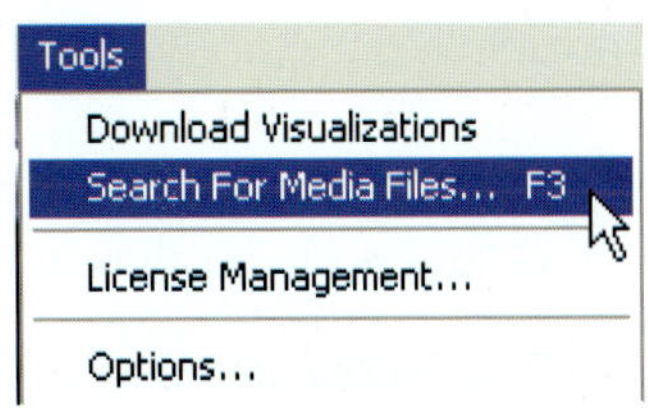

2 In the menu that opens, determine where Windows Media Player should look for multimedia files. The best selection is the option *All Drives*, because it guarantees that everything is found. If all interesting files are located on one drive, you can restrict the search to a certain drive and even directory, thus speeding up the

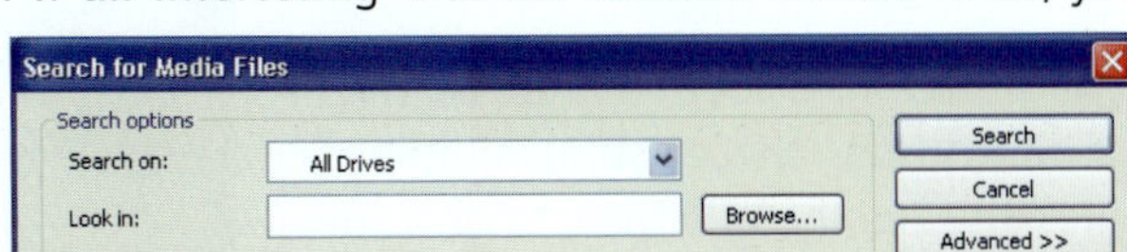

search process. Click *Advanced* to view further options, like determining the minimum size of the clips to be captured.

3 Click *Search* to start capturing and analyzing files. This process might take a while depending on the number of files. In the meantime, Windows Media Player entertains you with a status window. Once the analysis is completed, the status window displays the number of found files. Click *Close* to exit this function.

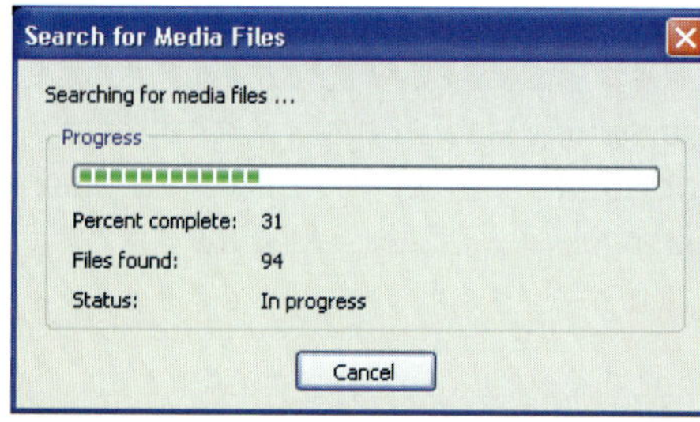

4 You then return to the previous search window. Here you can start searching a different drive, for example. The results of this search are then added to the previous results. End the search by clicking *Close*.

Using the Media Library in Windows Media Player

Windows Media Player manages all captured multimedia files in the so-called Media Library. In principle, the Media Library is a database comprising all media clips on your computer. You can view the clips in different views and search the database using different search criteria. The Media Library also allows you to open any available file quickly if you know its information, such as the title or artist.

1 To open the Media Library, click the button with the same name in Windows Media Player.

2 The Media Library functions according to the same principle as Windows Explorer. On the left, you have several categories (or folders). When you select a category by clicking it, its contents are displayed in the right half of the window. In addition, the categories often contain subfolders that you can open by clicking their icons.

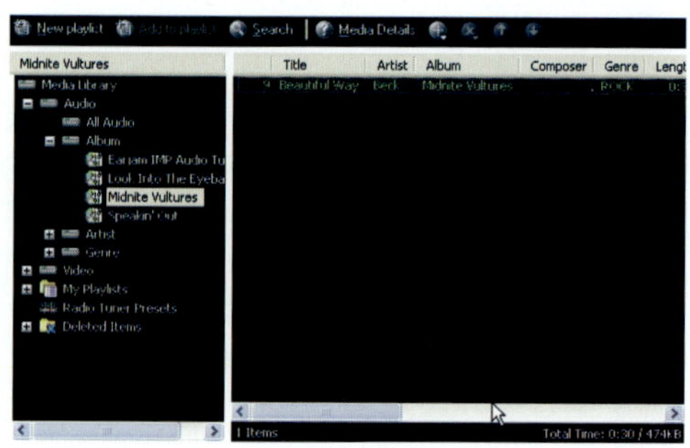

3 On the first level, Windows Media Player divides the existing multimedia files into *Audio* and *Video*, to give you a better overview. Inside these categories, you can find subcategories that give you different access avenues to the same content.

4 Under *Audio*, you can call up an alphabetical listing of all filenames by clicking *All Audio*. Choose *Album* to organize the individual songs by album, as far as this information is available (for example, for MP3 files). Click *Artist* to sort the songs by artist. Under *Genre*, the audio files are organized by such genres as *Rock*, *Classical*, *Jazz*, and so forth

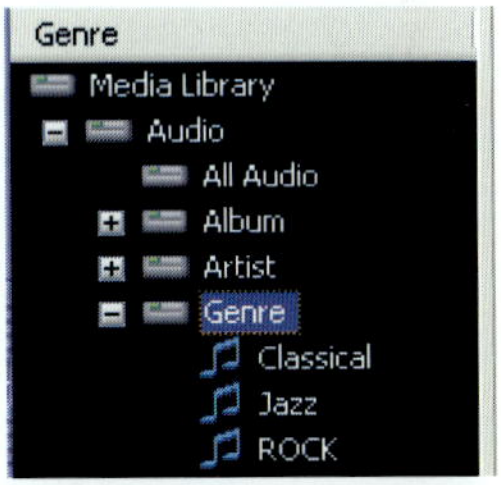

5 Because video files usually don't list as much information, you can sort these files only alphabetically with *All Video* or by *Author*.

6 All other categories are there for the sake of organization. Thus, under *My Playlists*, you can organize playlists that unite several clips by one group (for example, clips from one album). Here, you can also find M3U playlists, for instance. All deleted files go into the *Deleted Items* folder.

The Media Library thus offers a whole range of options for finding media clips. To play a clip, you only need to select it in the right half of the window and click the *Play* button.

Creating your own playlists

If you always want to listen to the music for which you are in the mood at the moment, you can create as many playlists of your own as you'd like.

1 In the Media Library, click the *New playlist* button on the top left.

2 In the dialog box, enter a name for the playlist. Use a meaningful designation, so you can find your playlist later.

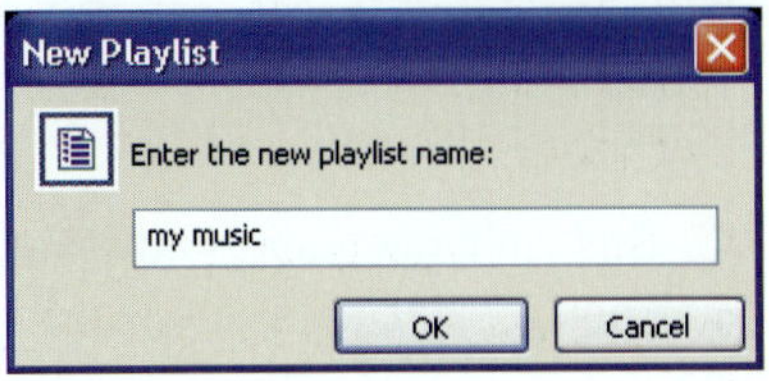

3 Your list now appears as a new entry in the category *My Playlists*.

4 To add content to the list, simply drag and drop into this playlist audio and/or video clips from other playlists and categories.

5 In the playlist, the clips are sorted in the order in which you have added them to the list. You can change the order, however, by displaying the list contents in the Media Library and by dragging the individual titles to the position in which you want them.

Copying audio CDs to the computer

More and more users are switching to copying their audio CDs to the PC. Doing so has a number of advantages. For one, you can thus play the stored music on the computer without having to search for the original CD anymore. You can also create and play your own music lists or even CDs (more about this in the next section). Finally, those who own a portable player with digital storage (for example, a MP3 walkman, and so forth) must copy the music from the CD and then compress it, before transferring it to the portable player. All these actions can be conveniently undertaken in Windows Media Player.

1 To copy an audio CD to your computer, insert the CD into the CD-ROM drive and start Windows Media Player.

2 From the navigation bar on the left, select the category *Copy from CD*.

3 Windows Media Player displays an overview of the CD contents. If the program doesn't recognize the CD, the overview doesn't help you much, because everything appears as "Track X" and "Unknown Artist". Now you can enter the information about the *Title*, *Artist*, *Composer*, *Genre*, and so forth by hand.

4 This isn't necessary, however, if your PC is connected to the Internet. In that case, a Wizard helps you find all necessary information online. To call up the Wizard, click *Get Names*.

5 This starts a Wizard in the bottom half of Windows Media Player. In the first step, you need to choose whether you want to search by *Artist Name* or *Album Name*. Click one of the option fields and a text entry field appears, in which you can enter the desired search term. A third option allows you to type in the album information yourself if the CD is your own compilation.

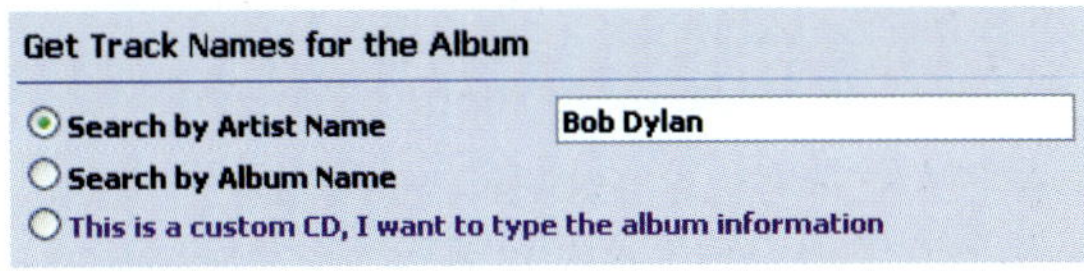

6 If exact matches occur, the Wizard then gives you the option of selecting from the matches, according to genre. If no matches occur, you can select *Artist not found* and, out of the kindness of your heart, add the relevant information for your CD to the form that follows by hand and submit it to the server for others.

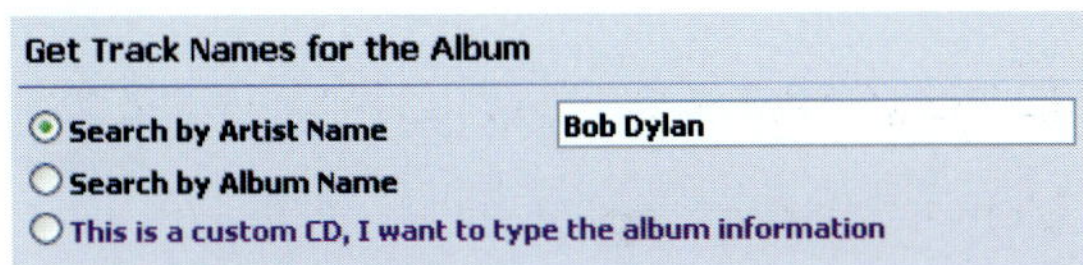

7 The Wizard searches for CDs by this artist and presents an overview of the search results. From the overview, select the CD you have inserted into the computer.

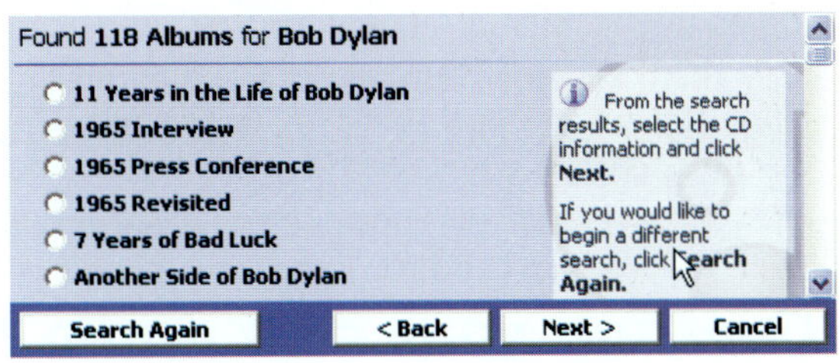

8 When you click *Finish*, the Wizard downloads the information and completes the entries in the display.

> **Note**
>
> **No matching data available?**
>
> The Wizard can't always find the desired information for you. This is the case especially with unusual music not found in the mainstream. In this case, you might have to enter the data by hand after all. Unfortunately, the database at Gracenote, from which you can download practically any CD information, does not support Windows Media Player.

8 Click the *Copy Music* button to transfer the songs from the audio CD to your PC.

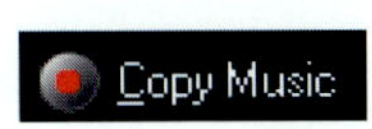

9 Windows Media Player first notifies you about copy music protection. If you want to play the copied music on other players (for example, a portable player), you should enable the option *Do not protect content*. You should still note the information about property rights, however.

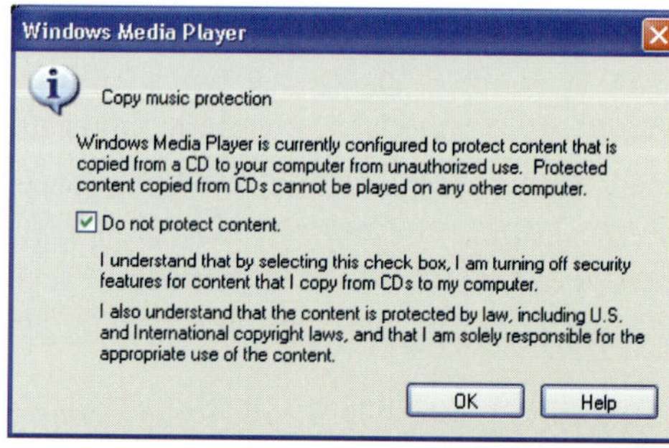

10 Then, Windows Media Player starts copying the songs from the CD. You can monitor the progress in the *Copy Status* column.

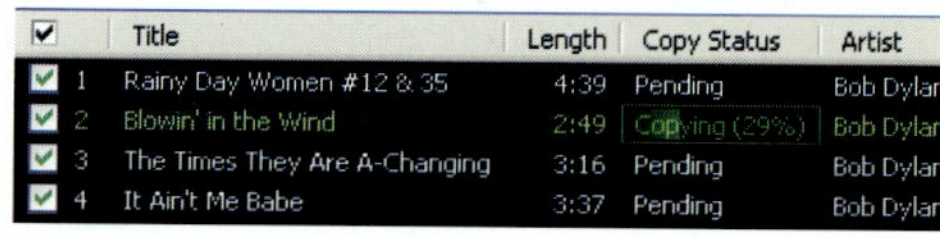

When the copy process is complete, the songs from the CD are stored as digital copies in the Media Library. You can play them directly, use them in playlists, or copy them to other devices. The copies are in Windows own WMA format, not in the popular MP3 format. Windows XP doesn't allow you to create MP3s (for more information, see also chapter 9).

Creating your own audio CDs

Because you can organize your entire music collection so well with Windows Media Player, it would be a shame if you couldn't also create your own music CDs with it. This is no problem, however, if your computer comes with a CD burner.

1 First, create a playlist in the Media Library especially for the CD, as described above. While creating the playlist, you should pay attention to the order of the songs. You should also pay attention to the *Total Time*, which cannot exceed the capacity of your blank CD.

2 Next, select the playlist and switch to the Windows Media Player category *Copy to CD or Device*.

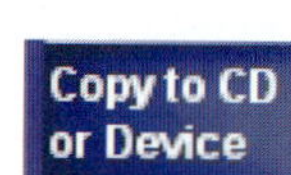

3 There, you can find the contents of the playlist displayed on the left. Mark the tracks you want to include on the CD. Checking the box in the *Title* bar affects the selection of the entire list.

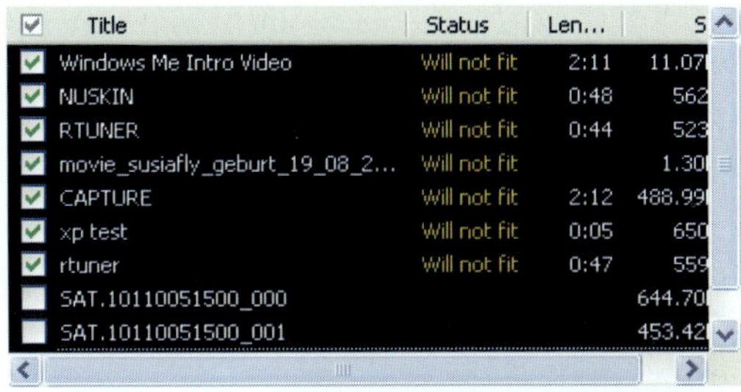

4 In the right half of the window, select the device to which you want to copy the tracks. You must definitely select the CD burner, if you also use other devices (for example, portable player) with the program. If the CD burner is the only device, it is selected by default.

5 Once everything is prepared, click the *Copy Music* button on the top right.

6 Because only WAV files can be played on a CD, Windows Media Player now has to convert all non-WAV files. The program informs you if it cannot convert some files and offers to quit the procedure.

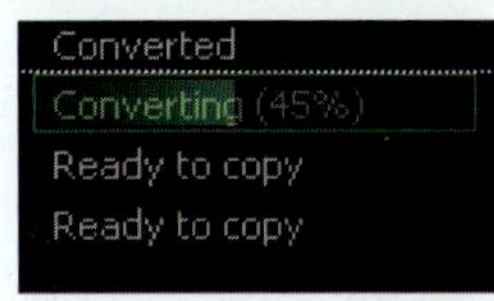

7 Then, Windows Media Player starts burning the songs to CD one by one. During the burn process, you should avoid disturbing the computer with complicated tasks, so the CD can be created without problems. How long this takes depends on the length of the tracks and on the write speed of the CD burner. The estimated time is displayed in the status bar.

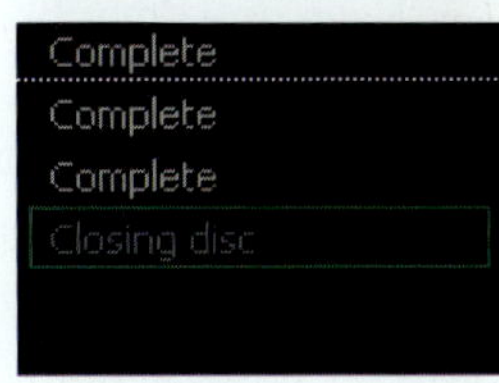

8 Once the creation of the CD is complete, the CD is ejected from the burner, and you can enjoy it immediately.

As a last step, you can verify, if you like, the CD. Of course, it is possible to play the CD not only on your computer, but on any commercial CD player, Discman, or car CD player.

Burning pictures, documents and files to CD

You have just seen how to compile and burn an audio CD of your favorite songs. Yet music CDs aren't the only kind of CDs you can create in Windows XP. On the contrary, if your computer has a burner, you can write any files or folders to a CD-R or CD-RW. This way, you can create CDs of your vacation pictures or backup copies of important documents. This feature is also easy to use. You only need to drag the files to the CD burner drive, just as you would if you wanted to place them on a diskette or the hard drive. Once the files are on the drive, a Wizard helps you burn them to the blank CD in no time. Windows XP writes data to CD-Rs in such a way as to allow you to add data at a later time until the CD is full.

Transferring data to the CD burner drive

To write files to a CD-R or CD-RW with the CD burner, simply copy or drag the files to the CD burner drive. There are different ways of getting the files there.

1 Windows XP displays the CD drive like any other drive under My Computer. This means that you can save any document directly on the CD burner drive, if you select it in the *Save As* dialog window of your application.

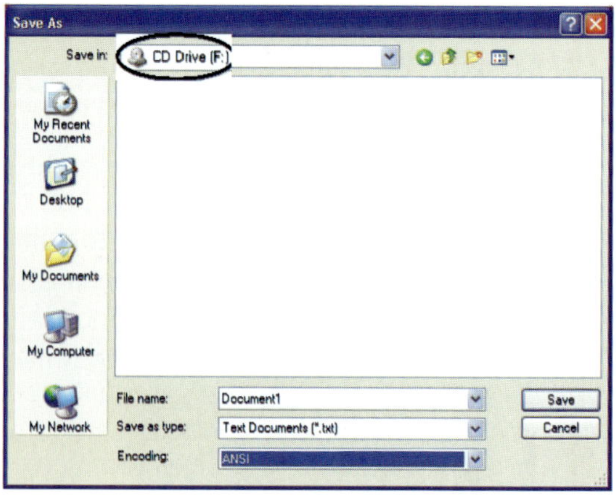

2 You can also drag and drop the file and folder icons to the CD burner drive.

3 In addition, every pop-up menu that opens when you right-click a file or folder provides you with the option *Send To/CD Drive*. Thus, you can designate any object for saving on a CD.

Note

How saving on CDs works

As you may know from your own experience with burning CDs, in reality writing data to CDs doesn't go very fast. Windows XP employs a trick here. The files are first written to a temporary directory on a hard drive. Thus, the data can be saved without any appreciable delay. The actual CD is created only when you have selected all files and have confirmed this. In the meantime, you can turn the computer off without worry. The files are permanently saved until you burn the CD or remove the data yourself. When Windows XP starts, it reminds you of any data you have designated for burning on CD.

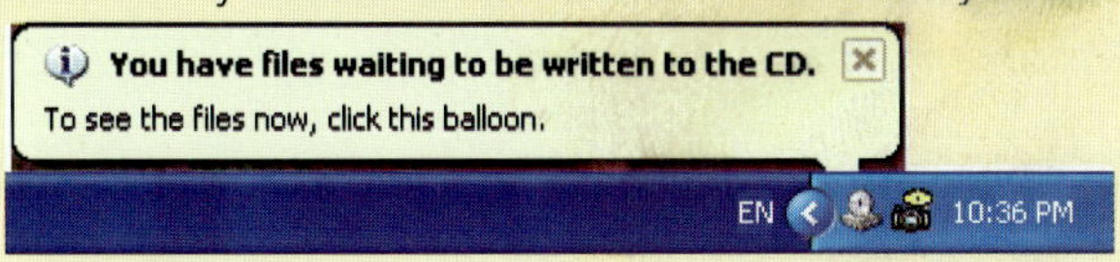

Writing data to CD

Once you have accumulated all the files you want to burn to CD, you can create the latter at any time.

1 Open the CD burner drive in Windows Explorer to display its contents. In the *Tasks* area, you can also find all the important information about the blank CD.

2 The *Total Size* of the blank CD and the available *Free Space* on it are displayed under *Details*. If you are using the same CD several times, this information lets you know if there is still enough storage space available.

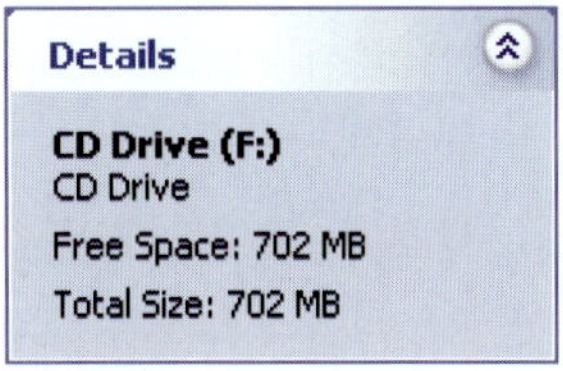

3 In the *CD Writing Tasks* area at the top, notice the two tasks *Write these files to CD* and *Delete temporary files*. With the latter command, you can delete the files if you decide not to burn the CD. This deletes only the copies (shortcuts) created for the CD, of course; the original files are preserved.

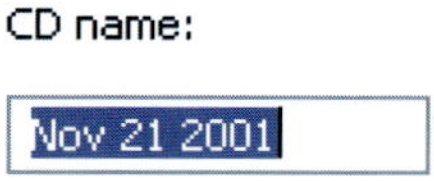

4 To create the CD from the files you have saved, you must select *Write these files to CD*. This opens the CD Writing Wizard.

5 The Wizard first prompts you for a CD name. It suggests the current date by default, but you can enter any name you want. However, the name cannot be longer than 16 characters and shouldn't contain any special symbols.

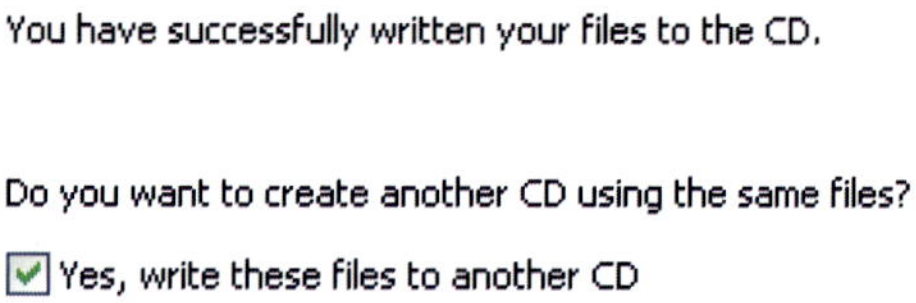

6 The Wizard begins writing the data to the CD. How long this takes depends on the amount of data and the speed of your CD burner. You can monitor the progress in the status bar.

7 In the end, the Wizard confirms the successful writing of the CD with the message *You have successfully written your files to the CD*. You can create another copy of this CD by checking *Yes, write these files to another CD*.

8 Quit the Wizard by clicking *Finish*. The temporary files created for the CD are then deleted from the hard drive.

6. Home networking with Windows XP

Local area networks (LAN) - whether at home or at the office - are becoming more and more popular. This is easily understood, given that increasing numbers of users employ more than one computer. In an office, every employee needs his or her own computer,but many users are even joining home computers. One of the reasons for this growing society of PCs is the need to regularly upgrade to a more powerful computer to keep up with modern applications (for example, current computer games). The "old" PC might then be used for standard applications (like word processing), which do not require the display of the newest 3D graphics. Once you own a few such PCs, it makes sense to connect them to each other to share data more easily and use available devices such as printers from any computer. In addition, a LAN allows you to play many computer games (multiplayer games) with others over the network, opening new playing and communication possibilities.

Building a local area network

You have a local area network if two or more computers are connected with each other in such a way that they can share data. For PCs, the most usual kind of network is the Ethernet, in which each PC is connected through a special extension card called a network adapter. The network adapter has external connections that receive the connection cable. The network adapters can then share data over this cable. For the user to benefit from this exchange, software in the form of network protocols must also be installed. These protocols allow the network connection to be used for transferring files and other information.

Hardware requirements for local area networks

If you want to connect several computers to a network, you should settle for an Ethernet network, which is not only price worthybut also offers a lot of flexibility and high speed. Serial or parallel cables are a cheap solution, but they are considerably slower and usually allow only simple file transfers and no real network functions. If you want to connect only two PCs, you only need a network adapter for each PC and a connection cable, which you can buy for about $50. However, for about the same amount, you can buy a networking starter kit that includes not only the network adapters, cables, and necessary software, but also a router or hub that makes your life easier if you want to connect your network to the Internet using a broadband connection. If you want to connect more than two computers, you definitely need a hub. The latter is a sort of central distributor for the network that looks like a small box with a certain number of network connections. Instead of connecting the computer network adapters with each other, you must now connect all network cables to the hub. The hub is now responsible for the correct distribution of cables. If you want to avoid fumbling with the computer, you can buy external network adapters that are easily connected to the USB port.

Note

The right speed

Before buying Ethernet-components, you should think about the connection speed you desire. The cheapest components support a rate of 10 Mbps (megabit per second). This is enough for many applications, but if you need to transfer larger amounts of data, you might have to wait a bit. Newer components already support 100 Mbps (that is, about ten times the speed). Because such Fast Ethernet devices really aren't much more expensive than the older components, you should probably start with one of these directly. It is only important that the hub and the network adapters support the higher speed, because the hub adjusts to the speed of the slowest component. There are also hubs out there that work with different speeds simultaneously. These hubs are more expensive, however, and it makes more sense, therefore, to exchange a slow network adapter for a faster one. In the meantime, you can already get Ethernet components in the gigabit range, but it isn't worth buying these for private home networks, as they are still expensive.

If the network components are already there during the Windows XP installation, the Installation Wizard generally automatically recognizes them and configures them accordingly. If you are setting up your network after having installed Windows XP, you should follow the instructions for the network components and install the included software. Should you have any problems with the network hardware, take a look at chapter 3 for further instructions. One way or another, the network driver is initially configured during installation to function only at its lowest level. Windows XP also needs to be configured to use the network connection.

The basic network configuration

To access your local network through Windows XP, you must first configure the system for the network functions. A convenient Wizard is of course available to help you. It adjusts all the settings according to your instructions and installs all the necessary components. Once the Wizard closes, you might need the installation CD-ROM.

1 To call up the Network Setup Wizard, go to Start/All Programs/Accessories/Communications/Network Setup Wizard. You can also find the Wizard under Setup a Home or Small Office Network in the Network and Internet Connections category of the Control Panel.

2 The Wizard greets you with a short overview of its functions. Click *Next* to continue.

3 The Wizard notifies you of the steps you need to take before configuring the network. These include such obvious steps like sketching out the network, buying and connecting the components, as well as installing the network adapters. If you have already completed all of these steps, confirm this by clicking *Next*.

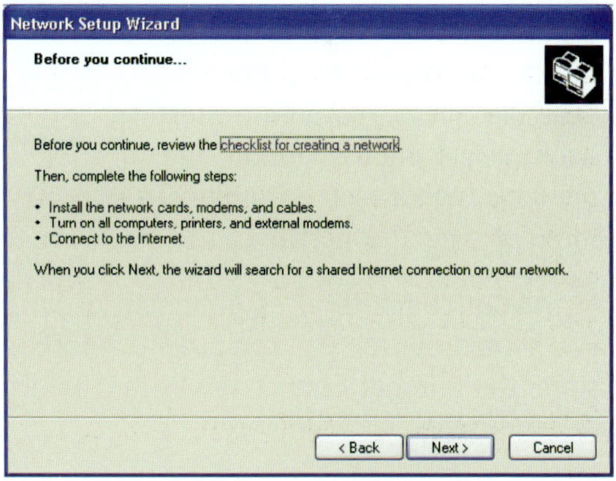

4 The next step is to select a connection method. The question here is how the computer should connect to the Internet. If you want the computer to use the Internet Connection Sharing feature of Windows XP, you need to select one of the first two options. This case is dealt with in more detail in the last section of this chapter. Instead, select the option *Other*, if you want your PC to dial into the Internet, or if you don't want to use it to access the Internet at all. (Even if you want to use Internet Connection Sharing, you should initially select the third option. You can select direct access later, as described in the last section of this chapter).

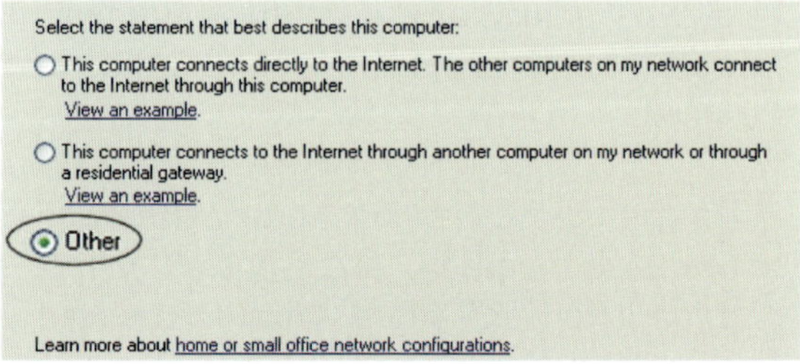

Note

Examples help you make a decision

In the step just described, as well as in the next one, most options come with examples. The Wizard displays a neat little sketch for each configuration, so you can select the most fitting option.

5 If you selected *Other* in the previous step, the Wizard displays further Internet connection options. If your computer is part of a network connecting to the Internet over a dedicated line (for example, in a corporate network), select the first option. The network is then set up in such a way as to allow your computer to access the Internet over the network.

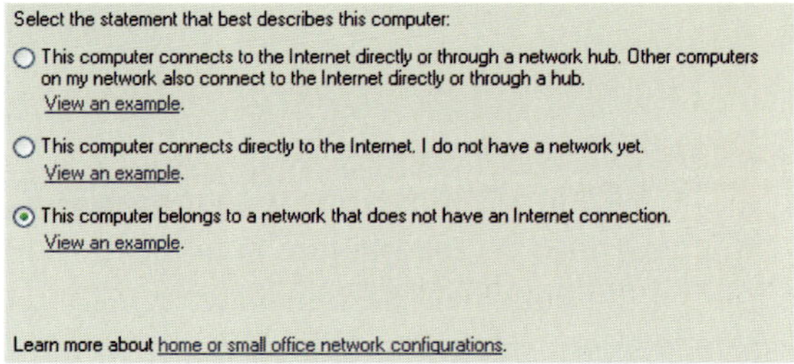

6 If your computer uses a modem or an ISDN adapter to dial into the Internet, you should opt for *This computer connects directly to the Internet.* The Wizard then starts the Internet Connection Wizard, which is presented in more detail in chapter 7.

7 If you don't want to use the Internet on this computer at all, simply choose *This computer belongs to a network that does not have an Internet connection*. Then the

Wizard stops trying to establish an Internet connection and concentrates on the other network functions.

8 Next, the Wizard asks you the name under which the computer should be recognized by other computers in the network. Enter the *Computer name* in the designated field. You can also add a short *Computer description,* which can help establish a better overview of computers in a larger network.

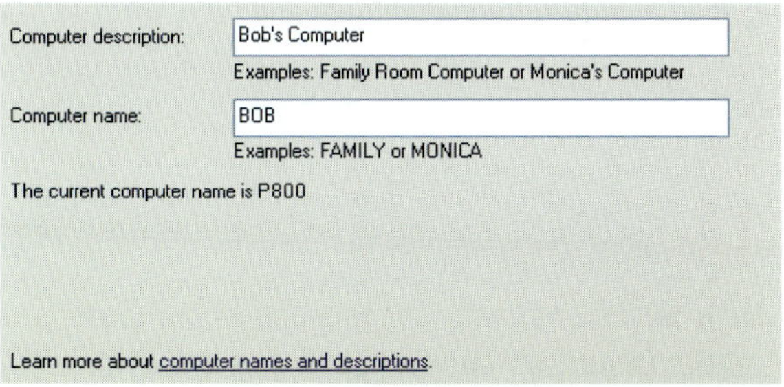

9 Next, you also need to name the network. Enter the *Workgroup name*. Important: All computers to be linked together in a network must use the exact same workgroup name!

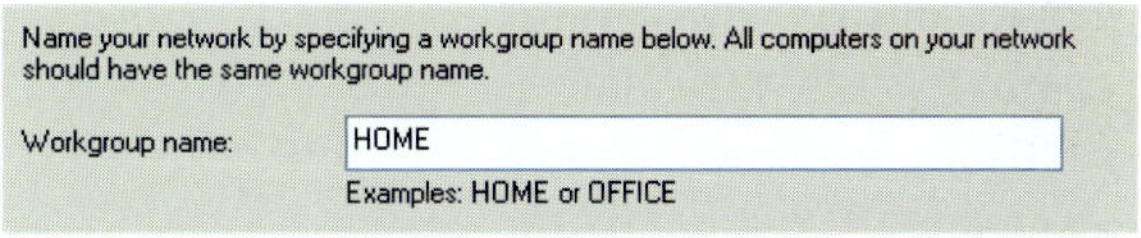

10 Now the Wizard shows you a summary of the selected settings and asks you to confirm them. If you click *Next*, the Wizard applies the changes. This might take some time, depending on the extent of the changes. If the Wizard needs to install additional components or drivers, you might have to insert the Windows XP installation CD-ROM at this point.

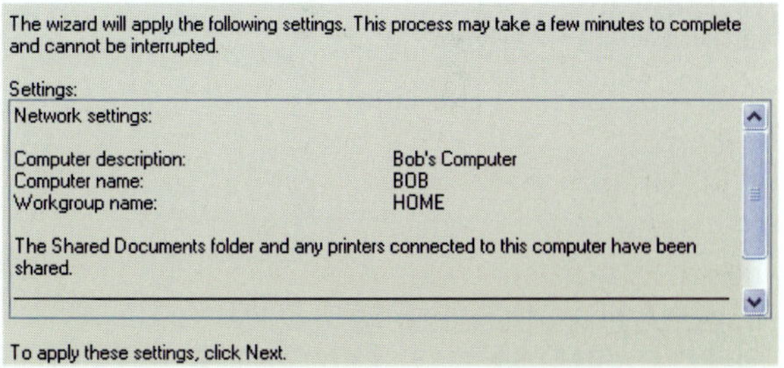

11 After you have finished configuring this system for networking, you might have to repeat the procedure on all other participating computers. Other

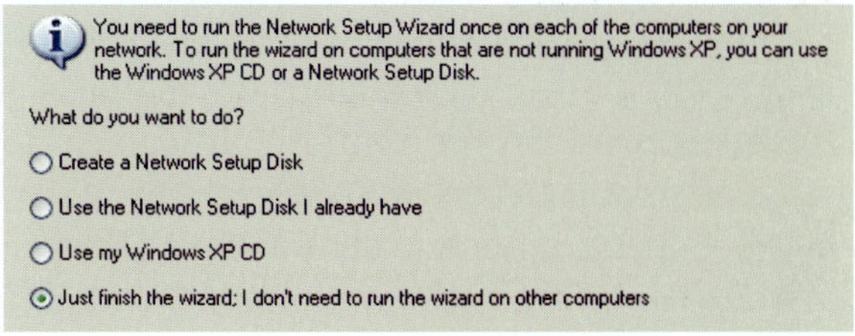

computers in the network don't necessarily have to use Windows XP but can run an older version of Windows. In that case, you should select the option *Create a Network Setup Disk* in the next step. The Wizard then creates a diskette containing all necessary changes for other Windows systems.

12 You can also use the relevant configuration tools on the other Windows PCs, however. The decisive thing is that all computers use the same workgroup name. In this case, select *Just finish the wizard; I don't need to run the wizard on other computers.*

13 Click *Next* and then *Finish* to quit the Wizard.

Now this PC is ready for the network. Please be aware that you need to set up all other computers connected to the network in this or a similar way. You can then easily test how well the network functions. Open the network folder of your computer by going to *Start/My Network Places*. The folder displays all accessible network resources. If your network consists of several computers, all their names should be listed here. If only the name of your computer appears here, the network is not functioning properly yet. Check the settings as well as the physical connections between the computers.

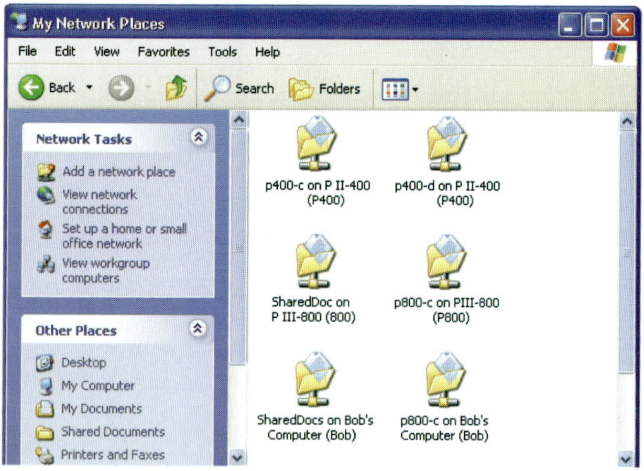

Sharing your folders with others

Having several computers linked to each other in a network doesn't automatically mean that you can access all of the resources located on one computer from all the other ones. On the contrary, the folders that are meant to be accessed by other network members must be explicitly shared. When the Wizard configures the network, it sets up one folder for shared documents. All other folders are initially inaccessible to the network. However, you can share any folder or drive over the network at any time. When you decide to share certain folders over the network, be careful how you set the network sharing security functions, so the data is really only accessible to those authorized to view it. Otherwise, unauthorized persons could abuse the sharing function. If a folder is only read-enabled, the files and documents can "only" be viewed and copied. If a folder is also write-enabled, the files can be secretly changed, and new files can be deposited on your computer, together with viruses or Trojans.

1 To share a folder, open Windows Explorer and display the folder.

2 Right-click the folder name to open the pop-up menu for the folder. Select the *Sharing and Security* function.

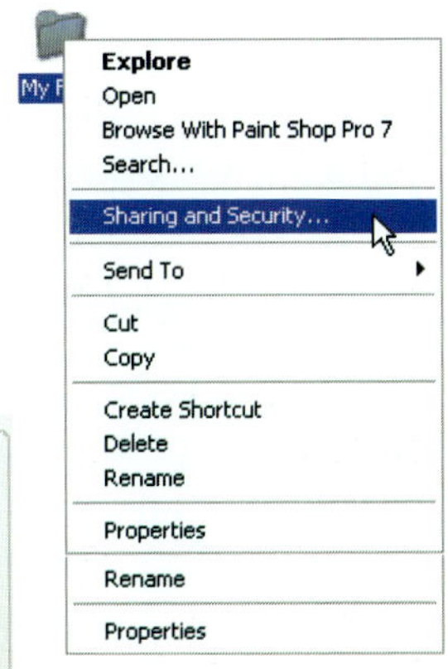

3 In the menu that opens next, enable the *Share this folder* check box in the *Share* tab. Windows automatically enters the folder name as the *Share name*, but you can choose a different designation, of course.

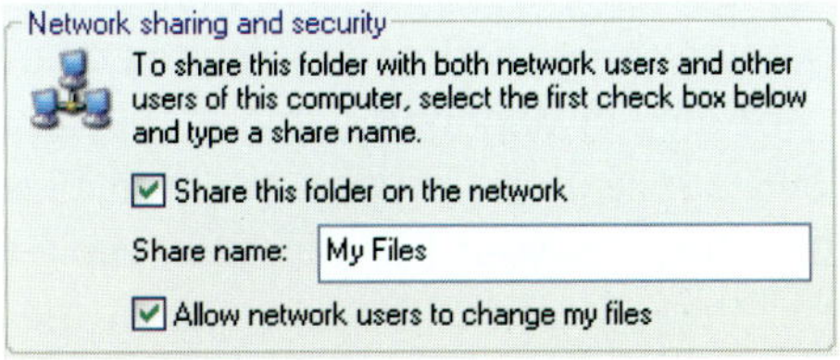

Note

The trick with the $

To make sharing your folders more secure, you can use a simple trick when choosing the folder designation: add $ to the end of the share folder name. The symbol ensures that the folder is not listed. This is true for the network neighborhood in Windows, but also for many of the network analysis tools often employed by hackers. It is still possible to access such a hidden network drive, but only if you know the exact share name. Thus, if instead of the share name "Data", you use "Data$", this shared folder would remain hidden and accessible only to insiders.

4 Now you must decide what kind of access to your data you want to allow. Generally, shared folders are read-only. If you want the other members to also be able to write into your files, enable the option *Allow other users to change my files.*

5 To share the folder with the chosen settings, click *OK* or *Apply*.

You can then take a look in My Network Places to make sure the new shared folder is visible (unless you have added $ to the end of the name, in which case the folder is not listed).

Accessing other network drives

In the same way in which you share your own drives and folders over the network, you can also access the folders and files that other network members make available on their PCs. No preparation and no special software is necessary. However, there are two different ways of accessing shared folders, depending on how often you want to access the data.

Opening network folders when needed

First, every folder shared over the network is a normal folder for you. You can always find it in the network neighborhood described above. You can view the network neighborhood not only in Windows Explorer, but also in any *Open* dialog box of any other Windows application. To open and edit files on the network, you don't have to first transfer them to your PC; you can simply call them up over the network. The following example uses the *Open* menu of the text editor WordPad, which is similar to the same menu in most other Windows applications.

1 Open the file menu by going to *File/Open* or by clicking the *Open* icon on the toolbar.

2 From the panel on the left, select the category *My Network*. Note a list of the available network resources (just as if you had opened the network neighborhood directly).

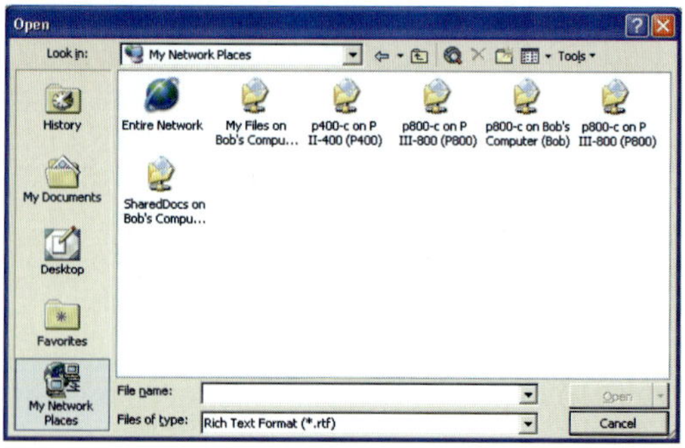

3 Double-click the resource you want to access. It is opened like a normal document, and its contents is displayed. Now you can open one of the files contained within or switch to another subfolder.

You can also save the file as if it were on your computer. If you have opened the file from the network, you can simply go to *File/Save* or click the *Save* icon on the toolbar to save the changed contents. If you want to save a newly created file to a network folder, open the *My Network* category in the *Save As* dialog box and search it for a suitable storage place. The only limitation when saving is if the selected folder is read-only. In that case, an error message appears when you tr to save changes. Find a folder that allows the changing and saving of files or change the settings for that folder.

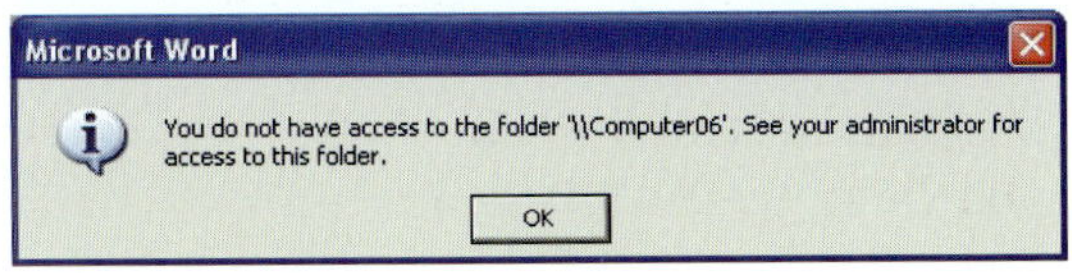

Permanent access to network folders

The method described above is very flexible, but it can also be awkward. If the network neighborhood is large with many shared resources, or if you need only certain data from a folder of a subfolder, finding the relevant folder can be tedious. Searching for this folder might be acceptable, if you only need it once in a while. However, if you need a shared folder regularly, searching for it every single time becomes annoying. Windows XP gives you the option of making individual network resources permanently accessible. Such resources are assigned one of the free drive letters and are thus accessible directly through My Computer. This shortens the path to the needed documents.

1 To permanently assign a drive letter to a shared folder, open Windows Explorer and go to *Tools/Map Network Drive*.

2 This opens the *Map Network Drive* dialog box. Here, you need to first select the drive letter you want to assign to the network resource. The *Drive* list box gives you all available drive letters that don't belong to any physical drive or to another network drive.

3 In the *Folder* field, enter the shared folder you want to access with the drive letter. You must enter the name in a certain way: \\ followed by the name of the computer where the resource is located, followed by another \, and, finally, by the name of the resource. Thus, if you want to assign the letter to the folder *Data* on the computer *OLAF*, you must enter the following name: *\\OLAF\Data*.

4 For an easier method, click *Browse*. Then you can select the folder from a dialog box displaying all available network resources.

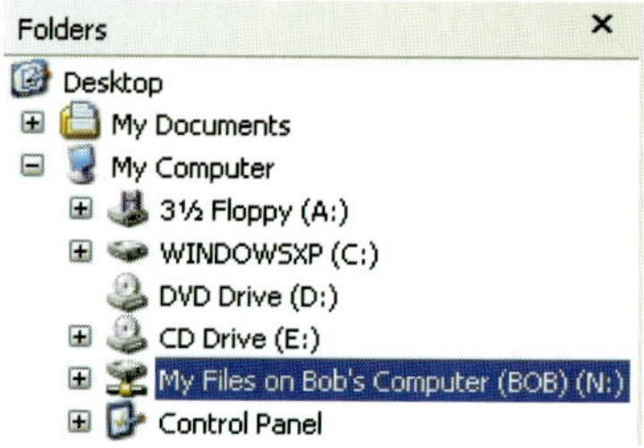

5 Finally, click *Finish* to create the network drive and assign it the drive letter. You can find the shortcut in the list of drives in My Computer, and you can access it like any other drive.

The nice thing about creating a network drive in this way is that Windows automatically sets up the connection every time it starts (unless you have disabled the option *Reconnect at logon* in the *Map Network Drive* dialog box). Once you have created the drive, you can always find it there whenever you turn on the computer and start Windows. The only exception occurs when the network is down or when the computer on which the resource is located is turned off.

Disconnecting network drives

Of course, you can also undo a permanent connection you have created.

1 Start Windows Explorer once again and go to *Tools/Disconnect Network Drives*.

2 Windows then shows you an overview of all connected network drives. Select the drive you want to disconnect and click *OK*.

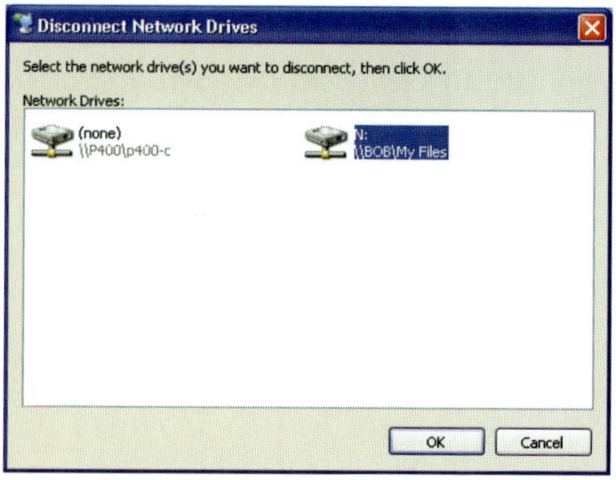

3 If there are open folders or files on this network drive at this time, you could lose data, and Windows warns you against it. Check whether all files in question are properly saved and confirm the message by clicking *Yes*.

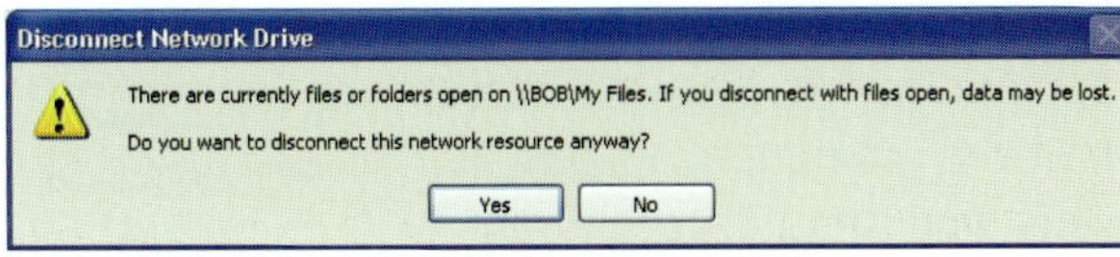

4 Windows then disconnects the network drive.

Printing over the network

Sharing printers is another very practical opportunity provided by a network. A printer connected locally to one computer can also be used by all other network members. If you have several PCs but only one printer, you can use a network instead of buying further expensive printers. In offices, too, it is practical to have a networked printer. For instance, you can have one expensive but superior printer for an entire department instead of cheap printers for each individual workstation, which is more sensible and cheaper in the long run. Like drives or folders, printers, too, need to be explicitly shared to be accessed by other network members, but this is easily done.

1 Open the Windows system settings by going to *Start/Control Panel* then; click the *Printers and Other Hardware* category.

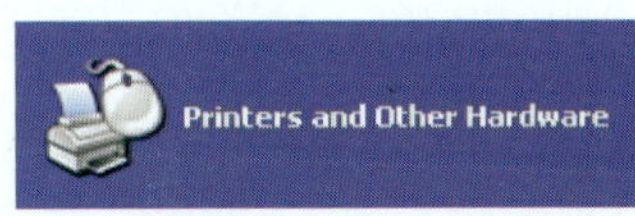

2 Select the task *View installed printers or fax printers*.

3 This opens an overview of the installed printers, which should display at least the printer model installed on this computer. If there are other printers connected to computers on the network, they are also listed here.

4 Select the local printer you want to share and click *Share this printer* in the task panel on the left.

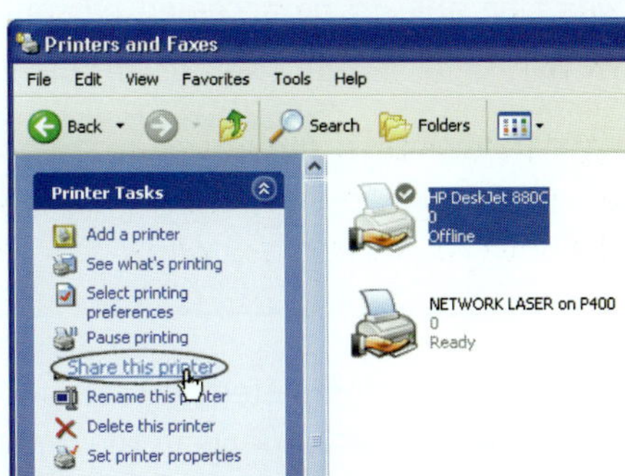

5 This opens the *Sharing* tab in the *Printer Properties* window. First, enable the option *Share this printer* and then enter a *Share name* for the printer. The name appears in My Network Places on every computer on this network and should be chosen in such a way as to immediately inform the users which printer it designates.

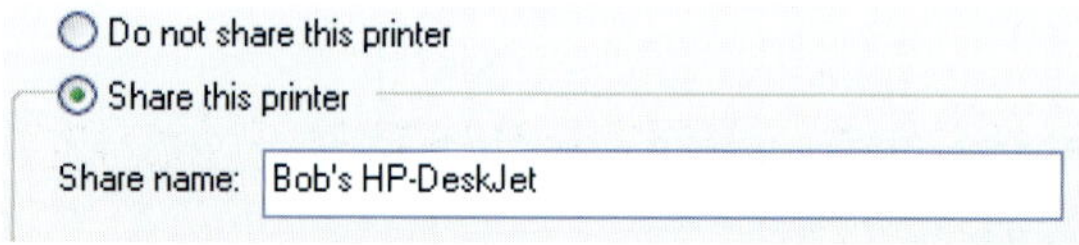

6 If your network also includes computers with a different Windows operating system and you want them to also use this printer, click *Additional Drivers* at the bottom to install the printer for these operating systems as well.

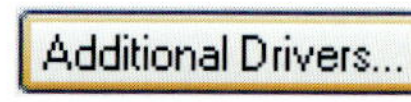

7 Select the additional printer drivers from the menu that opens. During selection, pay attention to the *Environment* for each system. PCs generally have an *Intel* environment.

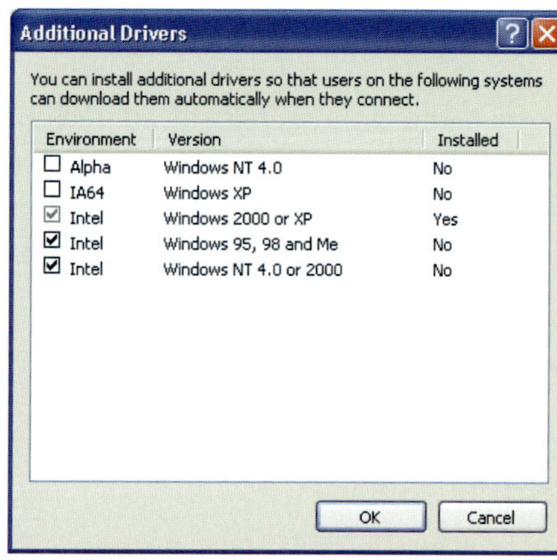

8 Next, enter the path for the corresponding printer drivers. You can usually find the path on the CD-ROM that comes with the driver.

9 Back in the *Sharing* tab, apply the settings by clicking *OK*.

10 If you have used spaces or special characters in the share name, the printer won't be able to be accessed by some MS-DOS workstations. If there are no such workstations in your network, you can ignore this warning and click *Yes*.

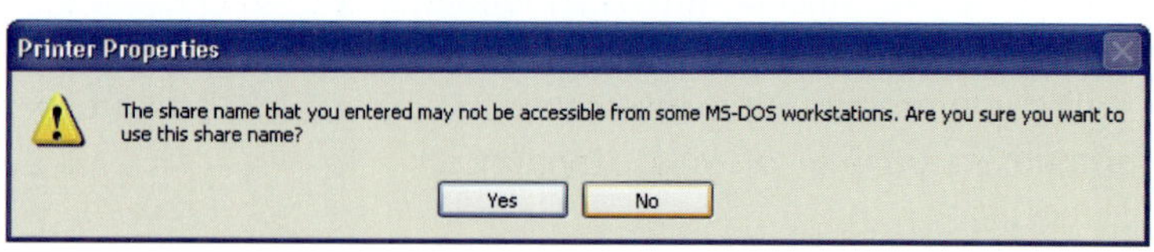

You have now completed the setup for sharing your printer over the network. The networked printer appears in the network places and printing options on all PCs in the same workgroup. All users of these computers can print their documents on your printer just by clicking its icon.

Connecting several PCs to the Internet over a network

If you have set up a Windows PC network at home or at your office, you now have the option of connecting all the networked PCs to the Internet. Normally, each computer would need its own modem or ISDN card and phone connection to connect to the Internet. Internet Connection Sharing allows you to equip only one of the computers with this hardware, thus obtaining Internet access. The Internet connection can then be shared with all other computers over the network, just like a folder or a printer (that is, the other networked PCs can get into the Internet using the connection over the network). This way, you can avoid investing in additional modems or ISDN cards and fumbling with telephone cables.

> **Note**
>
> **Networking PCs for shared Internet access**
>
> Internet Connection Sharing might interest you, even if you haven't yet networked your computers. If you have a computer with Internet access and another one without, it may be cheaper to network the two than to buy another high-speed modem or ISDN card. Simple network starter kits cost about as much as a modem. Networking also has other advantages in addition to Internet connection sharing, such as fast and convenient data sharing between computers and sharing of a local printer, described above.

Configuring the host computer

For Internet Connection Sharing, you need a computer with its own Internet connection (the connection must be independent of the network). This computer should have the necessary hardware (for example, modem, ISDN card, and so forth) installed plus functioning Internet access. Then you can share this access with the other PCs in the local area network.

1 Open the Network Setup Wizard by going to *Start/All Programs/Accessories/Communications/Network Setup Wizard*.

2 Acknowledge the Wizard's greeting and introduction by clicking *Next* both times. In the third window, select the option *This computer connects directly to the Internet. The other computers on my network connect to the Internet through this computer.*

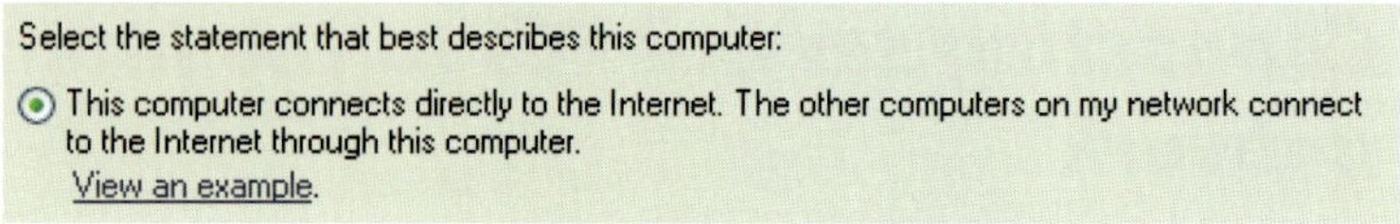

3 In the next window, select which of the configured Internet connections you want to share with the network.

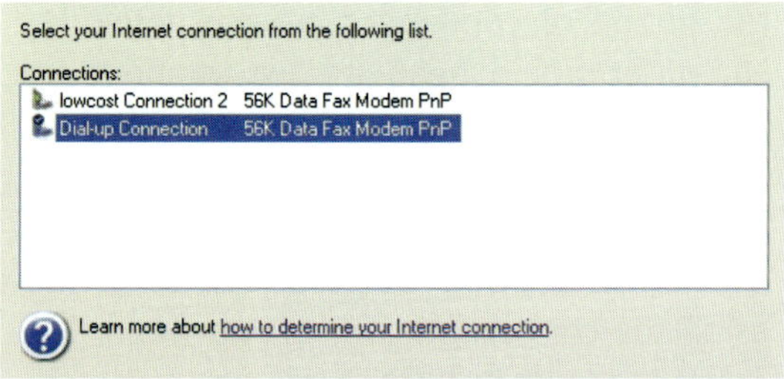

4 The Wizard then goes through the other steps for setting up the network, as already described at the beginning of the chapter. The most important steps are choosing a *Computer name*, *Computer description* and *Workgroup name*. If your network is already configured to your satisfaction (with the exception of the Internet connection sharing), you should apply the values you had already set, to avoid influencing the performance of the network.

5 As a last step, Windows offers to create a network setup disk with which you can configure all other PCs on the network as needed.

6 Finally, click *Finish* to complete the Internet connection sharing.

The PC is now configured for Internet Connection Sharing. Now you must configure the other computers to use this PC's Internet access over the network.

Setting up other PCs for Internet use

Every computer that uses Internet Connection Sharing must be configured accordingly. Therefore, you need to repeat the following procedure for every computer.

> **Note**
>
> **Internet Connection Sharing in other Windows versions**
>
> Basically, all versions of Windows starting with Windows 98 support Internet Connection Sharing, although other Windows versions might require you to configure different settings. In such cases, you should definitely use the network setup disk, which Internet Connection Sharing can create on your PC.

1 Once again, start the Network Setup Wizard by going to *Start/All Programs/Accessories/Communications/Network Setup Wizard*. Skip the first two windows by clicking *Next* each time.

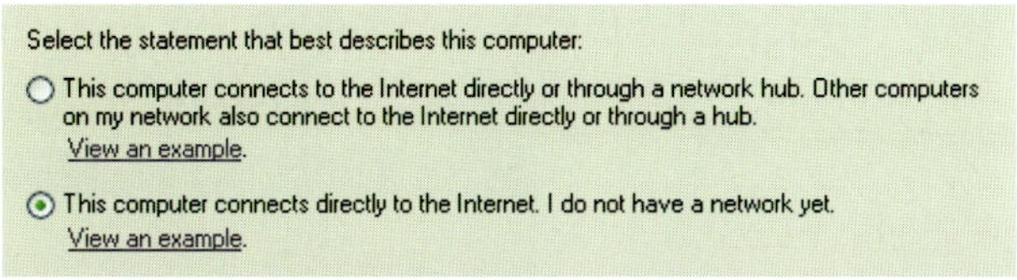

2 In the third window, select the connection method *This computer connects to the Internet through another computer on my network or through a residential gateway*.

3 Now follow the usual steps for setting up the network (enter the computer name, computer description, and workgroup name). Please make sure that the computer is in the same workgroup with the host computer.

4 As a last step, choose the option *Just finish the wizard; I don't need to run the wizard on other computers*. Now you can quit the Wizard by clicking *Finish*.

When Internet Connection Sharing is set up on all computers, Internet queries from other PCs are sent to the computer connected to the Internet. This computer thus becomes the mediator between the Internet and the local area network. Whenever necessary, it creates an Internet connection and uses it to send data to the Internet. It also distributes incoming data to the individual network computers. Because this mediation happens at the lowest level of the Internet protocol, it functions without restrictions with all kinds of Internet applications.

Monitoring network connections

If you have connected your computer to a network and are sharing your resources, it is important that you keep the overview of the use of your resources.

1 Open the system properties by going to *Start/Control Panel*.

2 Open the *Performance and Maintenance* category, and double-click the *Administrative Tools* icon.

3 In the *Administrative Tools* folder, double-click *Computer Management*.

4 Here, you find an overview of what is being shared on your computer in the *Shared Folders* category. In the *Shares* folder, note all the shared resources.

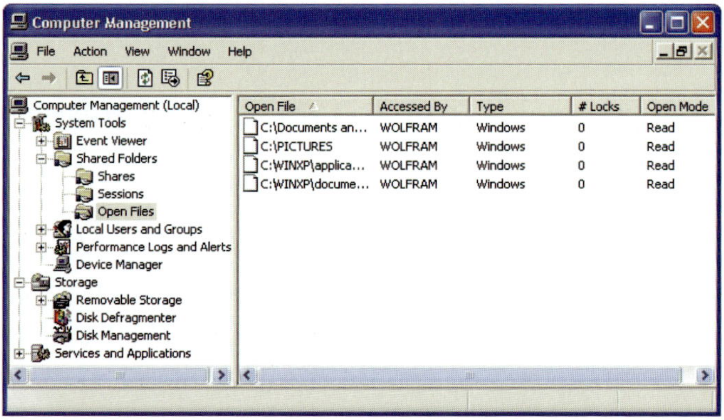

5 In *Sessions*, you can monitor which network members are using your computer's resources just now.

6 Finally, the *Open Files* folder details which members are accessing which files right now.

If you don't agree with the activities of other users, you can always deny them access quickly. In the *Action* menu, locate the appropriate commands for closing a file, terminating a session, or canceling sharing.

7. World Wide Web! – Online with Windows XP

Of course, the Internet isn't missing from the new Windows XP! Microsoft has endowed its new operating system with updated versions of Internet Explorer and Outlook Express. As usual, these components have been integrated into the Windows interface, which makes them easy to use. In this chapter, you learn how to best set up your Internet connection with Windows XP, and how to surf effectively and safely with Internet Explorer. In the next chapter, you can examine Outlook Express and e-mailing in more detail.

Establishing and optimizing Internet connections

To establish Internet access for your computer, you need two things:

- First, you need a hardware component that secures the physical connection between your computer and the Internet. The most usual solutions for private access are modems and ISDN adapters. Companies often use network adapters for more efficient direct connections.
- If the hardware functions correctly, you need to set up the actual online connection only. For dial-up connections with a modem or ISDN card, you need a dial-up network connection.

Windows XP puts a handy Wizard for setting up online connections at your disposal. The New Connection Wizard opens automatically when you want to access an Internet connection that isn't there. However, you don't have to wait for the Wizard to start automatically. You can open it manually anytime (for instance, to enter additional data) by going to *Start/All Programs/Accessories/Communications/New Connection Wizard*.

Entering location information

To establish a connection, the operating system needs to know your dial location. You must enter this information once. If you have just installed Windows XP and are setting up the first Internet connection, this is probably your first connection of any kind, so the following query appears automatically.

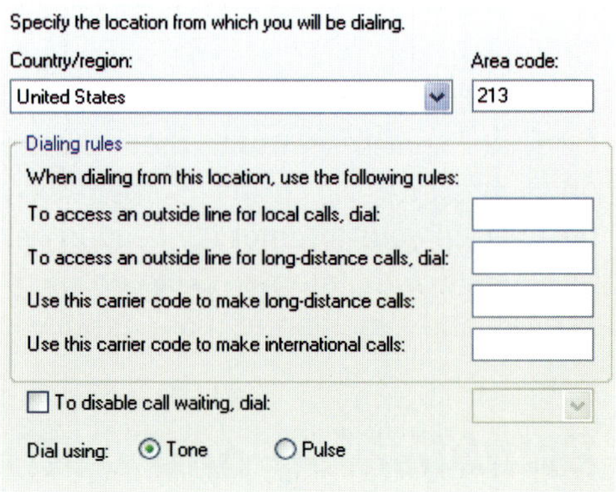

1 In the *New Location* window, first enter a *Location name*. You should select a name that helps you identify the location later.

2 Underneath, enter your *Country/region* and your *Area code*.

3 You need to enter only access digits or carrier codes under *Dialing rules* if your phone connection requires them. For example, if your phone is connected to a switchboard and you need to dial a certain digit (for example, 9) for an external line, or if you are using a local or long-distance carrier different from the one common for your area code. Windows then dials these numbers automatically before establishing a connection.

4 If you don't want incoming calls to interrupt your connections, check the option *To disable call waiting, dial*, and enter the number in the text entry field.

5 Finally, choose whether you want to dial using *Tone* or *Pulse* and then double-click *OK* to confirm your settings.

Windows uses this dial location information for all connections by default. If the information changes, or if you want to create a connection with a different set of data, you can adjust the settings by going to *Start/Control Panel/Network and Internet Connections/Phone and Modem Options*. Here, you can make changes or add further dial locations, for example, for your cell phone.

The New Connection Wizard

Once you have entered the dial location information, the New Connection Wizard automatically opens. This Wizard is in charge of all types of Internet and network connections.

1 Acknowledge the Wizard's greeting by clicking *Next.*

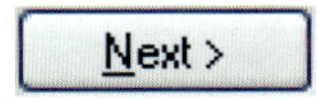

2 In the second window, choose the network connection type you want to use. Select *Connect to the Internet* to create a new Internet connection then click *Next.*

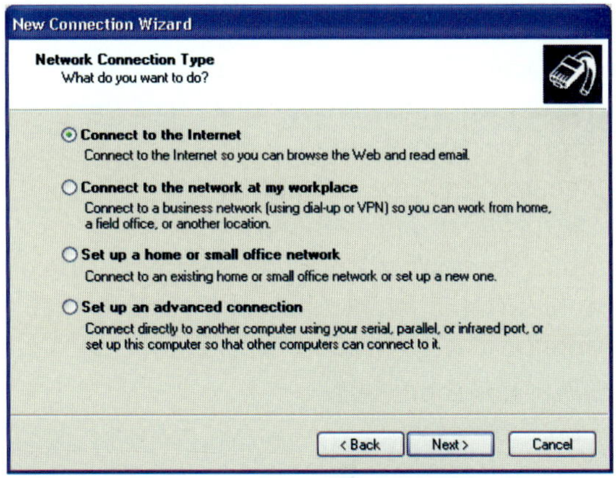

3 In the next step, tell the Wizard how you want to create the Internet connection. If you don't have an Internet service provider (ISP) yet, select the option *Choose from a list of Internet service providers (ISPs)*. The Wizard then displays a list of providers for your area and helps you with the selection.

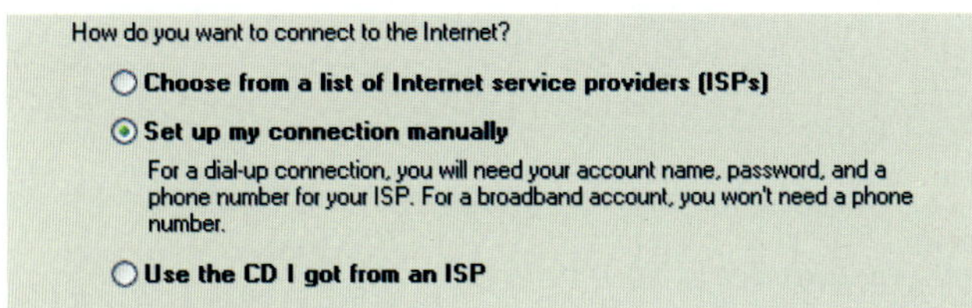

4 If you already have a provider and know the relevant connection information, you are best off selecting the option *Set up my connection manually*. This way, you can enter all the relevant data by hand. The advantage of this is that the Wizard doesn't incur any expenses by establishing a phone connection with Microsoft's reference service. In the following, you can pursue this option, because it represents the most usual scenario.

5 You can of course also select the option *Use the CD I got from an ISP*. In that case, you only need to insert the relevant CD-ROM (for example, from a magazine) into the drive. The Wizard opens the installation program found on the CD-ROM.

6 If you have selected to set up the connection manually, the Wizard first asks you how you want to establish the connection. If you want to dial into the Internet using a modem or ISDN card, select *Connect using a dial-up modem* (this works for both modems and ISDN adapters). The other two options are for users with broadband Internet access through DSL or cable. The difference between them is that the first option configures broadband connections as needed, whereas the second option is for permanent connections (broadband flat rate).

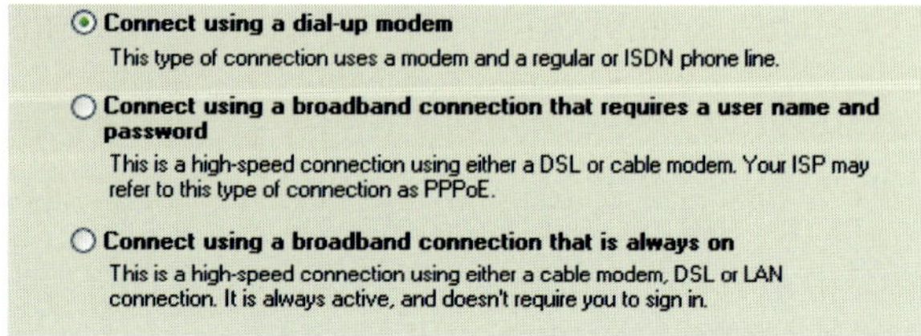

7 Next, enter the name of the ISP to which you want to establish a connection. Windows XP uses the name to designate this Internet connection. You can really designate the connection by any name you want.

8 In the next step, enter the *Phone number* of your ISP, that is, the number the computer must dial to make the connection.

9 The Wizard now wants to know your *Internet Account Information*. Enter your *User name* and *Password*, which you must confirm. Once you have entered this information, the computer can dial into the Internet automatically.

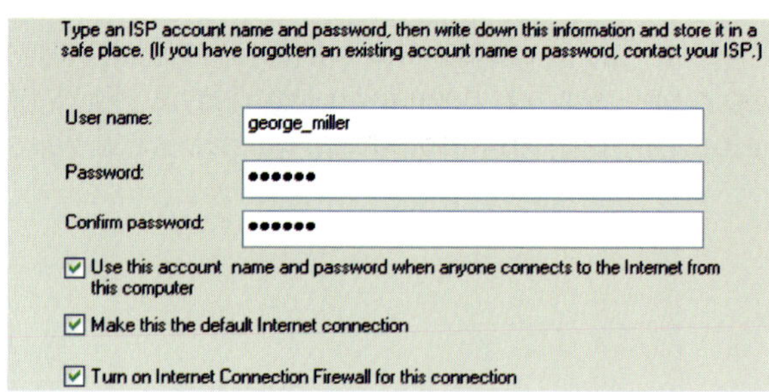

10 Underneath, you can find a few options for regulating the use of the connection you have just set up. Enable the option *Use this account name and password when anyone connects to the Internet from this computer* to give all users access to this connection. Otherwise, every user has to establish his or her own connection.

11 Enable the option *Make this the default Internet connection* if you want the computer to select this connection every time it dials into the Internet.

12 If you don't want to take any risks while surfing, you should also enable the option *Turn on Internet Connection Firewall for this connection*. Windows XP then uses a special safety mechanism for this connection, which protects you from attacks from the Internet while online.

13 The setup for your connection is now complete. Click *Finish* to create the permanent connection. If you enable the option *Add a shortcut to this connection to my desktop* first, you can afterwards find a desktop icon over which you can establish the connection at any time.

Establishing and closing Internet connections automatically

Once an online connection has been established, you can create a connection to the Internet at any time. You can, for example, allow Windows to do it completely automatically. This is definitely the most convenient method: whenever you require a connection to the Internet (when, for example, you want to request a Web site in Internet Explorer or to check your e-mail), Windows XP automatically establishes the necessary connection when set in this mode. If more than one dial-up adapter is available, the default is selected.

The operating system then monitors the online connection, registers it, and, once no more data has been exchanged for a while, breaks it off. Naturally you can also manually end an automatically established connection at any time.

Note

The problems with establishing an automatic connection

Establishing an automatic connection, unfortunately, also has its problems: many Internet programs work on a schedule by which they automatically accomplish certain tasks (for example, the Favorites subscriptions in Internet Explorer or the automatic e-mail update in Outlook Express). If the computer is set up to establish a connection automatically, a connection is also automatically created to meet these requirements. Therefore, you should definitely use a test phase to monitor and control which programs establish an Internet connection and when.

1 To enable and set Windows XP to establish a connection automatically, go to *Start/Control Panel/Network and Internet Connections/Internet Options* to open the Internet settings; switch to the *Connections* tab.

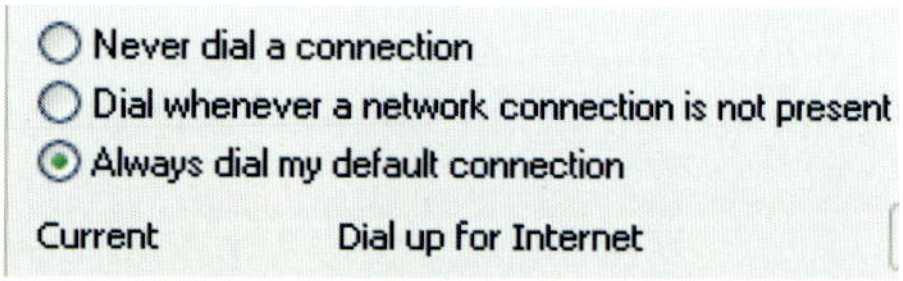

2 In the *Dial-up and Virtual Private Network settings* area, you can find all the essential settings. First enable the *Always dial my default connection* option for establishing a connection automatically.

3 If several dial-up connections are available to choose from, you must indicate which one should be used by default. To do so, select the corresponding connection from the list and click the *Set Default* button. The selected connection is then displayed with the extension (*Default*).

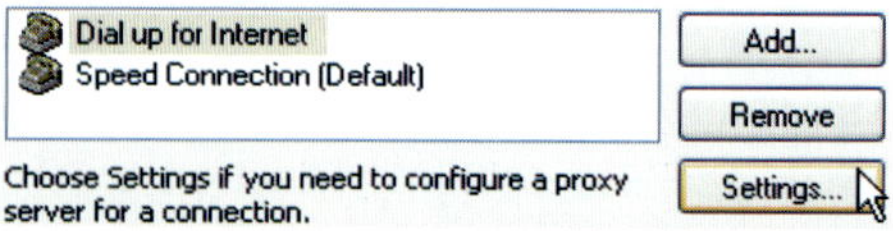

4 Up to this point, all the steps for establishing the connection have been completed. It is now necessary to request the automatic connection. To this end, select the default connection and click the *Settings* button.

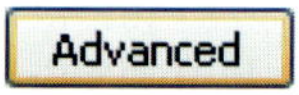

5 In the *Dial-up Connection Settings* menu that follows, click the *Advanced* button in the *Dial-up settings* area at the bottom.

6 The *Advanced Dial-Up* dialog box opens. Here, you can find the two decisive settings for establishing a connection.

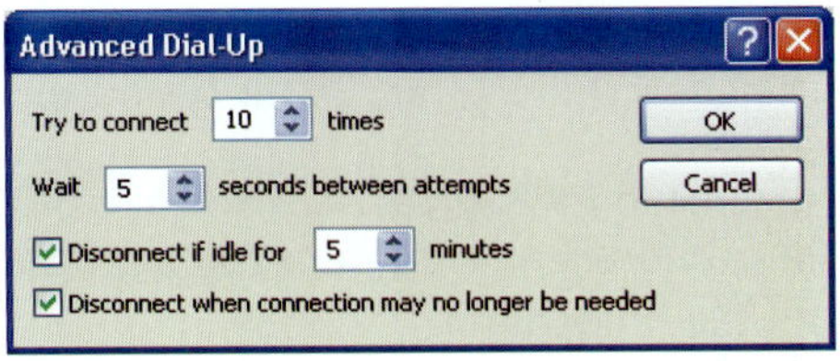

7 In all cases, enable the *Disconnect when connection is no longer needed* option. Doing so enables the creation of the actual automatic connection. It should take care of breaking the connection when it is no longer in use.

8 Because the automatic connection does not unfortunately always work reliably, you can enable the *Disconnect if idle for X minutes* option as a safety measure. If this setting is enabled, Windows always monitors the connection for data exchange. The connection is immediately terminated if no activity occurs for the indicated period of time.

9 Finally, click *OK* three times for each of the menus to apply the new settings.

As of now, you no longer have to think about establishing a connection. Simply start the Internet application of your choice and go for it. Whenever an Internet connection is required, Windows XP registers this and creates it. Expect a short pause before the connection is established. If you have finished working on the Internet, Windows closes the connection automatically.

Remedying problems with Internet connections

The most important aspect of using the Internet is a working online connection. When your computer has permanent access to the Internet through a network adapter (in an office environment, for instance), there is usually no problem. The computer sets up the connection whenever it is started. If there is a problem, you can usually go to the system administrator. The case is slightly different if you want your home computer to dial up to the Internet over a modem or an ISDN adapter. A whole slew of sources of error occur here, and, for the most part, no one is around whom you can ask. If it turns out your online connection doesn't work, the following tips help:

1 First, verify the connection information for your Internet service provider. To do so, open the Network Connections in the Control Panel and display the properties of the troublesome dial-up connection. Compare the information with that of the provider. Quite often, small typing mistakes with large consequences occur.

2 Take a look at the hardware for the connection: Are all connections (telephone line, and also the power supply for the modem!) run and connected correctly? Are all the plugs tight?

3 External modems generally have a row of control lights that display the status of the device. Pay attention to these when you are trying to establish a connection. If possible, turn on the speaker for your external modem. If nothing occurs, there is already a problem with the communication between the modem and the computer. With ISDN adapters, a monitoring program is usually included that serves a similar purpose. If possible, use an existing test program.

The connection is successful, but log-on is rejected by the provider ...

... check especially the access information (use name and password). Perhaps a little mistake occurred here? If nothing is apparent, consult with your provider. Notice for new connections thatthey are often "switched on" at a certain time, even if you have already received the access information.

Are you using the correct access number?

Pay attention for a possible country or area code to dial first. A simple test is to dial the exact same number using a normal phone. With modem connections, you should be able to hear the same familiar monotone carrier sound as with fax machines. With ISDN connections, you usually hear a busy signal. If a human-sounding voice picks up, you have most likely misdialed. However, use the opportunity to ask.

Is your provider's dial-up node overloaded perhaps and therefore permanently busy?

This will most likely lead to an error message in Windows. In this case, it is also useful to test the connection by phone.

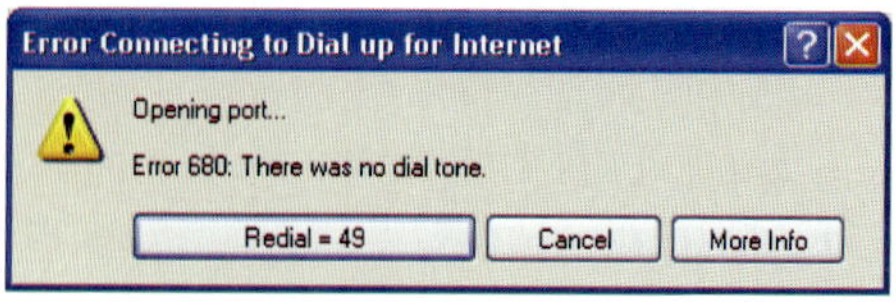

If you cannot make any progress by yourself in any case, it might help to ask acquaintances who are customers of the same Internet provider. Perhaps they have experienced something similar and have the knack to remedy the problem.

For the completely confused and unabashed, try the Internet provider's service hotline. If long waiting time and high telephone costs don't scare you and you even have a thing for hold music, you should try your luck with the hotline. Prior to doing so, be prepared to provide the information about your computer, the operating system, and the communications devices you are using.

When Web sites do not load – What the error messages mean

Even if the online connection can be successfully established, not everything is necessarily perfect. Even the Internet connections that are used to load Web sites have their hiccups. Some typical error messages and what they mean follow.

The page cannot be displayed

An error message that you might encounter often is *The page cannot be displayed*. It means that Internet Explorer could not contact the desired Web server. Perhaps the indicated server doesn't exist. Check the address given for any possible typos. This error message occurs more frequently because a connection to the Internet is not operating error-free. Therefore, check your computer's Internet connection to make sure it is active.

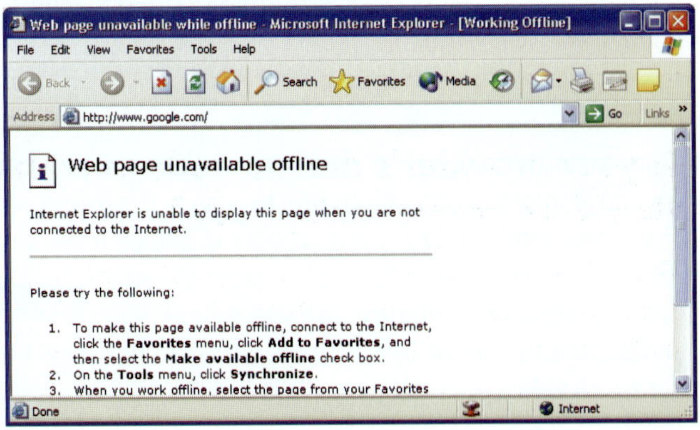

Object not found

The other important error message is directly displayed in the browser window and is called *Object Not Found*. The message means that, although Internet Explorer could connect to the desired Web server, it could not return the requested Web site, as it doesn't exist. Instead, it produces a Web site containing an error message as a response. One reason for this error could be a typo. It is also likely that you have entered an old address that, in the meantime, is no longer correct because the structure of the Web site has been altered. In such cases, try only the server name without indicating a particular Web site address. This action brings you to the host start page, from where you might be able to find the information you are looking for.

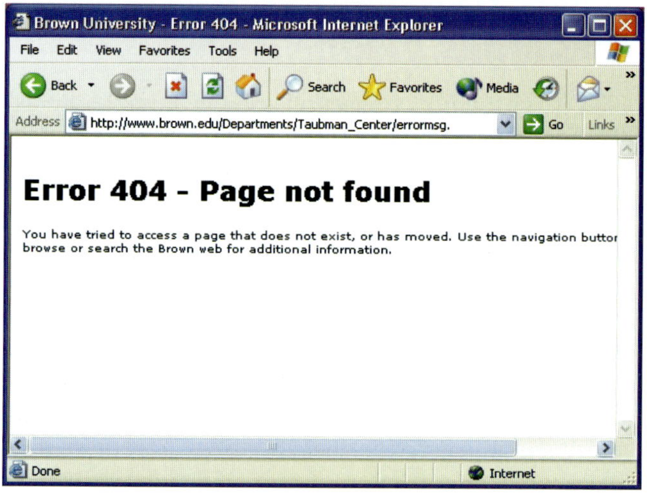

Requested URL not available in offline mode

If you regularly use the offline mode in Internet Explorer, you can encounter another error message (*The requested URL is not available offline*). This means that you have requested a Web site that is not present in the cache of the browser. Therefore, Internet Explorer can only grant your request if you establish an online connection. Before it connects, it prompts you. Choose *Connect* to request the site online. You can choose to stay offline; however, you cannot access the desired Web site.

Finding information on the Web

Surfing through the World Wide Web presumes that you have some suitable entry point into the Web from which to begin surfing. You can get these starting points from numerous sources, such as computer magazines, advertising boards and displays, business cards or tips from acquaintances. Even if that is not the case, and you have an interest in a topic without knowing the relevant address, Internet Explorer does not leave you high and dry. With the built-in search function, you can find the necessary entry points in the blink of an eye.

1 To use the search function, display the search bar. Go to *View/ Explorer Bar/Search* in the menu or, even quicker, click the *Search* icon.

2 Thereupon, Internet Explorer divides the browser window vertically and displays the current Web site only in the right half. The area on the left contains a search form.

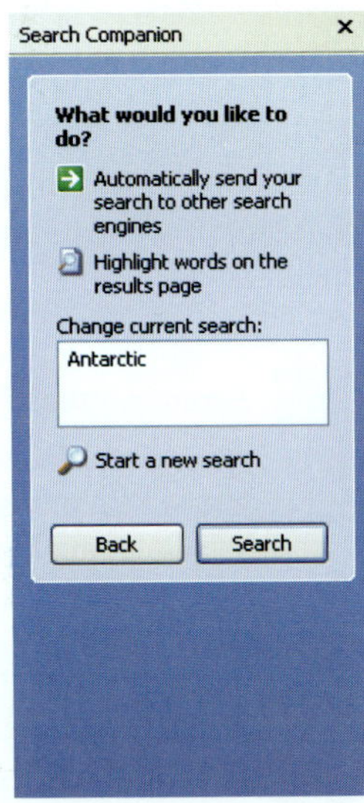

3 Leave the default option *Find a Web page* selected. If you have previously already performed a search, you can go back to those results with *Previous searches.*

4 In the *Find a Web page containing:* text entry field, type the search term that you want to find. The example looks for information about Antarctica. When you have entered the query, click *Search* to begin the search.

5 Internet Explorer directs your request to a search engine and waits for the results. If there are hits, the search results appear in the *Search* window. For each entry, the title of the found site is given.

6 To view one of the found sites, click the title shown for the site, which is a link that immediately takes you to the Web site. Internet Explorer displays this page in the right half of the browser window, so that the search results are retained. This way you can also inspect any of the other results at any time.

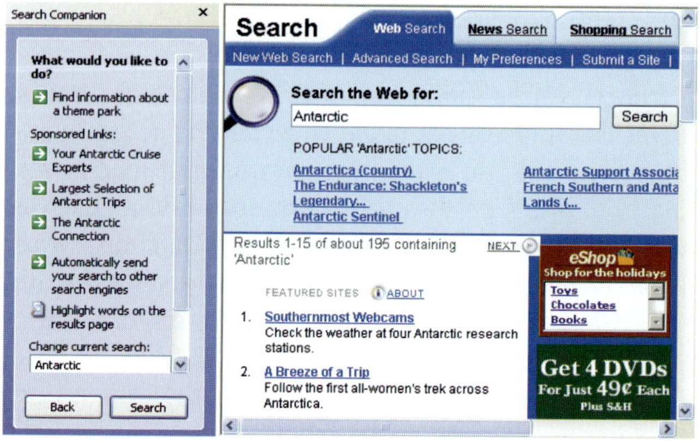

7 If you are not happy with the search results, click *Next* >> at the bottom of the list. This way you receive details on other Web sites, where you can perhaps find the desired information.

8 If you have found a suitable entry point on the topic you are searching for, you can close the search bar by clicking the *Search* icon. Internet Explorer then removes the *Search* window and once again makes the entire browser window available for viewing Web sites.

Note

Extensive search terms restrict the results

The example shows a simple search query with only one word. Such searches give an abundance of results, so that you don't know where to start surfing. If you wish to find something more specific, you can, enter more search terms. To find, for example, Web sites particular to boat cruises in Antarctica, you could use the search term "Antarctica boat cruises". The search function then finds only those Web sites that contain all of these terms. As a result, you receive more specific and usually more exact results.

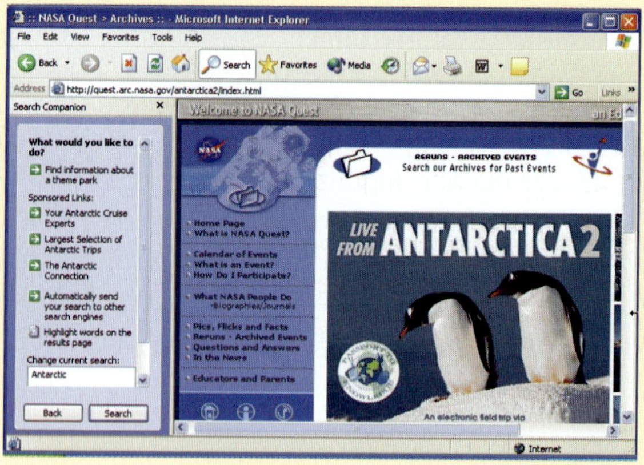

Downloading files safely and problem-free

When you are surfing the Internet, you encounter a significant risk from viruses that hide in files made available for download from Web servers or FTP archives. The actual downloading of an infected file is in itself not risky. If you execute the file, the virus can become active, infect other files and multiply itself, spreading throughout your computer. The consequences range from harmless but bothersome effects to damage and complete loss of files. Therefore, if you download files off the Internet, it is absolutely necessary to check them for viruses immediately afterwards.

1 Files that are offered for download on a Web site appear no different from hyperlinks at first. In general, their names appear in blue and are underlined. Similarly, an icon can be used to link to the file. If you move the mouse pointer over the link, it changes to a hand symbol. In addition, the file that the link references is displayed in the status bar at the bottom edge of the Internet Explorer window.

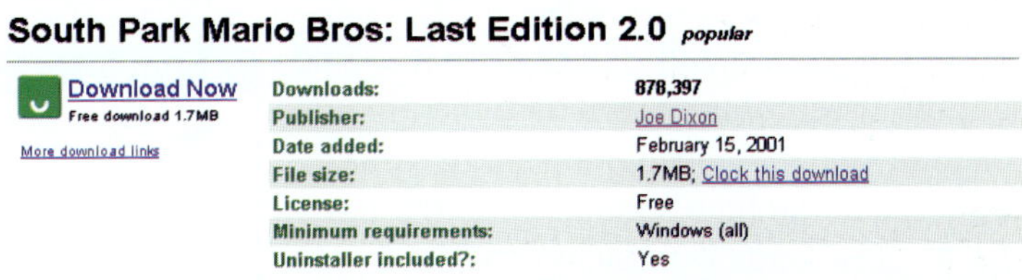

2 To download a file, click the corresponding hyperlink. Internet Explorer then requests the document from the Web server to which the link points. The program automatically recognizes if you are dealing with a file download and changes its approach. A prompt informs you about the file and inquires how you would like to proceed.

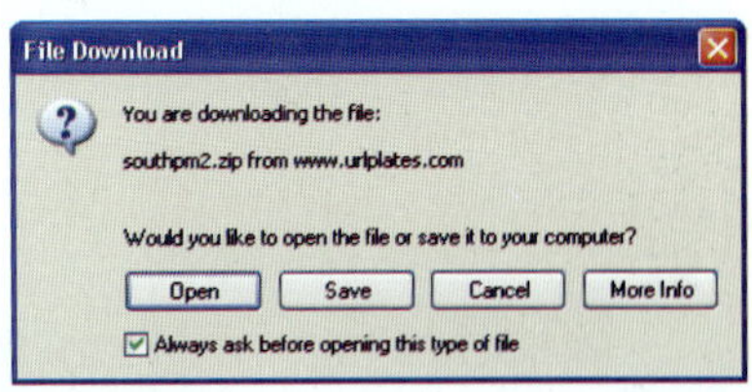

3 To download the file and immediately execute it, click *Open*. This is not recommended for security reasons, because, should there be a virus inside, it could infect your computer without impediment.

4 Using the *Save* button is safer. The file is then downloaded and a local copy is created on your hard drive. You can take your time to check it for viruses before opening it.

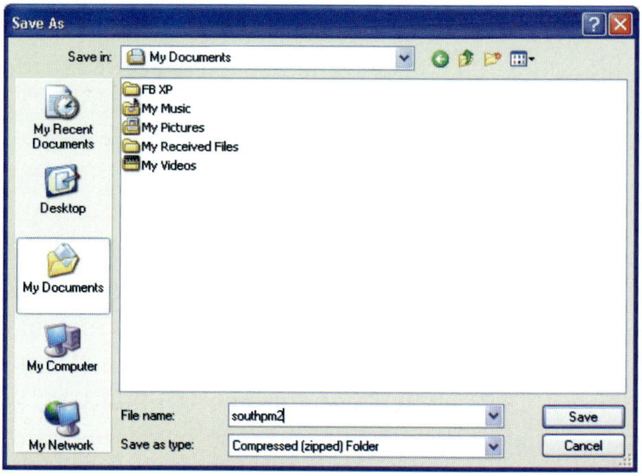

5 If you decide to save the file, Internet Explorer queries where and under what name it should be saved. A *Save As* dialog window opens, where you can indicate the folder and the file name. The browser normally suggests the name of the file, but you can choose another description.

6 Start downloading the file by clicking *OK*. Internet Explorer displays a status window during download. You can use it to find out the speed of the download, the amount of data that has been transferred, and an estimate of the time remaining for the transfer. If downloading is taking too long, you can interrupt the process and, if necessary, try again later.

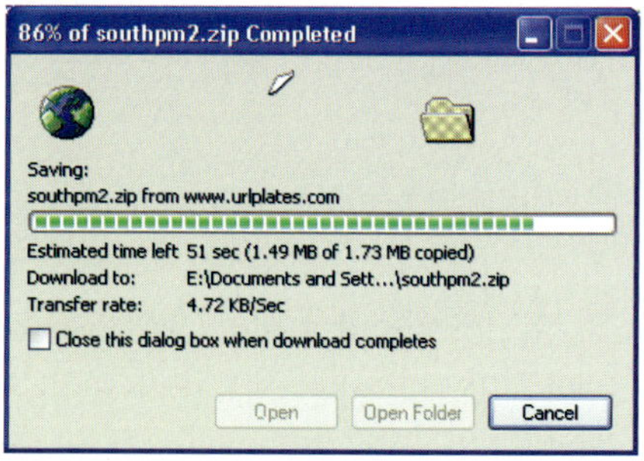

Note

Downloading files takes place in the background

The downloading of files for the most part takes place in the background, that is, once the download has started, you can continue surfing with Internet Explorer. The file is automatically transferred to the background. However, the two processes (downloading the file and at the same time surfing the Net) share the capacity of the online connection. Both processes might run slower than normal. In addition, you cannot exit Internet Explorer before the download is complete, as the transfer is then aborted.

7 Once the file download is complete, Internet Explorer saves the file to the designated location. The buttons *Open*, *Open Folder*, and *Close* are then enabled, and you can use them to access the downloaded file immediately.

Before you execute/open the downloaded file, you should check it for viruses. Every virus scanner is capable of analyzing any file. Unfortunately, no virus protection is included with Internet Explorer, so you must depend on additional software. Many commercial virus scanners integrate themselves into Windows Explorer. With such a protective program, it is enough to right-click the downloaded file and select the scan function from the context menu that appears. The virus program checks the selected file and confirms its harmlessness, where applicable.

Surfing securely with Internet Explorer

Security is extremely important when surfing the Internet. Dangers are awaiting you left and right. Thus, you can infect your computer with dangerous viruses by not being careful with the files you download. Likewise, active Web content such as Java applets, ActiveX controls and cookies threaten your data and your privacy. Internet Explorer offers a series of functions and settings with which you can increase your security while surfing.

Inform yourself about the security status

While surfing, you can inform yourself about the security status of your connection. This way you can know at any time if you can harmlessly pass on confidential information. You have several possibilities:

1 Internet Explorer has reserved a place for the security status display in the status bar at the bottom edge of the window. It is the far right group of three small, quadratic fields. As long as the connection is insecure, it is simply gray.

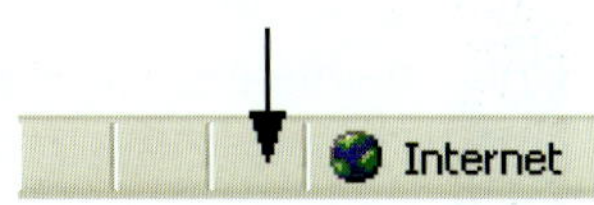

2 When you switch to a secure connection, Internet Explorer displays a lock in this field, which symbolizes the secure connection. It appears until you once again leave the secure connection.

3 You can find out more than if a secure connection is available. You can also find out more detailed information about the provider, the site, and the security status. Double-clicking the security field in Internet Explorer's status bar opens the *Certificate* properties.

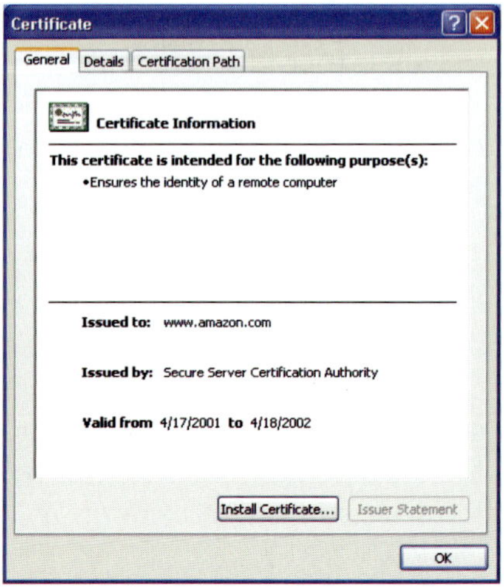

4 There, you find a summary of the most important information in the *General* tab: for whom the certificate was issued, who the issuer is, and how long it is valid. You can find even more detailed information in the *Details* tab.

Internet Explorer security zones

Internet Explorer uses a concept of four security zones to protect users from dangerous Web content. It is based on the idea that all the Web sites requested by the user can be categorized into one of these four zones. The user can determine certain access restrictions for each of these four zones; for example, allowing or blocking dangerous content such as ActiveX. Thanks to these various zones, such restrictions no longer have to be made globally for all Web sites. Instead, you can set different levels of security that Internet Explorer then applies to the different Web sites, depending on the security zone assigned.

1 Access to the four Internet zones of Internet Explorer can be found on the *Security* tab under *Tools/Internet Options*. There, at the top, you can choose between the various security zones.

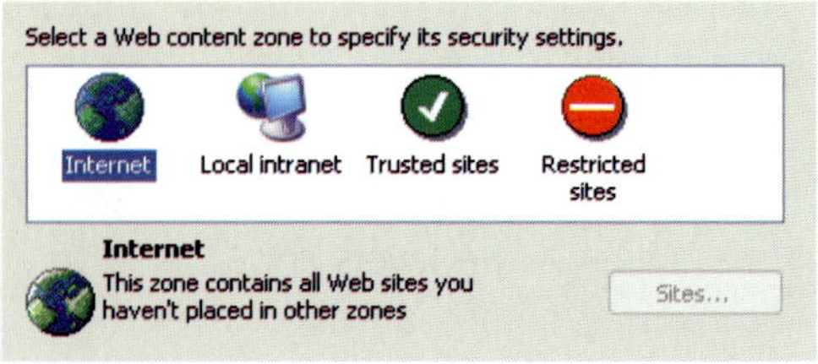

- All the Web pages that stem from your computer or from a Web server in the same subnet (for example, a company intranet) are included in the *Local intranet* zone. You can assume these pages present little danger, for damage (or at least intentional damage) from the immediate vicinity is not expected.

- The *Trusted sites* zone contains the addresses of sites that you consider harmless. For Internet Explorer to change to the trusted zone when requesting such sites, you must assign the addresses to this zone (see further below). You should assign only trusted sites here, because relatively large security risks are associated with it.
- The *Restricted sites* zone is intended as a quarantine area. It generally has restrictive security settings so that destructive content doesn't have a chance. If you suspect genuine danger from a site, you should enter its address in this zone, before you call it up for the first time.
- *Internet* contains all the remaining sites that are not automatically, based upon your manual assignments, allocated to one of the first three categories. If Internet Explorer requests a site that is not assigned to one of the other zones, it automatically switches to this zone, in which strict security measures should be undertaken.

Note

How the security zones work

With Internet Explorer, you can determine your own settings for each security zone. This way it is possible to allow ActiveX controls contained in Web pages on your own Intranet to execute, for example. In contrast, the browser, to keep out possible dangers, blocks active content in other Web pages. Regardless of the Web page requested, Internet Explorer automatically switches to the appropriate zone in each case. The assignment takes place according to the address of the Web site. If it is located on your own intranet or a local site on your computer, the browser enables the security measures for the local intranet. If the requested address belongs to one of the trusted or restricted site zones, the corresponding restrictions are applied. If the address hasn't been assigned to any of these three zones, Internet Explorer uses the security measures for the Internet zone.

By default, Internet Explorer assigns predefined security levels to each security zone. Each of the levels contains different restrictive security settings. The following table provides an overview of the default security levels enabled and their action.

Zone	Level	Action
Local intranet	*Medium*	The user is warned before potentially damaging content is executed.
Trusted sites	*Very low*	There are practically no restrictions. All content is executed without warning.
Restricted sites	*High*	The browser disables potentially damaging content from executing.
Internet	*Medium*	The user is warned before potentially damaging content is executed.

When surfing with Internet Explorer, you can determine at any time and at a glance which security zone you are in. The browser indicates the current zone on the far right of the status bar at the bottom of the window.

Determining the correct security levels

The default security levels have settings that make sense for the various zones. However, you can also freely change the attributes, if necessary. For instance, if might be necessary to set the security level of the local intranet to low if you want to work with ActiveX controls or Java applets that are distributed over your local network.

1 To select a different security level for a zone, open the settings in Internet Explorer by going to *Tools/Internet Options* and switching to the *Security* tab.

2 First, select the security zone to which you would like to assign a different security level, such as *Local intranet*, for example.

3 Under *Security level for this zone*, Internet Explorer shows you which levels have been allocated to this security zone. Select the new level here.

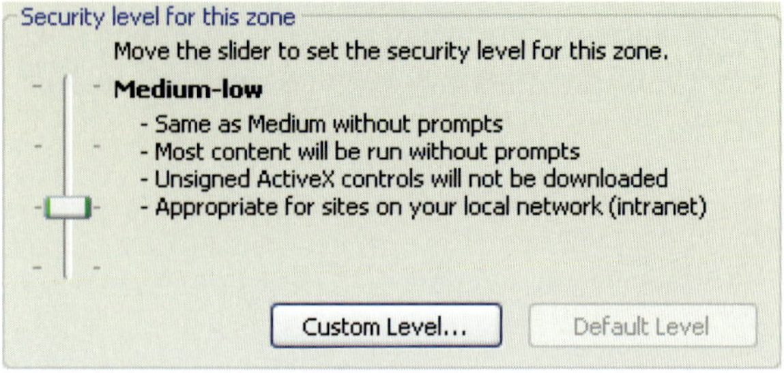

4 Internet Explorer has doubts about some of the combinations of security zones and levels. These are communicated through a warning message. To ignore the warning and to implement the new settings regardless, click *Yes*. If you do not want to take a risk and would rather rely on Internet Explorer's security rules, discard the changes by clicking *No*.

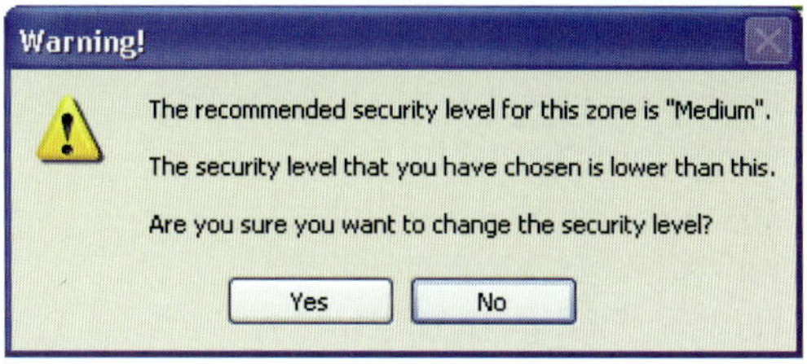

5 If you would like to go back to the original settings, click the *Default Level* button.

Protect your privacy from cookies

In recent times, privacy during use has become more and more significant because of two circumstances. In the first place, increasingly more companies and organizations are trying to obtain increasingly more - and more personal - information about Internet users for profit.On the other hand, the surfers' awareness of the dangers for their privacy is growing. Microsoft has therefore come up with a new concept for Version 6 of Internet Explorer, which is supposed to allow the users to flexibly protect their privacy. Microsoft has thus implemented the information protection protocol P3P that allows or hinders the individual and convenient surrendering of such personal information. Furthermore, the handling of cookies is now integrated into this function of Internet Explorer.

Note

Spying on information through cookies

"Cookies" is a weak description for small files that Web sites can place on your computer. With the use of the information contained therein, Web servers or their operators can save information about you and recognize you right away at a later visit. This technology is not without dispute. Many consider cookies a way of trespassing on protected information and privacy. It is possible to precisely trace saved cookies and the path they have recently taken through the Web. It is common for cookies to be used by online shops. Many online shops use cookies to ensure that at any given time a clear assignment of each user's virtual shopping cart occurs. You cannot go shopping in such stores if you have disabled the use of cookies. For the most part, other techniques have become available to the operators of online stores, so that customers do not necessarily have to live with these treacherous cookies.

1 To determine the guidelines for your privacy, open the Internet Explorer settings by going to *Tools/Internet Options* and switching to the *Privacy* tab.

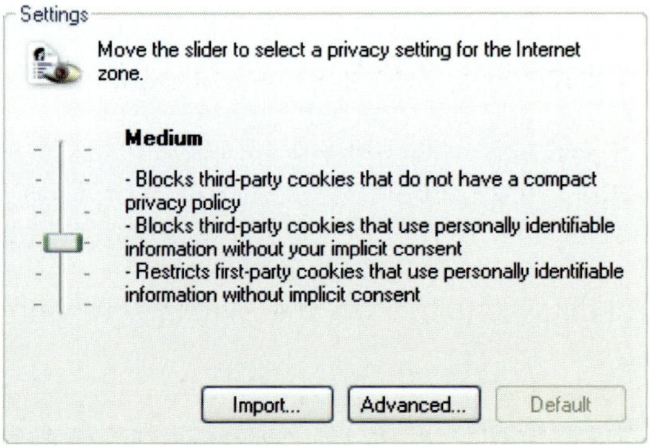

2 Here, you can select the guidelines you prefer from the *Settings* area. By default, the level is set to *Medium*. This level enables the P3P function, but also allows the use of cookies for the most part.

3 Alternatively, you can set the level to *Block All Cookies*, if you want more security. In principle, cookies are disabled. That might, however, lead to some Web sites using cookie technology not correctly working anymore. The weakest privacy settings, *Low* and *Accept All Cookies*, are never recommended!

4 Apply the changed settings by clicking *OK*. They are immediately active.

Individual cookie settings

In addition to the general handling of cookies within the framework of P3P options, Internet Explorer offers you the possibility to always accept cookies selectively or strictly forbid them from certain Web sites. Thus, you can work with cookies flexibly. If you have a skeptical nature, you can completely reject the acceptance of cookies and, for example, only allow them individually for certain Web sites (such as a favorite online shop with a cookie shopping cart).

1 To determine individual cookie privileges for certain Web sites, click *Edit* in the *Web Sites* category in the *Privacy* settings.

2 In the window that follows, enter the address of the Web site in the *Address of Web site* field.

3 Depending on whether you want to *Allow* or *Block* cookies for this site, click the corresponding buttons.

4 The address is then added to the *Managed Web sites* list underneath. Here, you can undo the individual settings by selecting to *Remove* the entry at any point in the future.

Handling cookies without P3P

If you preferred the old concept for handling cookies of Internet Explorer, where you could determine to always accept cookies, never do so, or do so only after being prompted, you can have IE6 revert back to it.

1 To do so, click the *Advanced* button in the *Privacy* settings.

2 In the window that follows, first enable the *Override automatic cookie handling* option. This enables the settings available underneath.

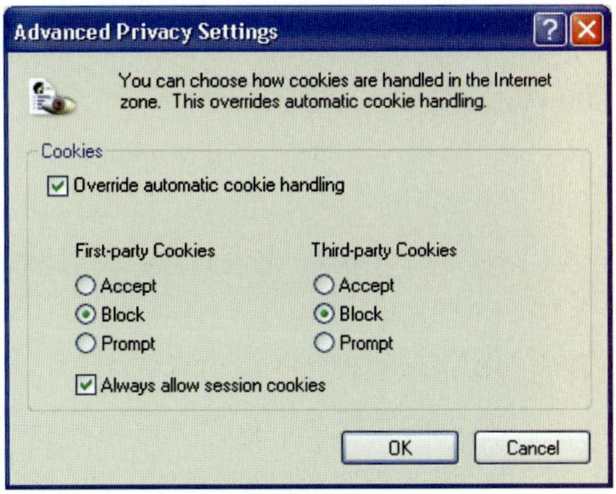

3 Here you can, as with early versions of Internet Explorer, select the options *Accept*, *Block*, or *Prompt*. The choice between cookies from a first party and a third party refers to cookies that come from the same Web server as the Web site or from a different one.

4 The *Always allow session cookies* option grants the unrestricted placement of temporary cookies that are stored only for the duration of the session.

Note

Everything about Internet security

A lot of dangers hide in wait for careless surfers exploring the Internet. You have seen some of these dangers and how you can use Internet Explorer to fight against them in the framework. If you would like more insights into the risks and preventative measures, we recommend picking up a copy of "The Hacker Report", written by the same author and published by DATA BECKER (ISBN 1-58507-053-X).

Receiving your favorite station over the Internet

Since version 5, Internet Explorer comes with a special Internet radio panel, so that you can listen to various radio programs as audio stream while surfing. In Version 6, this function is integrated into the Media panel. In principle, you can listen to Internet radio the way you did before, but the service has changed a little bit.

1 To listen to Internet radio, you must first display the Media panel by going to *View/Explorer Bar/Media* or by clicking the *Media* icon.

2 Here you must open the playback menu by clicking *Media Options* and requesting the *Radio Guide*.

3 Internet Explorer opens a Web site with a guide to the Internet radio stations registered with Microsoft. Here, you can select from the numerous radio stations and start *Play*-ing right away.

Note

Internet radio stations as Favorites

If you want to regularly listen to particular radio stations, you don't have to always make your way to the station overview over the Media panel. Instead, you can add the selected station to your Favorites list by using the command *Add to Favorites* and then later conveniently call it up using the Favorites menu. Internet Explorer then displays the Media panel and begins playing back the broadcast.

8. Worldwide mail – E-mail with Outlook Express

The current version of Outlook Express, used for e-mail communication, is also included with Windows XP, alongside of Internet Explorer 6. You can use it to create, send, and receive e-mail messages. In addition to these basic functions, you have other options, such as the sending files by means of e-mail attachments, creating e-mails using HTML formatting, or requesting confirmation that the e-mail has been received – a sort of registered e-mail.

Setting up an e-mail account

When starting Outlook Express for the first time, some connection information is required, such as your e-mail address, your name, but also the name of your provider's mail server. Thereby, the program starts the Wizard for accessing the Internet. It asks the necessary questions and, if needed, provides help.

1 The Internet Connection Wizard is automatically enabled when you start Outlook Express for the first time. It asks for all the necessary information in several steps.

2 First, the Wizard wants to know your name. It is best to enter your real name here. This is the name Outlook Express sends along with your e-mail address in outgoing messages.

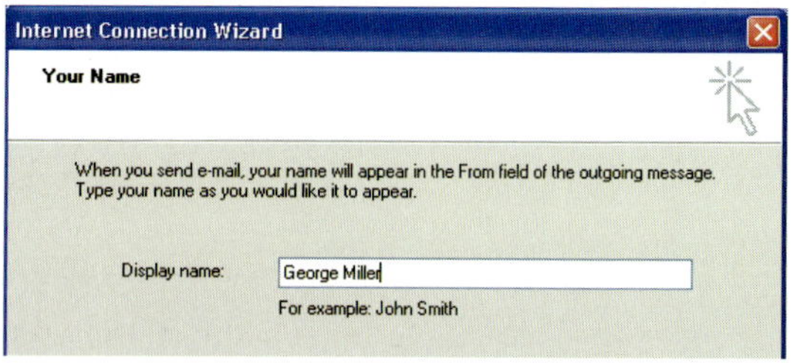

3 Next, you are asked for your e-mail address. You must get the necessary information from your Internet service provider (ISP). You can also obtain a secondary e-mail addressfrom a free mail service, such as http://www.hotmail.com or http://www.yahoo.com. Enter the address where you can receive e-mails in the *E-mail address* field.

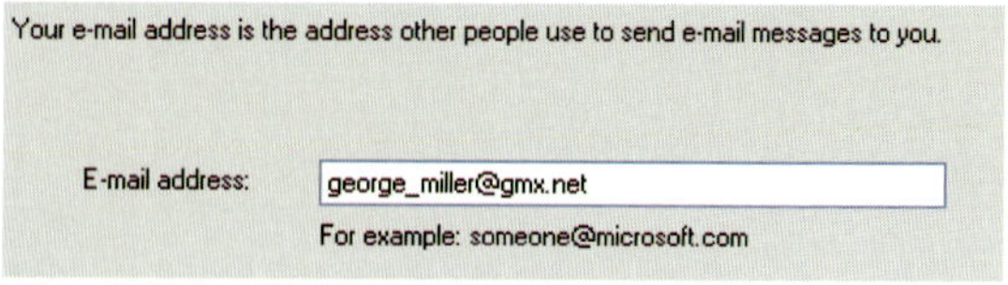

4 Then, the Wizard wants to know which method your Internet provider uses for picking up e-mail. In the *My incoming mail server is a XYZ server* field, you can select from Post Office Protocol (*POP3*), Internet Mail Access Protocol (*IMAP*) or access through the Web with the Hypertext Transfer Protocol (*HTTP*). Up to now, the most frequently used method is POP3. Here, too, you should contact your Internet provider to find out the correct settings, if you are in doubt.

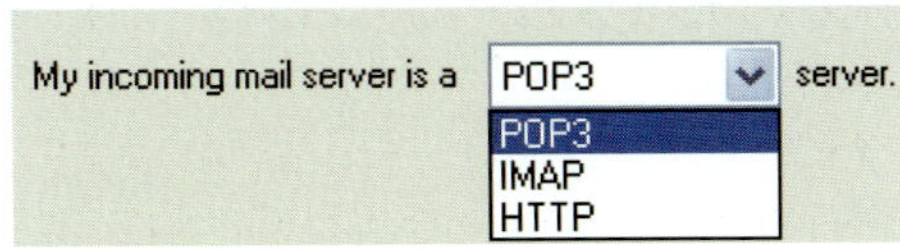

5 In the same step, the Wizard asks for the *Incoming mail server (POP3, IMAP or HTTP)*. Enter the name of the Internet computer used by your service provider to collect incoming messages for you.

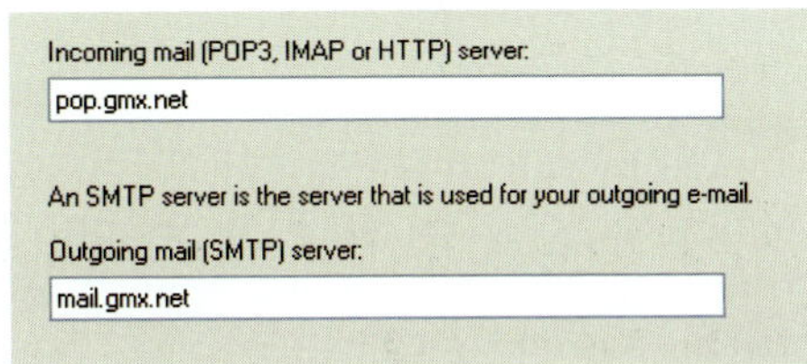

6 Directly underneath, you must enter the name of the Internet computer that acts as the outgoing mail server *(SMTP)*. This is the computer to which Outlook Express creates a connection to send your messages on their way. Internet computers usually perform both functions, so that you can enter the same name in both fields. If in doubt, it is better to check with your Internet provider.

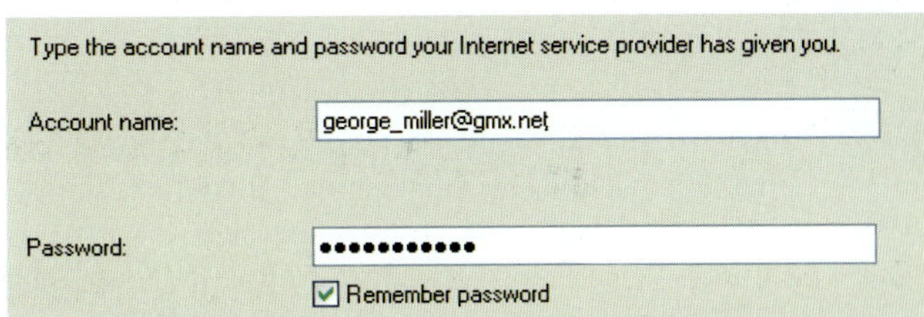

7 If you want Outlook Express to receive your e-mail completely automatically, enter your *Account name* as well as the corresponding *Password* in the next step. Using this information, the e-mail program identifies you to the mail server and thereby receives access to the messages saved for you. If you would rather identify yourself manually each time, forego entering the information.

Note

Save the password?

Outlook Express offers you the possibility to save the password for your mail server. You can thus completely automate the downloading of messages, that is, Outlook Express can, for example, automatically transfer your electronic mail at regular time intervals. This possibility is very convenient, as it saves you from continually having to enter your password. However, another person who has access to your computer can easily download and read your messages (for example, colleagues at work or children on your home computer). If your messages are so confidential that other users should not read them, disable the *Remember password* option and enter your password manually each time.

8 You have now entered all the necessary information and made the most important settings. Click *Finish* to set up the account according to your specifications. The name of the incoming mail server is initially used for the account name. You can always replace it with a more suitable description at any time. Afterwards, Outlook Express is ready for action.

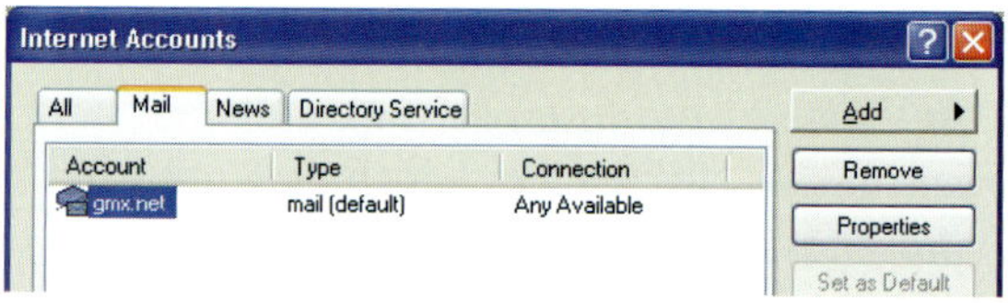

Note

Creating additional accounts

If you have several e-mail accounts from different providers, Outlook Express has no problem handling them. The program can manage several different accounts at the same time. When checking your mail, it contacts the various servers and collects all the messages for you. Similarly, you can decide when sending your message, which account and, thus, which sender's address to use. To create an additional user account, first go to *Tools/Accounts*, the manager for your Internet accounts. Then, click the *Add* button and, in the submenu, select *Mail*. The Internet Connection Wizard reappears, where you can enter your account information. Important: If you have set up several accounts, you should determine the default one. This is the account used when sending messages as long as you do not specifically select a different one when creating the message. To determine the default account, select an account in the account manger and click *Set as Default*. You can recognize the default account by the additional word *(default)* in the *Type* column.

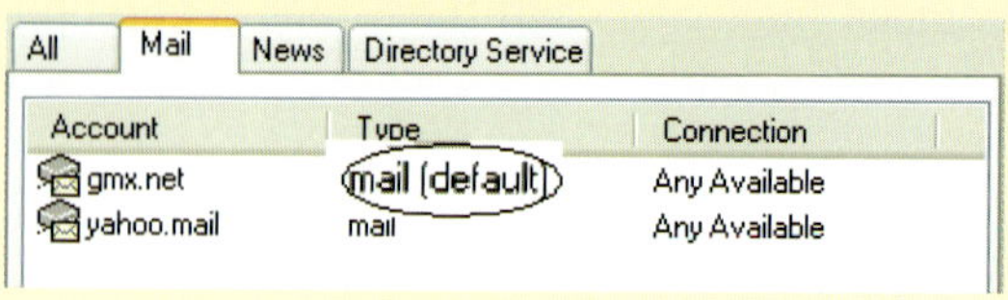

Sending and receiving e-mail messages

In Outlook Express, the sending and receiving of messages are functionally separated from the creating and reading of messages. The program thereby maintains as many offline functional capabilities as possible. Working on messages, be it writing them, reading them or responding to them, can take place completely offline. All of the composed messages are saved in the meantime. To send them and look for new messages on the mail server and, if there are any, retrieve them, as quick an online connection as necessary is established, which sends all the messages to be sent on their way. Similarly, incoming messages are locally saved and can afterwards be read in peace - again offline

1 To establish the connection to the mail server, go to *Tools/ Send and Receive/Send and Receive All* or to the *Send and Receive All* icon in the toolbar. If you only want to send written messages, without checking for new messages at the same time, go to *Tools/Send and Receive/Send All* instead.

2 Outlook Express contacts the server specified for outgoing messages and sends the ones out that are in the *Outbox* folder. You can monitor the progress in a status window.

3 Next, Outlook Express connects to the server specified for incoming messages and looks for new messages for you. If it finds some, it transfers the messages and places them in the *Inbox* folder. There, you can read the e-mails you have received.

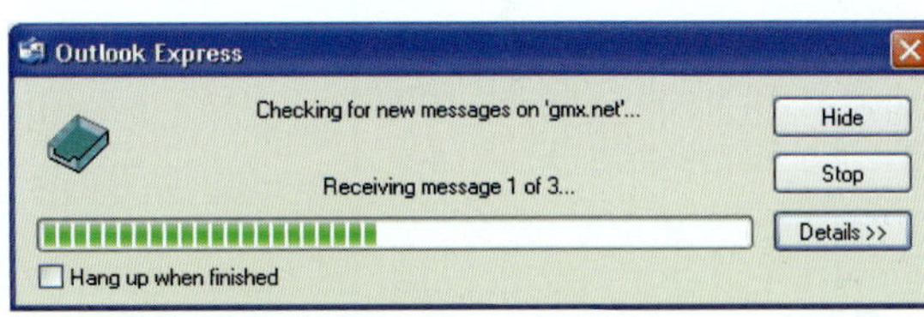

4 You can click *Details* at any point in time to view more precise information about the transfer. This is particularly useful should problems arise. You can view the exact error message in the details and determine which account or server has the discrepancies.

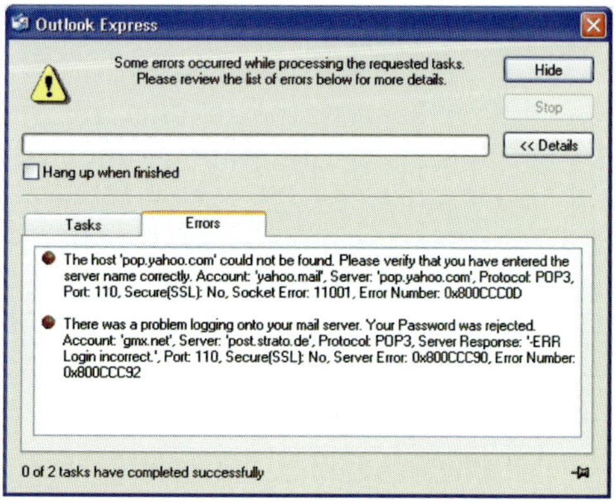

Sending files via e-mail

You can send more than just simple text files by e-mail. Because the messages are exchanged digitally, you can also send files, for example, Word documents, Excel spreadsheets, or multimedia files, in this manner.

1 First, open a new window for creating an e-mail message by going to *Message/ New Message*.

2 Fill in the letterhead with the recipient's address and the subject heading.

3 You should at least include a short blurb in the main text area so that the recipient knows what the file contains and what application he or she needs to view it. You can also include any additional text in the message.

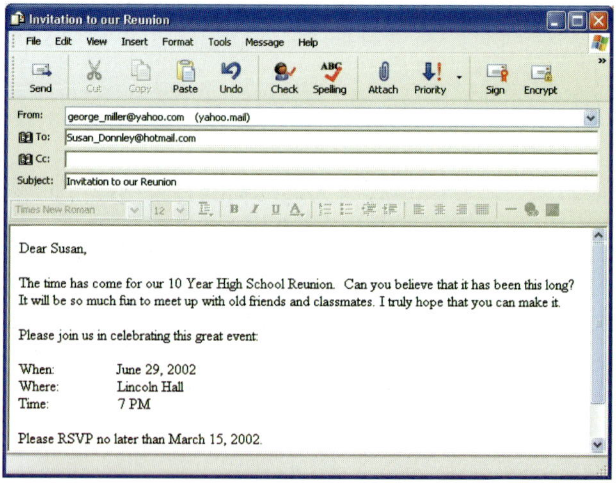

4 Next, use the *Insert/File Attachment* menu command or click the *Attach* icon to select a file to send.

5 Outlook Express opens an *Insert Attachment* dialog window in which you can select the file you want to send by e-mail. Once you have confirmed your selection by clicking *Attach*, the file is inserted into the e-mail as an attachment. An additional line appears in the letterhead called *Attach*, which displays all attachments. By repeating this procedure any number of times, you can add several files to one e-mail.

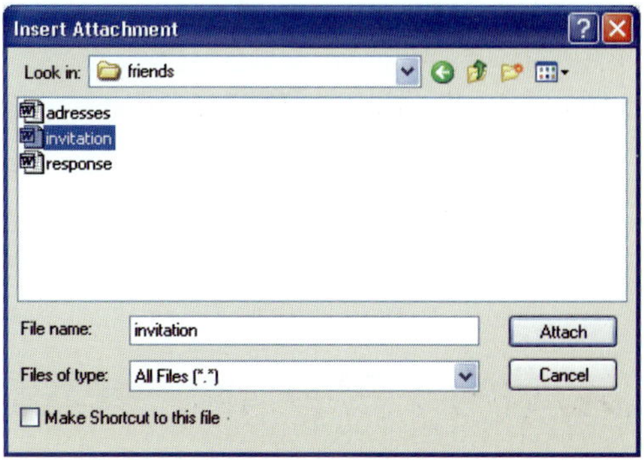

Note

Restrictions on sending files by e-mail

Unfortunately, the size of the files you can send by e-mail is restricted. The larger the file, the greater the chance that something might go wrong during delivery, and the message together with the file might not reach the recipient. This means that only file sizes up to 2 MB are valid. However, should the message be directed to someone using an online service, for example, even smaller files are risky. Therefore, try to make the files as small as possible. It is helpful to use Windows XP's compressed folders for this (see chapter 4), which can substantially compress the files. Using them, you can break considerable files into several pieces, which can then be sent without any danger and reassembled by the recipient.

Protection from e-mail viruses

A lot of hype has been created in the recent past about e-mail viruses , such as the famous/notorious "I love you" virus and similar ones. Because Outlook Express is integrated with Internet Explorer and the Windows operating system, it unfortunately belongs to the more virus-vulnerable e-mail programs. With the right settings, though, you can protect yourself from danger.

1 Open the program settings by going to *Tools/Options* and switching to the *Security* tab.

2 In the *Virus protection* area, you can find all the decisive security settings for receiving e-mail. First, *Select the Internet Explorer security zone to use* when dealing with HTML e-mails.

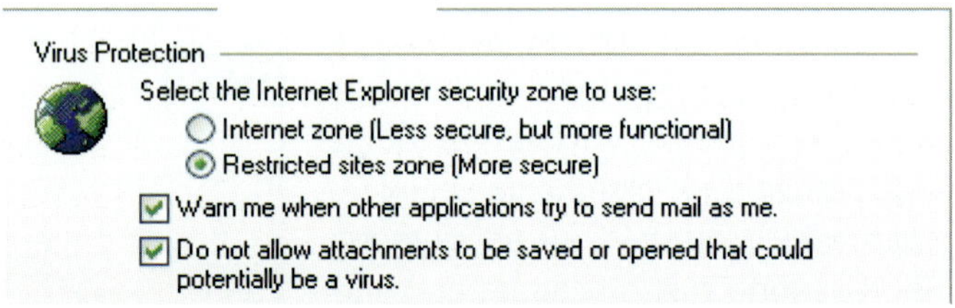

3 Outlook Express uses the settings of the *Internet zone* by default when an HTML formatted e-mail is displayed. It is safer in such a case to enable the settings for *Restricted site zone*. These are in general much more restrictive and don't allow active content such as scripts to be executed.

4 The *Warn me when other applications try to send e-mail as me* option is particularly helpful with viruses, such as "I love you", which try to automatically forward themselves. The option prevents an e-mail virus from accessing your address book and forwarding messages without your knowledge.

5 The *Do not allow attachments to be saved or opened that could potentially be a virus* option serves as protection specifically for file attachments. If you enable this option, there is practically no danger of receiving files that are infected with viruses or similarly dangerous components by e-mail. However, you can no longer receive a whole slew of file attachments through e-mail.

Confirmation of delivery for e-mails

Another fairly new procedure that expands the functionality of e-mails is is the delivery confirmation. In some respects it is the same as a return receipt for postal service letters. When the e-mail arrives or is read by the recipient, the sender is given a short notification that the message has arrived. That creates security, particularly with business or other extremely important messages.

The requirements for confirming receipt

Confirmation of receipt is not provided for in the "normal" e-mail protocols of SMTP, POP, and IMAP. Therefore, additional standards were created to harmonize the use of confirmation of receipt. To use it, you must use an e-mail program with the MDN standard (**M**essage **D**isposition **N**otification). In the meantime, most current e-mail programs have incorporated the MDN standard, including among others, Outlook Express. It is extremely important that both communication partiesuse software that supports the MDN, so that the confirmation of receipt function can be implemented. If the recipient's e-mail software simply ignores the prompt for confirmation of receipt, the function cannot work.

Requesting confirmation of receipt

If you send a message with Outlook Express, you can also request confirmation of receipt for each e-mail sent.

1 First, create the message as usual, without immediately sending it.

2 Prior to actually sending it, select the menu command *Tools/Request Read Receipt*.

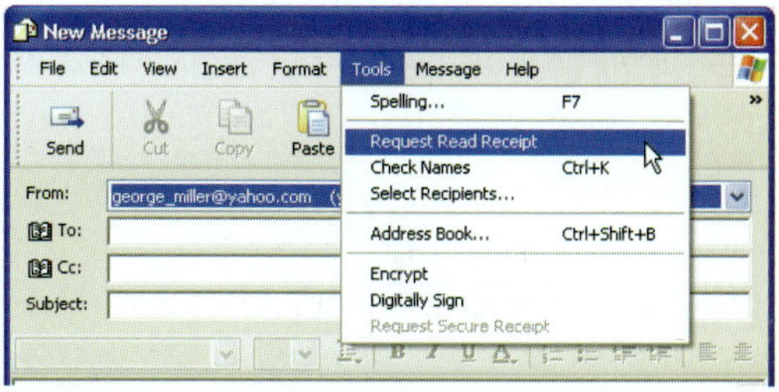

3 Then send the message as usual by clicking *Send*.

4 All you can do now is wait and hope that the recipient allows and his or her software supports the confirmation of receipt.

5 If this is the case, you receive a short confirmation message once your message has reached your correspondent's incoming mail server or has been read by the recipient.

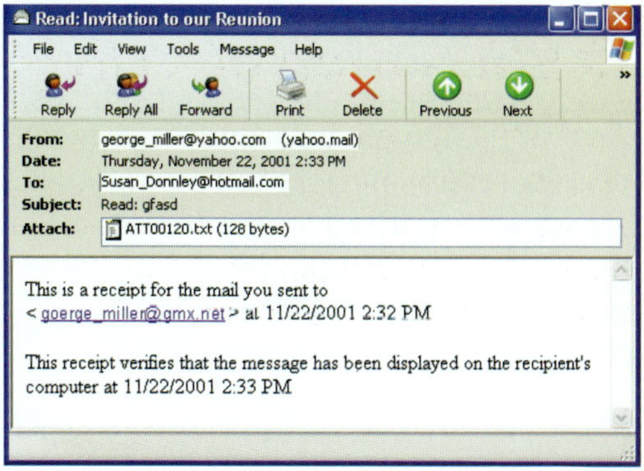

Requesting a confirmation of receipt at all times

If you request a confirmation of receipt for basically all the messages you send, you do not have to do it manually each time. Instead, you can set Outlook Express to automatically request a confirmation of receipt for each sent e-mail.

1 Open the settings for Outlook Express by going to *Tools/Options* and switching to the *Receipts* tab.

2 In the *Requesting Read Receipts* area, you can determine if the program should request confirmations. If you want it to do so, enable the option *Request a read receipt for all sent messages*.

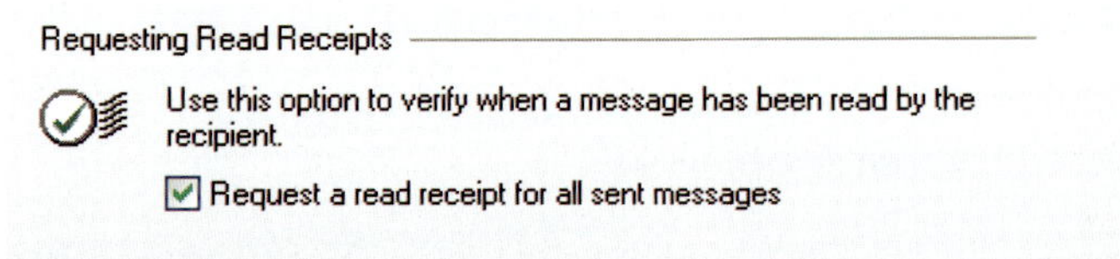

3 Apply the new settings by clicking *OK*. Outlook Express now furnishes all outgoing messages with a confirmation of receipt request.

4 If you do not want a confirmation at any one time, you can disable the feature in the e-mail creation window for the current message by going to *Tools/Request Read Receipt*.

Responding to confirmation of receipt requests

Much in the same way that you can make requests for confirmations of receipt, others can also ask you for confirmation when you have received a message. When this happens, Outlook Express can automatically respond to the confirmation request, if you adjust the relevant settings.

1 Open the Outlook Express settings by going to *Tools/Options*. Again, switch to the *Receipts* tab.

2 In the *Returning Read Receipts* category, you can determine the course of action when you receive a message a confirmation request.

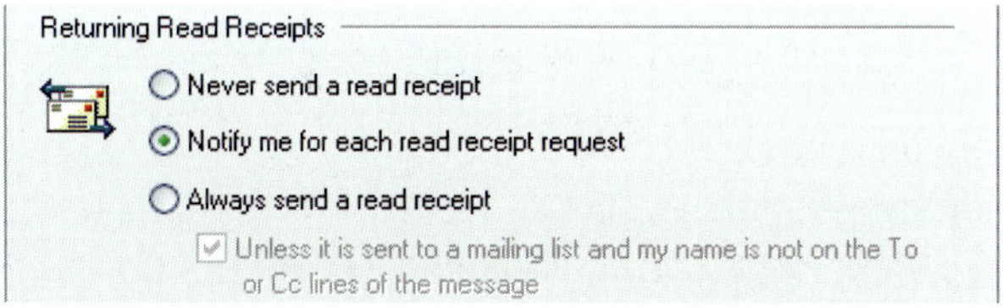

3 With the *Never send a read receipt* option, you decline sending confirmations of receipt. The e-mail program then simply ignores the respective prompts when it comes across such messages.

4 If you select *Notify me for each read receipt request*, you enable an interactive mode. The e-mail program informs you of messages that are requesting confirmation of receipt. You can decide if you want to send the confirmation or not.

5 The *Always send a read receipt* option ensures that the e-mail program automatically answers a confirmation of receipt request each time it is prompted.

6 With the *Unless it is sent to a mailing list and my name is not on the To or Cc lines of the message* option, you can restrict the program from responding to confirmation of receipt requests from anonymous mailing lists. This would otherwise be a good way for junk mailers to find out your e-mail address.

7 Apply the new settings by clicking *OK*.

If you have enabled the interactive mode and you receive a message with a confirmation request, Outlook Express informs you of it in a dialog box, asking you if a confirmation should be sent (*Yes*) or not (*No*).

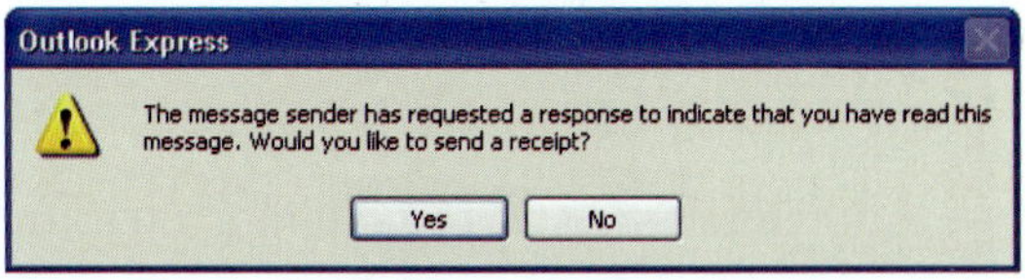

Adding a personal touch with signatures

Letterhead stationery is often used for traditional letters. This gives the letters a personal touch and also ensures that the important address information of the sender is contained within. Signatures in e-mails act in a similar way. Signatures are short blocks of text that can be freely created by the user. The e-mail program automatically attaches the signature to every outgoing message. Outlook Express even allows you to use several signatures, so that you can choose the appropriate one for each message, depending on the recipient of the content.

1 To attach a signature to your message, open Outlook Express settings by going to *Tools/Options* and then switch to the *Signatures* tab to set your e-mail signature.

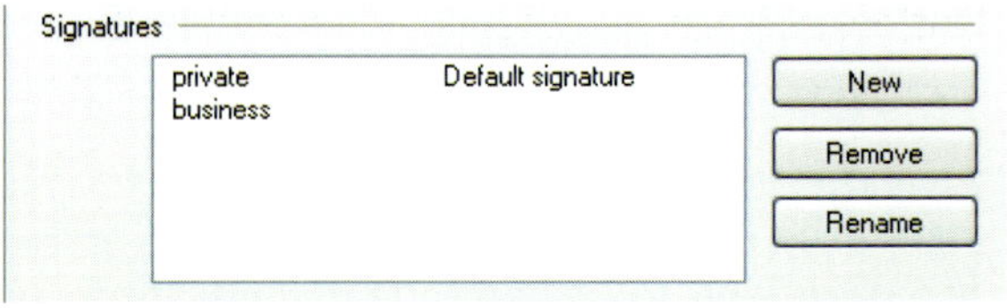

2 First, create a new signature by clicking *New* in the *Signatures* area. The new signature has a generic name (for example, *Signature #1*), which you can right away change by clicking *Rename*. It is best to use a meaningful description, so that when you are later selecting from the various signatures, it is easy to assign one.

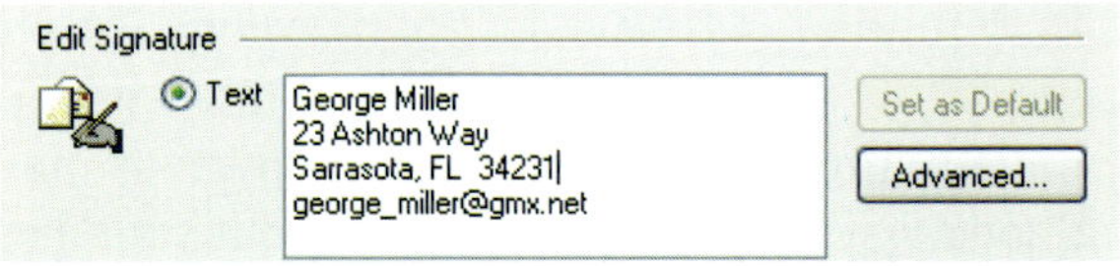

3 In the *Edit Signature* area, the signature currently selected above is displayed. Enable the *Text* option and, in the text entry field beside it, enter the text for your signature. In theory, the text can be anything. By selecting *Set as Default*, you can assign the signature currently being edited as the default one, meaning that unless you specify otherwise this signature is used. Clicking *Advanced* allows you to determine for which accounts this signature should be used.

How should signatures be designed?

As with many things on the Internet, no formal rules for how signatures should look exist - at least none that have been written down anywhere. In practice, the unwritten rule that a signature should be no longer than five lines applies for the most part. After all, this text is sent along with all of your messages. An excessively lengthy signature uses an unnecessary amount of transfer capacity and uses up additional hard drive space on the recipient's computer. As for the content , no rules exist at all. Most people usually include their name and their e-mail address. In addition, you can also specify other address information, such as your homepage. Others adorn their signature with a small ASCII graphic. In many cases, the text is also accompanied by a humorous or wise adage. When reading e-mails and news messages, pay attention to the types of signatures that others are using.

1 If you don't want to be restricted to using the simple editor available in Outlook Express, you can import the signature from a file you have previously created with a convenient text editor. Make sure you save the signature as simple text. Then, select the *File* option and enter the desired signature text file by clicking *Browse*. Outlook Express attaches the contents of the file as a signature to every outgoing message. Changes to the file are automatically applied without your having to import the file again.

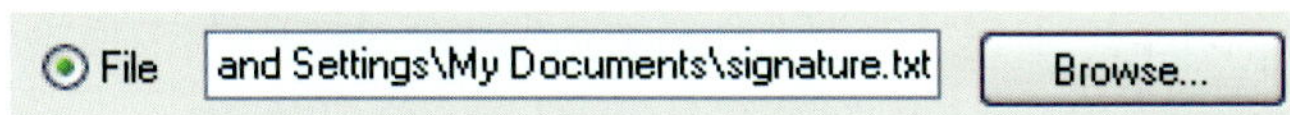

2 If you always want to use signatures with your messages, go to the above *Signature settings* region and enable the *Add signatures to all outgoing messages* option.

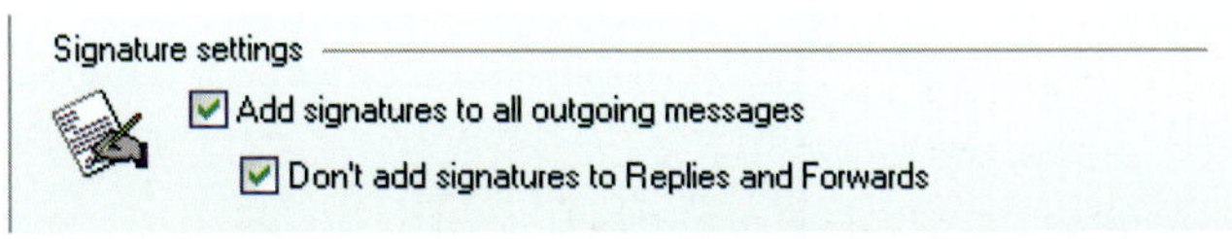

3 However, if you only want to attach signatures to newly created messages and want to refrain from doing so for replies or forwards, enable the *Don't add signatures to Replies and Forwards option*.

4 Clicking *OK* applies the new signature options. Depending on your selections, Outlook Express automatically inserts a signature into all outgoing messages in the future. This occurs in the window of the message you want to compose. This way, you can change the contents of the signature each time, if required, or completely remove the signature, if it is unnecessary or unsuitable for a particular message.

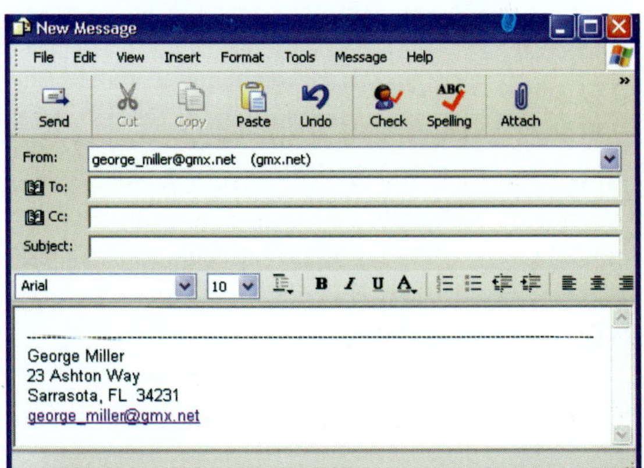

The e-mail is returned with an error message

Even when e-mailing with Outlook Express, you might find that not everything works the first time. Electronic letters, too, can be returned to the sender with an "unknown recipient" message. Usually, e-mails that come back with an error message contain information to help you determine the cause of the problem. You can find these error messages at the beginning of the e-mail, above a copy of your original message. The following table gives an overview of the most important error messages and their meaning.

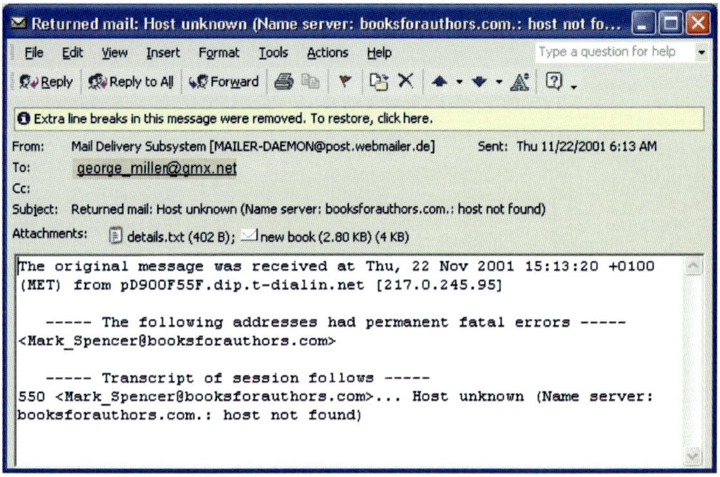

Error message	Meaning
Unknown User	The addressee, that is, the part of the e-mail address before the @ symbol, is not recognized by the specified Internet computer. The problem is usually a typo in the address (for example, *ferd@mail.art.com* instead of *fred@mail.art.com*).
Host Unknown	The Internet computer, that is, the part of the e-mail address after the @ symbol, could not be found. In this case, an error or a typo in the address is usually at fault (for example, *fred@mial.art.com* instead of *fred@mail.art.com*).
Unknown Domain	Here, too, the errors lies with the description of the Internet computer; more exactly, the description of the wrong domain (for example, *fred@mail.arf.com* instead of *fred@mail.art.com*).

Error message	Meaning
Unresolvable or *Unroutable*	No correct Internet address could be deduced from the e-mail address. The most likely reason is incorrect or missing punctuation (for example, *fred@mailart.com* instead of *fred@mail.art.com*).
Network Unreachable	The target computer described in the e-mail address could not be reached at the time. The cause is usually a technical problem. In this case, it is better to try again later.
Service Unavailable, *Connection timed out* or *Connection refused*	The target computer does not want to or cannot accept any e-mail. The cause behind it could be a technical problem or an incorrectly configured computer. Perhaps it was even deliberately set not to receive any e-mail. If the error continues to occur after several tries, you should double-check the validity of the e-mail address.

9. Questions, answers, and more ...

In the previous chapters, we have tried our best to get you better acquainted with the new functions of Windows XP. To adhere to the idea of a quick reference, we have at times concentrated on the most common procedures and left out one or two special cases. Not all special cases can be taken into consideration on the remaining pages, but we want to give you at least some answers to some typical questions that arise when working with Windows XP and when following the procedures described in this book. In addition, we provide you with some Internet addresses where you can find further information and tips about Windows XP.

Why can't I carry out the XYZ function as described in the book?

The user concept of Windows XP was fundamentally reengineered. As a consequence, an administrator, or a user with special rights, was added. This special user was determined during installation. Only the user possessing these administrator rights can undertake most of the system settings. In this case, you can log yourself on as the administrator, or you can bestow the necessary rights for administrating the computer upon your normal user profile. To do the latter, you must be logged on as the administrator.

1 Open the *Control Panel* and switch to the *User Accounts* category.

2 Select the user account upon which you want to bestow administrator rights.

3 For the next step, click the *Change the account type* entry.

4 In the account type settings, select the *Computer administrator* option and apply the new setting by clicking *Change Account Type*.

If you log on with this user name afterwards, you have unrestricted access to all the system settings and functions.

Should performing certain tasks still not be possible, it might be because of the hardware or software configuration. Functions such as burning CDs are only possible if your computer has a CD burner that is in working order. Otherwise, the options in question do not display. This applies to other components such as scanners, digital cameras, or network functions.

Why can't I record MP3s with Windows Media Player?

Microsoft has saved on the MP3 function for Windows Media Player. Although the program can play an MP3 file, the recording and copying of audio CDs only occurs in Windows own WMA format because Microsoft wants to push its own WMA format more. However, you can supplement the means of creating MP3 files with additional software. Certain companies offer a "Creation Pack", which is a type of plug-in for Windows Media Player. This software must be purchased, however. Plug-ins not only exist for the recording of MP3s but also for playing back DVDs in Windows Media Player.

You can find out more information about it if you go to the options in Windows Media Player (*Tools/Options*) and click the *MP3 Information* button in the *Copy Music* tab. Windows Media Player then opens a special Web site in Internet Explorer, where you can find out more information about MP3s and the corresponding Creation Packs and references to the Web sites offering them.

What do I do if the screen suddenly turns blue?

Supposedly, Windows XP is much more stable than the previous versions and, in particular, much more immune to driver problems. Blue screens almost always occur due to driver problems that completely knock the operating system out of stride. One thing is particularly important when such errors occur. Windows has recognized the problem and has somehow prevented a complete crash. Regardless, the system has become unstable. If you can still return to the usual interface after all the warnings have appeared on the screen, you must secure all the open files immediately. Then, close all the applications and restart Windows. This is the only way the system can return to a well-defined, reliable state. It doesn't make much sense to continue working after a blue screen appears, as the next, perhaps fatal error - according to experience - is not waiting far behind. Should this phenomenon start repeating itself all of a sudden, use the system restore to go back to an earlier, functional restore point. You can find more information on how to deal with crashes in Chapter 3. The system restore capabilities are explained in more detail in Chapter 4.

Are there really no more DOS functions?

As a matter of fact, Windows XP is the first Windows operating system for home users that is not based on the 20-year-old DOS architecture. Those who are well accustomed with the DOS method of input and don't want to lose it can always find it by going to *Start/All Programs/Accessories/Command Prompt*. Nothing has changed visually and with the underlying operation. However, not all pure DOS programs run under Windows XP without your making further adjustments. If an application is programmed to work very closely with the hardware, Windows XP blocks certain access to preserve its own stability. In this case, the DOS program does not function normally. If you have such a program, it is best to look for a Windows version or a similar application that works under Windows.

Where can I find more information about the topic of XYZ?

Windows XP has already included a contact that helps you with questions and problems during the installation on your computer: Windows Help. Here, all of the Windows functions are explained in more or less detail. In addition, a number of Wizards dealing with particular areas (for example, printing problems) have been integrated into Help. The Wizards are meant to help find the root of a problem through interaction with the user.

1 To start Windows Help, go to *Start/Help and Support*. In many cases, you can call up a pop-up Help within an application with the [F1] key or through the *Help* menu; this means that the Help program doesn't start with the general greeting but right away with special help for the particular situation (as far as possible).

2 To navigate through the Help topics, use the *Pick a Help topic* category in the left half of the window. Here, all the Help topics are listed and can be called up simply by clicking them. The tips and background information for the relevant topics are displayed in the right half of the Help window.

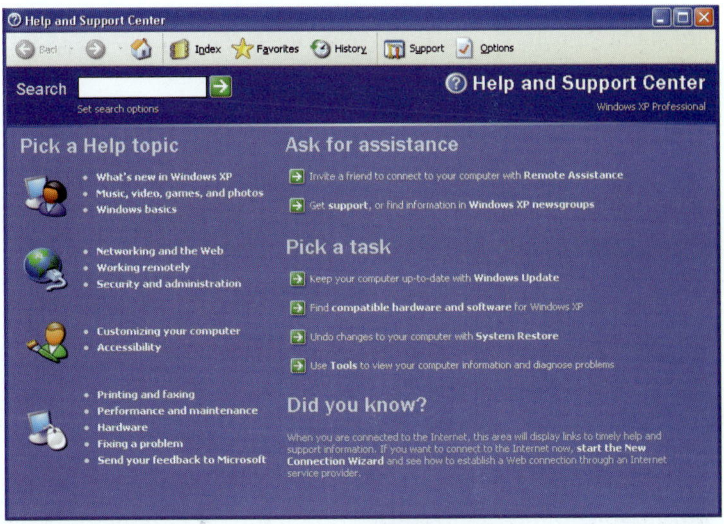

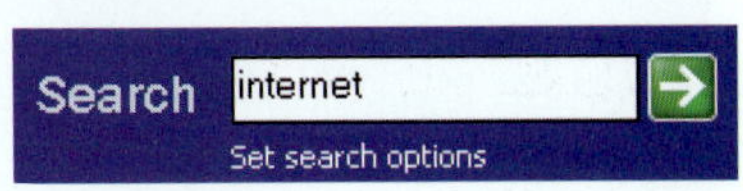

3 If you are searching for a particular term, you can undertake a complete text search through all the Help topics in the *Search* area. To do so, enter the term you are searching for. The search for this term in the Help topics begins once you press [Enter] or click the -> button.

If the term cannot be found in the Windows Help, the Internet offers an almost inexhaustible fountain of information, support sites, and tips. At the end of this section, you can find several addresses to use as a starting point for your own queries.

Do you still have questions?

Unfortunately, we cannot cover all the possible questions and difficulties in the framework of this quick reference. If you would like to know more about a particular function, something described in the book doesn't work for you, or you have other problems that the book did not address, feel free to contact me! I will gladly accept questions and suggestions at sawxp@gieseke-buch.de.

Internet addresses for Windows XP

Interest in the Windows operation system is great so a large number of Web sites are dedicated to it. We have selected a few useful international addresses about Windows in general and Windows XP in particular.

http://www.microsoft.com/windowsxp/

First, the "official" source. At this address, you can find information about Microsoft and their product, Windows XP. Once you filter out all the advertising, you can find some useful information here.

www.winsupersite.com

This Windows supersite from Microsoft insider Paul Thurrott belongs to the best-informed Windows Web sites on the Net. Here, you can find detailed information about all Microsoft products and especially the new Windows XP.

www.windrivers.com

Here, you can find an extensive international offering of drivers for Windows operating systems. In addition to multifaceted search functions, an archive is also available that, if needed, can be searched for drivers for older devices.

www.google.com

If you cannot find what you are looking for using the special Windows Web sites, try doing so with a search engine. Google belongs to the best agents in this field. Enter the search terms here that closely and precisely describe your problem. With a little bit of luck, you will find the necessary information.

Index

A

access digit 114
ACPI 73
activating 25
ActiveX control 53, 127
administrator 10, 150
applications
crashes 151
getting older ones to work 50
removing from memory 48
Task Manager 49
archive 69
area code 114
audio CDs 85
burning 92
copying 90
Gracenote 91
online information 91
WAV format 93
Auto-hide the taskbar 19
automatic cookie handling 133
automatic maintenance 78
AVI 85

B

background color 30
background images 28
from the web 30
position 29
Backup Utility Wizard 75
bad sectors 64
blue screen 151
broadband 116
burning CDs 94
busy signal 120

C

call waiting 114
carrier code 114
CD burner 85, 92, 94
certificate 128
cleaning up hard disks 66
Clear Type 15
closing applications 48
Command Prompt 152
compatibility 50
compatibility settings 51
Compressed Folders 69
compressed folders
creating with existing files 70
extracting 72
using 71
compressing files 69
computer administrator 150
computer administrator account 10
computer description 101
computer name 101, 110
confirmation ID 26
confirmation of delivery with e-mail 142
connecting PCs to a network 97
connection method 100
connection problems 119
Connection refused 149
Connection timed out 149
control panel 22
classic look 24
cookies 127, 131
automatic handling 133
blocking 132
individual settings 132
copy music protection 92
country/region 114
crashes 46, 151
removing programs from memory 48
creating compressed folders 70
Creation Pack 151

D

default e-mail account 138
defragmentation 64
desktop 11, 28
activating classic design 12
background 28
background color 30

desktop
- classic Windows user interface ... 32
- cleaning up ... 34
- control panel ... 22
- graphic effects ... 14
- icons ... 33
- notification area ... 20
- Start menu ... 16
- taskbar ... 18
- themes ... 31, 51

Desktop Cleanup Wizard ... 34
Device Manger ... 58
dial-up network connection ... 113
dial-up problems ... 119
digital cameras ... 81
disconnect due to inactivity ... 119
Disk Cleanup ... 66
driver ... 57, 151
- for networked printers ... 108
- signed drivers ... 61
- signature ... 61
- uninstallation ... 61
- updating ... 59

E

e-mail ... 136
- confirmation of delivery ... 142
- default account ... 138
- error messages ... 148
- saving your password ... 138
- sending and receiving ... 139
- sending files ... 140
- setting up an account ... 136
- signatures ... 145
- viruses ... 141

error messages ... 46
- e-mail ... 148
- with websites ... 121

error report ... 47
- customizing ... 48

error-checking ... 63
establishing a connection automatically ... 118
Ethernet ... 98
extensive search queries ... 124

F

Fade effect ... 14
Fast Ethernet ... 98
file system errors ... 63
files
- archiving ... 70
- burning to CDs ... 94
- compressing ... 70
- file task pane ... 36
- from compressed folders ... 72
- sending by e-mail ... 140
- sharing on the network ... 102

Filmstrip view ... 39
flat rate ... 116
folders
- accessing shared folders ... 104
- burning to CDs ... 94
- compressed ... 69
- for toolbars ... 39
- sharing on the network ... 102
- task pane ... 36

fragmentation ... 64

G

Gracenote ... 91
graphic effects ... 14
Group similar taskbar buttons ... 19

H

hard drive maintenance ... 62
hardware
- Device Manager ... 58
- driver signature ... 61
- drivers ... 57
- faulty compenents ... 59
- for the network ... 97
- hub ... 98
- uninstalling drivers ... 61
- updating drivers ... 59

Help ... 152
Help programs ... 62
home network ... 97
Host Unknown ... 148
HTML e-mails ... 142
HTTP ... 137
hub ... 98
Hypertext Transfer Protocol ... 137

I

I love you ... 142
icons
  desktop cleanup ... 34
  on the desktop ... 33
  selecting ... 34
images
  background image ... 30
  from the Web ... 30
IMAP ... 137
Inbox ... 139
incoming mail server ... 137
installation ID ... 26
Installed programs ... 68
Internet ... 129
  automatically connecting and disconnecting ... 117
  connection problems ... 119
  dial-up problems ... 119
  disconnect due to inactivity ... 119
  establishing a connection automatically ... 118
  establishing access ... 113
  firewall ... 117
  Internet radio ... 134
  one connection for several PCs ... 109
  searching for websites ... 123
  security ... 127
  shared connection ... 109
  website errors ... 121
Internet Connection Firewall ... 117
Internet Connection Sharing ... 100, 109
  configuring client PCs ... 110
  host computer ... 109
Internet Connection Wizard ... 136
Internet connections ... 113
Internet Explorer ... 34
  background images ... 30
  cookies ... 131
  Internet radio ... 134
  protecting information ... 131
  security concept ... 128
  security levels ... 129
  security status ... 127
  security zones ... 128
Internet Mail Access Protocol ... 137
Internet radio ... 134
Internet service provider ... 115
Internet zone ... 142
ISDN adapter ... 100, 113, 120
ISP ... 115

J

Java applets ... 127

K

Keep the taskbar on top of other windows ... 19

L

LAN ... 97
Layout Selection ... 84
local area network ... 97
Local intranet ... 128
location information ... 113
logging off ... 10
logging on ... 9

M

maintenance
  automating ... 78
  tools ... 62
manual update ... 53
Medial Library ... 88
memory ... 28
modem ... 100, 113, 120
MP3 ... 85, 151
MPEG ... 85
MS-DOS command prompt ... 152
multimedia ... 81
  searching for media ... 87
My Computer ... 34
My Documents ... 34
My Network Places ... 34, 102

N

network ... 97
  accessing shared folders ... 104
  building ... 97
  computer name ... 101
  configuring ... 98
  Ethernet ... 98
  hardware ... 97
  hub ... 98
  Internet Connection Sharing ... 109

network
monitoring connections ... 111
network drives ... 105
printing ... 107
sharing ... 103
workgroup name ... 101
network connection type ... 115
network drives
connecting ... 105
disconnecting ... 106
network monitor ... 111
Network Setup Wizard ... 99, 109
Network Unreachable ... 149
networking ... 97
New computer ... 42
New Connection Wizard ... 113
notification area ... 20

O

Old computer ... 42
online Help ... 152
online update, manual ... 53
online updating ... 52
optimizing the hard drive ... 64
Outbox ... 139
outgoing mail server ... 137
Outlook Express ... 136
confirmation of delivery ... 142
e-mail error messages ... 148
e-mail viruses ... 141
saving your password ... 138
sending and receiving ... 139
sending files ... 140
setting up e-mail ... 136
signatures ... 145

P

P3P ... 131
patches ... 52
Photo Printing Wizard ... 82, 83
pictures ... 81
burning to CDs ... 94
filmstrip view ... 39
from a digital camera ... 81
Picture Tasks pane ... 36
printing ... 83
reading in ... 81
pictures
slide show ... 82
thumbnails view ... 38
views in Windows Explorer ... 38
pictures from a scanner ... 81
playlists ... 89
POP3 ... 137
Position ... 29
Post Office Protocol ... 137
Power Options ... 74
power saving functions ... 73
printer, using over the network ... 107
printer drivers ... 108
privacy ... 131
problem solving, Safe mode ... 55
Program Compatibility Wizard ... 50
program crashes ... 46
removing applications from memory ... 48
programs
closing ... 48
crashes ... 151
getting older ones to work ... 50
removing from memory ... 48
Task Manager ... 49
protecting information ... 131

R

removable storage ... 82
restart ... 11
restore point ... 75
Restricted site zone ... 142
Restricted sites ... 129

S

Safe mode ... 55, 78
ScanDisk ... 62
Scanner and Camera Wizard ... 82
scanners ... 81
scanners and cameras ... 82
Scheduled Tasks ... 78
screen fonts ... 14
Scroll effect ... 14
searching ... 123
extensive queries ... 124
securing private information ... 131

security
- certificate ... 128
- cookies ... 131
- e-mail viruses ... 141
- Internet Explorer ... 128
- levels ... 129
- monitoring the network ... 111
- protecting information ... 131
- saving your password ... 138
- when surfing ... 127
- zones ... 128

security levels ... 129
security zones ... 128
Service Unavailable ... 149
sharing ... 103
Show Quick Launch ... 19
Shuffle ... 87
signatures ... 145
skins, Windows Media Player ... 85
slide show ... 82
smoothing edges ... 14
SMTP ... 137
Stand By mode ... 11
Start menu
- activating classic look ... 17
- customizing ... 16

start problems ... 78
Start-up, in Safe mode ... 55
support ... 152
Switch to skin mode ... 87
switchboard ... 114
switching users ... 10
System Restore ... 57, 69, 75
System standby ... 74

T

taks pane disabling ... 37
Task Manager ... 49
task pane ... 36
taskbar ... 18, 40
- notification area ... 20

temporary files ... 66
temporary Internet files ... 67
themes ... 31, 51
- classic Windows user interface ... 32
- online ... 32
- saving ... 32

Thumbnails ... 38
tone ... 114
toolbars ... 39
- customizing ... 40
- deleting ... 41

tooltips ... 14
transferring settings ... 42
transition effect ... 14
Trusted sites ... 129
Turn off computer ... 11
turning off ... 11

U

Unknown Domain ... 148
Unkown User ... 148
Unresolvable ... 149
Unroutable ... 149
Update Wizard ... 52
updating
- manually ... 53
- Windows ... 52

user ... 9
- administrator ... 150
- computer administrator account ... 10
- switching ... 10

using previously installed programs ... 50

V

videos ... 81
views ... 37
Virenschutz ... 142
viruses, e-mail ... 141

W

WAV format ... 93
websites ... 154
- certificates ... 128
- searching ... 123

Windows
- starting in Safe mode ... 55
- updating ... 52

Windows Advanced Options Menu ... 56
Windows components ... 68
Windows Components Wizard ... 68
Windows Explorer ... 35
- disabling the task pane ... 37
- filmstrip ... 39

Index

Windows Explorer
  task pane ... 36
  thumbnails view ... 38
  views ... 37
Windows Help ... 152
Windows Media Player ... 85
  burning audio CDs ... 92
  capturing media files ... 87
  controls ... 86
  copy music protection ... 92
  copying audio CDs ... 90
  Creation Pack ... 151
  Media Library ... 88
  MP3 ... 151
  playlists ... 89
  skins ... 85
Windows XP, activating ... 25
Windows-Explorer, burning files to CDs ... 94
Wizard
  Files and Settings Transfer ... 42
  Network Setup ... 99, 109
  New Connection ... 113
  Photo Printing ... 82, 83
  product activation ... 25
  Removable Storage ... 82
  Scanner and Camera ... 82
  Update ... 52
WMA ... 151
workgroup name ... 101, 110

Y

your own playlists ... 89

Z

ZIP ... 69